GREAT MOUNTAIN DAYS
IN THE
LAKE DISTRICT

ABOUT THE AUTHOR

The Cumbrian fells have held a lifetime's attraction for me, as they have for many others. Brought up in the far-flung west Oxfordshire countryside, the romance of the high fells tugged at my emotions from my youth. In 2001 my wife and I were able to up sticks and make a permanent home within sight of Lakeland. The move was triggered by a sought-after commission to write and produce the Lakeland Fellranger series, an eight-part guide for HarperCollins. The series was also soon to find its natural Cumbrian home, with Cicerone Press, thus assuring completion of my task and a long-term future for the series. *Great Mountain Days* was effectively created during this publishing transition.

My early experience of walking in fell country came in two guises. My mother's cousin was a farm manager on a fell estate near Kirkby Lonsdale. Hence summer holidays were spent gathering sheep and tending cattle. Though busman's holidays from my stockman's life in Oxfordshire, these were great experiences, developing my awareness of the magic of fell country.

By my late teens the lure of mountains for recreation had taken a real hold, and shortly after joining a mountaineering club I met, and became a regular house-guest of, Alfred Wainwright. Just being with such a gifted artist and writer was very special. We shared a delight in drawing and in poring over maps and walking guide ideas. He quickly saw my own appetite for pen and ink and my passion for the countryside, the fells in particular, and he encouraged me to consider creating my own illustrated guides.

My earliest guides were the *Cotswold Way* (1973), *Cornwall North Coast Path* (1974) and *Offa's Dyke Path* (1975). Cicerone commissioned a trio of hand-drawn walking guides to the Peak District which were published in the early 1980s (and subsequently revised). Other books followed, including – thanks to my fascination with historic landscapes – a guide to *Hadrian's Wall Path*. To mark the 1900th anniversary of Hadrian's accession to emperor I created Hadrian's High Way, a 100-mile route across the fells via Hard Knott, High Street and the Maiden Way.

After 14 years' dedicated research, I also completed the magnum opus Lakeland Fellranger series, with all eight individual volumes now available in a box set.

Mark Richards, 2016

↑ Author Mark Richards (far left) and Lesley Williams (far right) from Cicerone present the first cheque towards the Fix the Fells Project to Christina Smith from Nurture Lakeland and John Atkinson from The National Trust.

GREAT MOUNTAIN DAYS
IN THE
LAKE DISTRICT

by

Mark Richards

2 POLICE SQUARE, MILNTHORPE, CUMBRIA LA7 7PY
www.cicerone.co.uk

Printed by KHL Printing, Singapore.
A catalogue record for this book is available from the British Library.

Artwork and photographs by the author, except where otherwise credited.
Maps are reproduced with permission from HARVEY Maps, www.harveymaps.co.uk.

DEDICATION
To the three all-action outdoor adventurers in my family,
Daniel, Alison and Guy

WARNING

Mountain walking can be a dangerous activity carrying a risk of personal injury or death. It should be undertaken only by those with a full understanding of the risks and with the training and experience to evaluate them. While every care and effort has been taken in the preparation of this guide, the user should be aware that conditions can be highly variable and can change quickly, materially affecting the seriousness of a mountain walk.

Therefore, except for any liability which cannot be excluded by law, neither Cicerone nor the author accept liability for damage of any nature (including damage to property, personal injury or death) arising directly or indirectly from the information in this book.

To call out the Mountain Rescue, phone 999 or the international emergency number 112: this will connect you via any available network. Once connected to the emergency operator, ask for the police.

INTERNATIONAL DISTRESS SIGNAL

The recognised distress signal is six whistle blasts (or torch flashes in the dark) spread over one minute, followed by a minute's pause. Repeat until an answer is received (which will be three signals per minute followed by a minute's pause).

UPDATES TO THIS GUIDE

While every effort is made by our authors to ensure the accuracy of guidebooks as they go to print, changes can occur during the lifetime of an edition. Any updates that we know of for this guide will be on the Cicerone website (www.cicerone.co.uk/516/updates), so please check before planning your trip. We also advise that you check information about such things as transport, accommodation and shops locally. Even rights of way can be altered over time.

We are always grateful for information about any discrepancies between a guidebook and the facts on the ground, sent by email to updates@cicerone.co.uk or by post to Cicerone, 2 Police Square, Milnthorpe LA7 7PY, United Kingdom.

Front cover: Langdale Pikes from Lingmoor. Photo: Jon Allison, www.lakedistrictlandscapes.co.uk

CONTENTS

THE LAKE DISTRICT

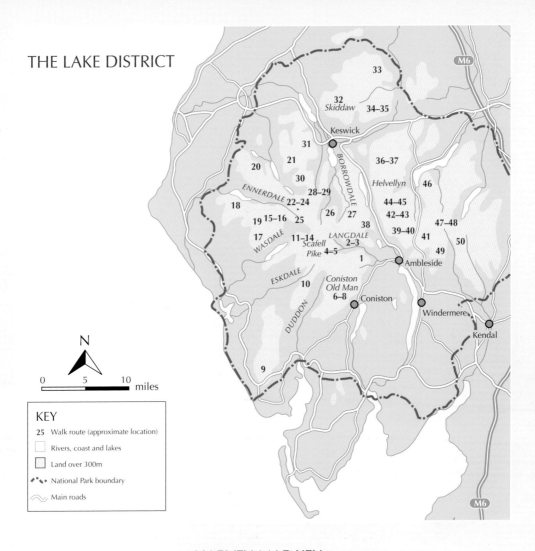

M6

33

32
Skiddaw   34–35

Keswick

31

20   21

30

36–37

Helvellyn   46

28–29

ENNERDALE   22–24

18

26   27

44–45

42–43

19   15–16   25

BORROWDALE

38

39–40

47–48

17   11–14   *LANGDALE*   41

WASDALE   2–3

Scafell   4–5   1

49   50

Pike

Ambleside

ESKDALE   10

Coniston Old Man
6–8   Coniston

Windermere

DUDDON

Kendal

9

N

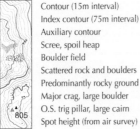

0   5   10   miles

KEY

25   Walk route (approximate location)

☐   Rivers, coast and lakes

☐   Land over 300m

•◦•   National Park boundary

〜   Main roads

M6

HARVEY MAP KEY

▰ •◦ •   Lake, small tarn, pond
〜〜   River, footbridge
〜〜〜   Wide stream
〜〜〜   Narrow stream
◠ ◠ ◠   Peathags
≈≈≈   Marshy ground

Contour (15m interval)
Index contour (75m interval)
Auxiliary contour
Scree, spoil heap
Boulder field
Scattered rock and boulders
Predominantly rocky ground
Major crag, large boulder
O.S. trig pillar, large cairn
▲▲ 805   Spot height (from air survey)

Contours change from brown to grey where
the ground is predominantly rocky outcrops,
small crags and other bare rock.

	Farmland
	Fell or moorland
	Open forest or woodland
	Dense forest or woodland
	Felled or new plantation
	Forest ride or firebreak
	Settlement
∨	Boundary, maintained
∨	Boundary, remains

On moorland, walls, ruined walls and
fences are shown. For farmland, only the
outer boundary wall or fence is shown.

═══   Dual carriageway
━━━   Main road (fenced)
•−•−•   Minor road (unfenced)
— — —   Track or forest road
- - - -   Footpath or old track
– – –   Intermittent path
⊢—⊣—⬛   Powerline, pipeline
•■ ◦ᵁ◦ ⌐   Building, ruin or sheepfold, shaft

Pike   Fell summits that feature as
chapters in this guidebook.

The representation of a road, track or footpath
is no evidence of the existence of a right of way.

SCALE 1 : 40,000

0 Kilometres   1
⊢+++++++++⊣

0 Miles   1

FOREWORD

by Sir Chris Bonington

For all my passion for high mountains played out on the world stage, Lakeland remains very much at the heart of my life – my emotional and physical home. I have lived around the Lakes for over 40 years, and in our present home on the edge of the northern fells for more than 30. Over the years I have walked and climbed on most of its peaks and crags. Although I have climbed in many of the world's greatest mountain ranges, however magnificent and high or wild they might have been I have never found anywhere that compares with the English Lake District, and always revel in its beauty on my return.

Here, in this guide, you can discover Lakeland hills for yourself. Typical of the man, Mark Richards has produced a book reflecting an exuberant affection for, and pleasure in, the exploration of the Cumbrian fells. Mark brings an artistic touch to the creation of a very practical and inspiring guide.

From a practical point of view, any walking day needs some planning. While I always regard a day on the fells as a relaxation, I never lose sight of the importance of thinking ahead. For me it is second nature to visualise where I am going, the potential effort involved, how long it will take me, and what I need to take with me. It's expedition planning in microcosm. A great mountain day begins in the mind, and your first steps are taken before you leave base. Good memories are built on the foundations of good planning. And this guide will help you to do just that.

It will enable you to plan fell-walking adventures in the four corners of the National Park that match your confidence and, hopefully, burgeoning ambition. While they represent the very best of fell walking, these Great Mountain Days are a big stride up from valley walking and several mighty pitches down from mountaineering. They will nurture your hillcraft skills, and in the process you will become more aware of the fell environment and learn self-reliance in high places. Always be mindful that the fells have all the characteristics of true mountains and deserve your respect. They can be savage, wild, remote and challenging, just as they can be playful, exciting, easy-going and fun.

For all I view the fells through the eyes of a cragsman, I have so often shared memorable days on them with good friends – just walking the high ridges and deriving my full measure of pleasure. Throughout this guide you will find rewarding walks to fill your mind with wonderful anticipation of hillwalking adventure and great days to come.

People have walked the fells for generations, but fell walking as a recreation has been a part of Lakeland life for barely 100 years. Its impact on popular routes to famous fells such as Blencathra, Helvellyn, Great Gable, the Langdale Pikes, Coniston Old Man and, of course, Scafell Pike has been immense. Hence, the co-ordinated work of the Fix the Fells project, a working harmony of the National Trust and National Park Authority, is very much to be applauded. I am delighted to see that Mark has given this project the prominence it deserves, and sought to encourage those new to the fells to play their part in their stewardship.

May I wish you many Great Mountain Days.

Sir Chris Bonington, 2008

← *Great Napes from the Lingmell Beck bridle path (Walk 16)*

PREFACE

The 50 Great Mountain Days I describe in this guide are very much a personal choice, selected to convey a rich flavour of the fells. They are derived, in part, from knowledge I gained while researching the first half of my Lakeland Fellranger series of guides (originally published by Collins) and the monthly 'Park and Stride' walks that I present on BBC Radio Cumbria. Otherwise the routes have been drawn from 30-plus years of devoted fell walking, first nurtured in the early 1970s during walks with Alfred and Betty Wainwright.

AW was a firm friend to the author, and companionship on the fells led to his mentoring me as I began to create my own hand-drawn walking guides. As the years have unfolded, the lure of Lakeland has drawn me irresistibly to also set my mark on the fells in a series of guidebooks.

In themselves these 50 Great Mountain Days seek to support and reassure readers in their mountain experience, while also cultivating the inventive confidence that brings the passion to explore to the fore. Above all else the walks confirm, irrefutably, the peerless beauty of the Lakeland fells. Rough or smooth, steep or sleek, each high rolling ridge, each combe, crag and tarn, has a character and quality all its own, frequently wild, often thrillingly dramatic, always rewarding on the eyes, body and soul – a tug on the heart when far away.

The rewards from a Great Mountain Day are there to find for those who seek them. Enjoy!

Mark Richards, 2008

A FEW WORDS

It was my first week presenting BBC Radio Cumbria's morning show. Into the studio swept one of the most effervescent men I've ever met. 'Today I thought we'd have a go at Blencathra,' enthused Mark Richards. I gently arched an eyebrow as he eventually sat down at the microphone.

Since then Mark's visits have become a monthly highlight, while the 'Park and Stride' series has become a firm audience favourite. Years of knowledge have gone into preparing this fresh take on some classic Cumbrian walks. Most important, though, is Mark's uncanny ability, while out walking, to sniff out 'scone' or 'real ale' from a mile or more away. Whichever path you choose, you'll have a great day and you're in safe hands.

Ian Timms
Presenter, BBC Radio Cumbria
July 2007

A family group ascends Jack's Rake (Walk 2) →

INTRODUCTION

'Only a hill, but all of life to me'
Geoffrey Winthrop Young

The beating heart of this guide is a love of the fells. These 50 fell walks have been specially devised to help readers get to know the fells and – with a new sense of confidence and adventure – to enjoy England's most majestic mountain environment to the full.

Each circular route, between 4 and 14 miles in length, is tailor-made to suit walkers early in their fell-walking careers – those confident in their country-walking fitness and prepared, when the elements conspire, to test their mountain navigation with map and compass – as well as more experienced walkers. What excitements lie in store! Feel yourself invigorated by breathing the good clean mountain air, stamping on firm rock, treading winding ridge-top trails, and gazing at richly patterned fellsides and across high-ridged horizons. From these and many more sensations progressively comes a oneness with this special place. In time Lakeland's mountain heritage becomes yours, treasured within unique memories of Great Mountain Days.

There is a buzz in fell walking that ordinary country walking cannot match. It requires effort and energy for a start. You might ask how on earth you are ever going to grasp the complexities of the fells,

the ridges and dales, the lakes and tarns, the rivers and becks, the maze of paths, and the individual fells themselves. The answer is that, surreptitiously, over the course of time, they begin to come together in your mind – you'll know them first from one angle, then another. The routes in this guide form the nuts and bolts of that discovery, a tapestry to follow or creatively embroider.

Clearly there can be no one definitive list of such walks – praise be for that! While many horseshoe routes are popular and have a natural symmetry, the real magic of Lakeland lies in the sheer diversity of choice, limited only by the imagination. Permutations on a theme abound. Some people have a systematic approach to their days in the hills and love ordered lists – hence the bagging of Birkett, Nuttall or Wainwright summits – so there will be those who choose to log all 50 walks in the same tidy manner. Whether you tick them off, or use them as an initiation by which you gain sufficient confidence to roam, by entering into the spirit of a Great Mountain Day you are assured of life-enriching experiences.

As confidence grows, so too does ambition; and with knowledge may come a yearning for special

Side Pike backed by Bowfell and the Langdale Pikes (Walk 1)

places to seek out beyond the range of this guide. Experience will give you the ability to craft bigger, bolder walks. One may even plan to walk the length of a range or engage in a tour of several days linking valleys or landmark summits. The magic in the creation of one's own walks soon takes hold, and this book will be consulted less frequently. But the selection will hold good as a fount of seasoned ideas quietly resting in your bookshelf in readiness for the moment you come calling again.

During your Great Mountain Days you will experience the pleasure of being in wild places and of sharing encounters with kindred spirits. There is a fellowship in the fells, both in the people you meet and in the fells themselves. They are dependable, always there – a shoulder to cry on in bad times, a haven of joyous elation at others.

About the Guide

The 50 walks in the guide are ordered in a clockwise spiral around the Lake District – the book starts from the springboard of the Langdales and gathers in the Coniston and Duddon Fells before heading north for Eskdale and the craggy giants of Wasdale. Sweeping further north via wild Ennerdale and sublime Buttermere the guide crosses Honister into Borrowdale, where the high fell ridges wrestle for attention, then ventures onto the sleek North-western

and Northern Fells before heading down Thirlmere to Ambleside. Switching north again the book strikes over Kirkstone for Ullswater, then back south over the Nan Bield Pass to end in the transitional dale of Longsleddale, where Lakeland horizons blend with the more benign Pennines. This arrangement gives a natural mountain focus from the common entry point of many walking visitors, arriving from the south via the M6 corridor.

At the start of each route description is a box containing all the key information for the walk: the distance, height gain, time and grade, as well as places for refreshment after the walk. Also provided near the start of the walk are details of suitable parking places. To compare and contrast the 50 walks, consult the Concise Walk Reference (Appendix 1), which summarises all the route information to help you fit the walk to the occasion.

Timings

Because of the variety of terrain encountered on these walks a clear indication of the time involved is given based upon how long it actually took the author, bearing in mind that he is no spring chicken and readily presses his pause button to capture a good view in his camera lens or consider the route.

Strong fell walkers will find the times very generous, but why rush? The fells are full of magical views and unexpected crannies to explore. The timings allow for these distractions – for me the heart of the walks.

Walk grades

In order to give a sense of the degree of effort and mountain craft involved in each route, three grades have been employed to categorise the walks.

- **Energetic:** devoid of serious hazard, requiring straightforward map-reading skills on largely secure paths, in normal circumstances involving up to 6 hours' walking.
- **Strenuous:** far more committing in terms of time and energy. Set aside a full 8-hour day and be prepared to be remote from valley bases.
- **Arduous:** an altogether rougher, tougher encounter with the possibility of mild scrambling. Scrambling requires composure and a good head for heights, and several optional scrambling sections occur on routes in this guide.

Scrambling

Numerous routes inevitably tackle steep broken slopes, and on occasion this turns into actual hands-on-rock scrambling. Unroped scrambling can be one of the most dangerous mountain activities. You should take great care, and if you feel unable to comfortably manage a route you should take an alternative.

Even modest scrambling can have the potential for hazard, especially for anyone unaccustomed to the mountain environment. Misty, windy, wet, icy or snowy conditions conspire to turn such encounters into serious mountaineering. Most caution is needed when rocky ground is encountered during a descent. At such times even walking poles can get in the way; always take your time and have confidence in your footing.

There are genuine, though invariably brief, scrambling encounters on the following 16 walks – 2, 3, 5, 7, 10, 12, 13, 14, 15, 16, 27, 30, 34, 35, 43 and 44. Any mountain walk can be hazardous in poor weather, so never dismiss the sound advice that retreat is always the greater valour.

If you are not confident scrambling, the walks nearly always provide an alternative walking-only route. Various local guides and outdoor centres offer training in straightforward mountaineering. Cicerone and other publishers have a range of books on techniques, and if you really enjoy scrambling sections, try Cicerone's *Scrambles in the Lake District* books (see Appendix 3).

Mapping

To aid visualisation the routes are depicted both on line diagrams and customised HARVEY maps (1:40,000). The former give an aerial impression of the walks, while the latter pin-point the key detail covered in the route description. The bold symbols of HARVEY maps make them well suited to outdoor use. HARVEY maps owe their origins to the dynamic sport of orienteering, and it shows. Note that key landmarks that feature on the maps and diagrams appear in **bold** in the text to help you plot the route.

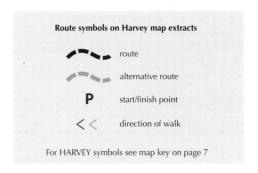

Route symbols on Harvey map extracts

- route
- alternative route
- **P** start/finish point
- << direction of walk

For HARVEY symbols see map key on page 7

Although the guide contains map extracts and diagrams, you are strongly advised to also take with you the relevant sheet map for the route – not only for safety, but also to help you get to know the wider area in which you are walking.

Six **HARVEY Superwalker** maps are required for the walks in this guide: Lakeland Central, Lakeland South West, Lakeland South East, Lakeland East, Lakeland West, Lakeland North.

Alternatively, four **Ordnance Survey** maps are needed: OL4 North-western area, OL5 North-eastern area, OL6 South-western area, OL7 South-eastern area.

Pike o'Blisco summit looking to Crinkle Crags and Bowfell (Walk 5)

Caring for the Fells

The contemporary overlay of tourism in the Lake District does not completely obscure the traditional interplay of dale and fell life. At one time, all was hard graft in a challenging climate, with sheep farming and mining holding dale communities in tight allegiance. The economic balance has swung, and outdoor recreation and tourism for the wider community hold sway. Nonetheless, there exists a culture of care for the fells.

The National Park Authority, National Trust, Friends of the Lake District, Forestry Commission, Cumbria Wildlife Trust, RSPB and others, together with individual farmers, seek to exert a continuing sensitive and positive influence on how the fells live and breathe. In some lights the landscape may look barren and untamed, but there is no utter wildness here. The fells have been managed through the grazing of sheep in recent times, but the fellsides were once richly wooded, and a far greater diversity of plants and animals made these fells teem with life. Now resources are being redirected to manage change, in certain instances allowing high sub-alpine meadows to bloom again, as is the intention in the Wild Ennerdale project. The transition in grazing regimes will inevitably cause changes to the flora and fauna, and there is a danger that if funding dries up and stock prices plummet the continuity of farming knowledge will be lost.

We are all beneficiaries of the care and efforts that go into managing the Lake District landscape – fell walkers perhaps more than most. However you get the first inkling that mountains are important in your life, once you get the bug you will be hooked for life and eternally grateful. You will be fitter and more appreciative of the natural environment too. You will also begin to perceive the importance of our wild places, sensing how they contribute to the balance of the wider ecosystem, and thus to the greater good of our human existence.

Born in Scotland, John Muir, whose fervent writings influenced the establishment of the world's first national parks in the USA, said 'Do something for wildness and make the mountains glad.' Well, with this guide you can do something for your own spirit and make yourself glad, and from this you may feel a resolve to play your part in making the Lakeland mountains glad too. There are ways and means at our disposal to get involved.

Over the last two centuries fell walking has grown and grown in popularity, with the last 50 years seeing the greatest recreational rise. This has inevitably had an impact on the state of fell paths. While a certain proportion of trails had historic purpose and were engineered to withstand heavy use, many more have developed from recreational impulse and do not have the benefit of a man-made base. Fell walking is now a year-round hobby and there is little relief in popular areas. Unchecked, the wear of boots progressively creates bare ground. Upland plants inevitably have slower growth and, importantly, regrowth characteristics, especially on the high fells, and this hampers natural surface recovery. On steep damaged slopes sudden flash floods can swiftly open up a fellside, irretrievably dislodging tons of rock and earth.

As dedicated Lakeland fell walkers we should applaud and support in whatever way we can the recent concerted commitment of resources for both capital projects and pre-emptive repair (see the Fix the Fells project, pages 18–19). While some seasoned walkers have poured scorn on the pitching work, the intensity of debate tended to lose sight of the real product, the long-term security of the walking environment.

The first wave of recreational pitching had a built-in flaw – it sought to replicate the historic pitched ways which had been constructed to ease the passage of sledges; hence their downward tilt. Anyone who wanders up the pitched path from Oxendale by Ruddy Gill to Red Tarn will witness the point of transition – the sudden change in the path marks the retirement of the National Trust's fell paths officer who determined the style of the first new paths! Plans to rectify this particular path are scheduled, so this may, in itself, become a historic footnote. (cont. p20)

Pikes Crag, Mickledore and Scafell Crag from Lingmell (Walk 14)

Main photo: *Stepping stones,
the best solution over peaty ground*

Inset photo: *Typical parlous state
of popular un-made mountain trail,
Broadcrag col – a case for modern pitching*

Fix the Fells

The Fix the Fells project, a working harmony of the National Trust and National Park Authority with Natural England, has many years to run in terms of workload, yet its current funding base will soon be spent. Future funding will inevitably rely on the ability of Cumbria's Nurture Lakeland (www.nurturelakeland.org) to gather money to keep some level of work running.

Hence the role of a voluntary donation scheme that encourages people who come to enjoy our beautiful natural places to give something back to the landscape. The voluntary donation is collected by participating tourism businesses, forwarded to Nurture Lakeland, and used to fund important local conservation projects. Major contributors are the Friends of the Lake District, and membership of that organisation is to be actively encouraged, so that by tangible means you can contribute to the care of the precious beauty of the Lakes. I would urge walkers to think seriously about putting their pounds where their pounding boots tread via www.fixthefells.co.uk. Resolve at the dawn of each new walking year to dedicate a given sum of your hard-earned cash – let's say the price of one decent post-walk pub dinner. Your soul has been enriched from the fell-walking experience; putting that modest sum back enables more soles to do the same.

Main photo: *Historic 'made' miners' path, Warnscale Head.* Top inset: *Rock for path repair and pitching brought by helicopter, the most efficient means of delivery, on the summit plateau of Helvellyn.* Bottom insets: (left) *Well-bedded modern pitching;* (centre) *Richard Fox, LDNPA Upland Path Officer, co-ordinator of the Fix the Fells project;* (right) *New pitching secures a route up shifting scree on Great Gable.*

We all learn through experience, and the Trust was able to adapt its pitching technique to give a firmer leading edge, effective both in ascent and descent. Many walkers comment that these set stones can be slippery when wet or icy. Care will always be needed, but the paths have hugely improved matters both environmentally and aesthetically, securing many a slope for another 100 years or more of boot traffic.

The other ancient path-construction technique re-invented, to save many eroding paths, has been soil inversion. A light-tracked digger is carried by helicopter onto the high fell, whereupon a trench is dug along the line of the worn path, emphasising gradient zig-zags. By flipping the subsoil a causeway of coarse substrate is exposed with drainage dykes on either hand. This was precisely how the Romans made their High Street ridgeway, creating a hard-wearing surface with no carting of heavy materials. The very presence of this causeway gives foot travellers a faithful line to follow in mist and rain (inevitably it is lost under drifting snow).

Weather to walk?

The fells are a world apart from lowland walking areas in terms of their weather and its consequences for the walker. For one thing, the fells create their own weather, and proximity to a western seaboard adds to the mix. Conditions can change in a trice. One minute the weather is sunny and the next palpably chilly, turning from cool to bitter, damp to dire, gusty to gale force, or furtive cloud to confusing fog in a twinkling, and sorely testing your navigation skills, confidence and comfort state.

So – a simple act – always pay particular attention to the mountain weather forecast both the night before and first thing on the day you intend to walk. The internet is the best recourse, and recommended sites include:
- www.metoffice.gov.uk/loutdoor/mountainsafety/lakedistrict.html
  Alternatively, ring 09068 500484 for the Met Office Lake District Mountain Forecast (at a higher per/minute rate).
- www.mountaindays.net/content/weather/lakes.php
- five-day forecast for the Lake District, www.lake-district.gov.uk/weatherline/index.htm
  tel 08700 550 575

Additionally, there are numerous good websites based in the Lakes providing all round information, advice and brilliant photographic galleries, such as: www.leaney.org and www.wasdaleweb.co.uk.

For a daily infusion of reports on great mountain days visit www.fellwalkingclub.co.uk, the Online Fellwalking Club.

Before you start

If you are new to fell walking visit a dedicated outdoor shop and seek their advice. Find shops in which the staff love outdoor pursuits and value good customer relations, and they will proffer sound guidance tailored to your precise needs.
- First and foremost wear comfortable **boots**, and do give them a chance to break in before you head for the hills. Customised insole inserts are excellent too.
- Wear woollen or mohair **socks** – the latter do not harbour the sweaty smell of the former after use and yet are just as fit for purpose.
- **Walking trousers** these days are not expensive and dry quickly in the breeze, unlike cotton; give denim the widest possible berth.

← *Gareth Browning, forester to the Wild Ennerdale Project, and Tony Beatty (fencing contractor) on the summit of Caw Fell prior to the construction of the temporary ridge fence for grazing management of the sub-alpine meadows (Walk 18)*

- Just as you would not drive without checking the fuel, oil and engine coolant consider your own physical needs. Carry **water** to replenish body fluid; fancy drinks or a hot toddy in a flask come a poor second to pure water. Drink regularly, preferably hourly, to avoid dehydration. Carry **food** in two forms – the casual reviving snack to enjoy quietly from a summit cairn or impromptu viewpoint (this can be just a sandwich, nuts and raisins and/or fruit); and high-energy restorative sources like Kendal mint-cake, marzipan or dextrose.

Preparation

The very fact that you are consulting this guide gives you a head start. Reviewing the walk in advance and properly 'looking' at a map – seeing precisely where the day's endeavours will lead – is always the first step on any walk. Too many walkers embark upon their mountain day with only the most casual of glances at a map and trust that they will auto-pilot round, following in the footsteps of the many who have blazed the trail before. You cannot rely on doing this, so it is a fundamental wisdom to develop a thorough navigational competence with large-scale maps and a conventional magnetic compass. Being able to work out grid references is an absolute must. See 'Appendix 3: Further Reading' for some useful books to help develop these skills.

It is also a smart move to let a responsible person know where you intend to go (and make sure you let them know when you've arrived). For example tell them you intend to follow Walk 43. Then if you don't arrive, at least the mountain rescue team's search will be precisely focused and get to you with minimal loss of time. Keep a whistle in the pack for just such an occasion. The recognised distress signal is six whistle blasts (or torch flashes in the dark) spread over one minute, followed by a minute's pause. Repeat until an answer is received (which will be three signals per minute followed by a minute's pause).

These days it is possible to find your way with a GPS handset, having pre-loaded the route's key

- Wear a series of light **top layers** – modern fabrics are excellent at wicking perspiration away, keeping you dry and therefore warmer. By wearing layers you can instantly effect change to suit your physical state. A light woollen jumper never goes amiss.
- The vagaries of the weather demand you carry a decent **waterproof top** and a pair of **over-trousers**.
- **Gloves** and **hat** help you face any squall – the latter is like a lid on a kettle, keeping you really warm, as so much heat is lost off the top of your head.
- **Gaiters** are excellent at keeping your trousers clean and your feet doubly dry.
- **Walking poles** are a real boon, especially during steep, slick or unstable descents.
- Use a moderate **daypack** – don't fall into the trap of carrying a monster sack that you feel obliged to fill – the author's preference is Macpac, its construction and fabric are perfect for the British climate.
- Modern **torches** are so small and light that they deserve a place in any daypack.

IN CASE OF EMERGENCY

For information on the 12 volunteer mountain rescue teams based in Cumbria visit: http://homepages.enterprise.net/ldsamra.

If you need the services of a Lake District Mountain Rescue Team:

- Call 999 and ask for POLICE. Ensure that you are put through to Cumbria Police and not another Emergency Service.
- Tell the police operator that you need MOUNTAIN RESCUE.
- Tell them where you are (grid reference if possible) and the nature of the incident.
- Give them a contact phone number.
- If an ambulance is needed the police or the rescue team will ensure one comes. You do not need to ask for the ambulance service as well.
- Stay by the phone or in the place where you can receive a signal on your mobile.
- A rescue controller will call you back at the number you have given.
- He will take further details and mobilise the team. They will be with you as quickly as possible.

grid references into it from a PC via specialist software. However, the author places all his confidence in a conventional compass – there's less to go wrong, and it makes one really READ the map while on the fell.

A word on mobile phones. I sometimes chance a phone call home during a day's walk. But the important word here is chance, for while I am frequently surprised by the locations where reception is possible, more often I am frustrated by the message 'no network'. Take heed: a mobile is only a string in a bow – to be carried but uncertain in an emergency.

Car parking

For all we may gripe at the cost of car parking and the paucity of casual parking places, it is still our responsibility as visitors to use formal car parking and be careful and considerate when slipping the car in impromptu fashion onto verges. Bear in mind that several of the shorter walks can be achieved using the regular bus services. For more information see www.traveline.org.uk or call 0871 200 2233.

If you've read this much of the introduction it's either raining very hard, or your partner insists you read every morsel of advice before embarking upon your first mountain walk together. Good thinking!

Blencathra, Catbells and the Newlands valley from Robinson (Walks 24 and 30)

Lingmoor Fell
from Little Langdale

A superb introduction to a regal array of majestic Lakeland fells. The walk takes fullest advantage of Lingmoor Fell's remarkable position which shows off to great effect the contrasting dale-heads – Great Langdale, dominated by the Pikes, Bowfell and the Crinkles; and its junior namesake, Little Langdale, focused on Little Langdale Tarn and no less grandly rimmed with fine fells. The route climbs onto the spine of the north-westerly-trending ridge and crosses the 470m/1542ft summit before heading down via the Fat Man's Agony access to Side Pike. It then swings round the beautiful bowl of Blea Tarn to reach and follow the Wrynose Pass road down by Fell Foot and Bridge End to pass under the slate quarries by Low Hallgarth and cross the utterly delectable Slater Bridge.

Lingmoor is heavenly favoured, at the centre of the Langdales. The ridge walk genuinely offers a new dimension to one's appreciation of the much adored twin dale-heads of Little and Great Langdale. Great expectations are fully rewarded with a gallery of fabulous outlooks. For all the slate quarrying, the fell remains largely wild and in part luxuriantly clothed in heather, hence the 'ling' in the fell name.

↑ *The Langdale Pikes from the north-west ridge of Lingmoor Fell*

ROUTE INFORMATION

Distance	10km/6¼ miles
Height gain	410m/1350ft
Time	4½ hours
Grade	energetic
Start point	GR319033
Maps	(Harvey Superwalker) Lakeland Central (Ordnance Survey) OL6 South-western area and OL7 South-eastern area

After-walk refreshment

Three Shires Inn at Little Langdale

The Start

For all the paucity of parking in the tiny community of Little Langdale there is a short stretch of road able to discreetly absorb a handful of cars close to Greenbank at GR319033, 200m east of the Three Shires Inn. The main car parking facilities for the Langdales lie in upper Great Langdale, but they are of little value to this walk. The National Trust has a small car park servicing access to Blea Tarn GR296043, which can efficiently play into this walk.

The Route

The walk begins by leading west along the narrow valley road from the **Three Shires Inn**. The volume of traffic as the season unfolds means that the walker needs to keep alert. Rise by the up-the-steps first-floor chapel and adjacent post office. Take the right-hand bridle lane, passing through Dale End Farm. After a gate watch for a gate left, rising to a hand-gate. The path contours to a further hand-gate before turning up the combe, zig-zagging on a partially pitched path and making steady progress onto the ridge. Here it meets up with a path from Banks Quarry, on the Elterwater side. There are isolated cairns to visit (left) on top of **Bield Crag** and (right) over a ladder stile on the

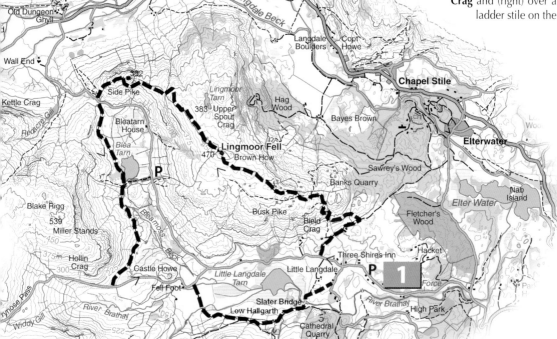

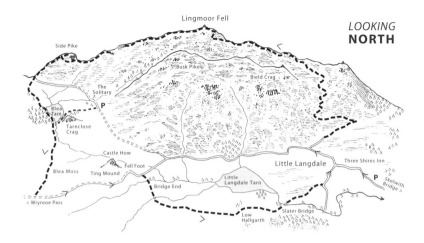

LOOKING **NORTH**

The squeeze on Side Pike

eastern end of the ridge. Both offer lovely outlooks – the latter towards Windermere over the wooded vale. It's largely grassy all the way.

To get to the summit walkers can follow a lower path from the Bield Crag cairn on the south side of the main ridge, passing along a high lateral valley and, at a wall, turning sharp right up to the summit. However, it is easier by far to stick to the ridge path proper beside the well-constructed ridge wall, running a switchback course. The path crosses a causewayed marshy hollow before taking a hairpin turn onto **Brown How** and crossing the light fence stile to reach the summit plinth.

This is **Lingmoor Fell** living up to its name – there is certainly more heather here! The differing grazing regimes between the north and south sides of the ridge are starkly apparent. Bravo for the survival of the heather, which looks stunning come August. For the rest of the year one can live with its brown tone, hence 'Brown How', knowing how its purple bloom will duly arrive to greet summer holiday visitors.

Follow the ridge fence and broken wall, with the Langdale Pikes direct ahead, the wall pointing straight towards Dungeon Ghyll. Catch a glimpse of the irregular and isle-decked Lingmoor Tarn, sitting in a lower hollow of the fell to the north of the ridge.

The path takes a sharp turn right to avoid a steep pitch of the wall and then switches back left to a stile at the wall junction. Follow the wall steeply down at first – the inviting spur leads only to a viewpoint and requires you to return to this point. The path eases down towards the abrupt crag of **Side Pike**. Cross the fence stile and follow the path initially up and then slightly down to the left of the cliff. The key to progress is a flake of rock that for most walkers requires them to take off their rucksacks and thread it and themselves through. If you fail this test then perhaps you need to do more walking to lose the weight! Alternatively, should you feel apprehensive about the manoeuvre, then backtrack over the stile and follow the fence down to the road, turning right to reconnect with the route or left to pass **Bleatarn House** and join the access path to Blea Tarn from the small car park.

Otherwise, having passed through the Fat Man's Agony, the path naturally curves round and up onto the west side of Side Pike, with the pleasing option of completing the modest ascent to its prim summit, a quite unrivalled viewpoint for the Langdale Pikes. Pike o'Blisco, Crinkle Crags, The Band and Bowfell demand a slice of the scenic attention too. Follow the ridge path down, crossing the broken wall and,

25

lower down, stepping over rock bands to reach a ladder stile onto the road. En route you can glimpse the new zig-zag path climbing up from the National Trust camp site in Great Langdale.

Step straight over the road to go through the kissing-gate and follow the rough, but hugely popular, path leading down to the woods screening the west side of **Blea Tarn**. The view back north from the south shore is a photographer's delight, with Harrison Stickle beautifully framed by Side Pike and reflected in the tarn. Continue south via the hand-gate, gaining a lovely view of the rich shrub and tree growth in **Bleamoss Beck**, which tumbles through a small gorge beyond **Tarnclose Crag**. The path sweeps across the damp lower slopes of **Blake Rigg** to reach the Wrynose Pass road. Turn left with the open road, with an enclosure wall to the right. The road twists where the shapely crag **Castle How** intervenes.

Make a point of looking over the wall to the right during this descent to spy the shallow grassy platform behind Fell Foot farm. Of little obvious consequence, this is the remains of a **Ting Mound**, a rare survival from a Viking settlement. The term describes a meeting-place, or moot point, akin to the Tynwald (or Tingwald) on the Isle of Man, the oldest continuous parliament in the world, founded in AD940.

Follow the road as it winds past the farmhouse, the projecting porch a chicane for cars. This provides a lovely foreground subject for another good view north to the Langdale Pikes. The road bears left, and then you cross the bridge right, following the gated lane to cross **Greenburn Beck** at a second bridge and passing Bridge End, a simple house and lathe (integrated stock-barn) National Trust holiday let. The track merges with the old copper miners' path out of Greenburn and keeps to the left fork to reach a gate entering a narrow walled lane. Little Langdale Tarn is seen across the rush-filled pasture shielded to the right by a larch-crowned knoll. Notice the ageing yew short of High Hallgarth. The lane becomes even tighter during its descent to **Low Hallgarth**. Both former farmhouses are now club huts, the latter belonging to Yorkshire Rambling Club. Slate tip invades between. The lane leads on beneath the massive slate tips associated with **Cathedral Quarry**, now enchantingly screened by natural silver birch

Slater Bridge

growth. Go left at the hand-gate / wall-stile down to a further wall-stile and cross **Slater Bridge**, without question the most beautiful workaday bridge you will ever encounter.

It is rare indeed to have this place to yourself. It's an open secret, so just be thankful that visitors have to walk to the spot. One may ponder how old it is – several centuries at least. The rustic single-arched footbridge and clapper slate with metal handrail has no peers in Lakeland for sheer visual poetry. The sparkling waters of Little Langdale Beck weaving through the bedrock complement the whole.

Follow the wall to the second gap and traverse the pasture over the brow to reach a hand-gate onto the road, where you go left. There will be some pleasure that the walk ends as it began, at the **Three Shires Inn**, and now the bar door will beckon.

← Little Langdale and Little Langdale Quarry

Pavey Ark and Harrison Stickle from the New Dungeon Ghyll

*T*he emphatic heart of the Langdale Pikes, and a route with perennial appeal. The route climbs by Stickle Ghyll to the hanging valley tarn for a walk or scramble to the top of Pavey Ark before working its way round the head-combe onto Harrison Stickle, a major Lakeland landmark summit. The walk can so easily be embroidered to include any number of fell tops – Thunacar Knott, High Raise, Sergeant Man, Loft Crag and Pike o'Stickle – dependent on conditions and your state of readiness.
The world's your oyster and the skylarks are singing on high!

The Start

Either the National Park Authority Great Langdale car park or the National Trust Stickle Ghyll car park GR295064 (both pay and display). As an alternative, during summer months the Langdale Rambler bus service 516 runs the 8 miles between Ambleside and the Old Dungeon Ghyll Hotel.

The Route

Either follow the lane that leads to a gate between **Stickle Barn** and the **New Dungeon Ghyll Hotel**; or, from the National Trust car park, depart from the information shelter close to the toilet block, passing by the hand-gate into the small paddock to the rear of the buildings. Go through the copse passage and keep beside the rising beck, where a tree-shaded paved path leads to a footbridge spanning **Stickle Ghyll**. The farm below once harnessed the powerful flow – hence its name 'Millbeck'.

↑ *The Langdale Pikes from Chapel Stile*

ROUTE INFORMATION

Distance	6km/3¾ miles
Height gain	677m/2220ft
Time	4½ hours
Grade	energetic
Start point	GR295064
Maps	(Harvey Superwalker)
	Lakeland Central
	(Ordnance Survey)
	OL6 South-western area

After-walk refreshment

The New Dungeon Ghyll Hotel and the Stickle Barn, in the shadow of the Langdale Pikes

Stickle Ghyll, which means the 'steep ravine', has a succession of exciting falls to enjoy, some requiring short diversions from the well-paved trail to properly view. The path-pitching work has made this still rough route remarkably secure. In even recent memory it was an awful mess – its state a testimony to the popularity of this approach to the Pikes.

The stone staircase works up beneath **Tarn Crag** and close to a lovely series of cascades spilling from near the outflow of **Stickle Tarn**. Arrival at the tarn is a moment of well-earned rest. Attention is immediately caught by the magnificent cliff of Pavey

Ark reflected in the dark, shining waters. Such a mountain prospect deserves contemplation, as does your decision on whether to climb the North Rake or Jack's Rake to the summit of Pavey Ark.

The **North Rake** is the uncomplicated route to the top of Pavey Ark, hidden from view – a 'round the corner' ridge. Follow the path right along the shore of the tarn, fording a minor marshy gill that then follows and fords **Bright Beck** to begin the ascent of the prominent gully in the midst of the broad, somewhat indefinite north-east ridge. Wainwright coined the name North Rake; pedants might think it the East Rake. Whatever the name, there is only loose gravel underfoot to in any way handicap a steady climb. Make a point of glancing left at the head of Easy Gully for a fine view of the tarn. The outlooks otherwise are limited.

Jack's Rake, on the other hand, is far from limited; in fact it is elating. Be mindful that in wet, windy and/or icy conditions it enters the realms of serious mountaineering. At other times, when dry and calm air drifts across the crag, the scramble is an all-enthralling and memorable experience. The old-time favourite approach lies left from the tarn outflow, by the remains of the dam, the path swinging round from west to north to embark upon a steady, if a trifle loose scree incline, passing a prominent memorial cairn inscribed 'SWS 1900'. Reaching the

Upper section of Jack's Rake

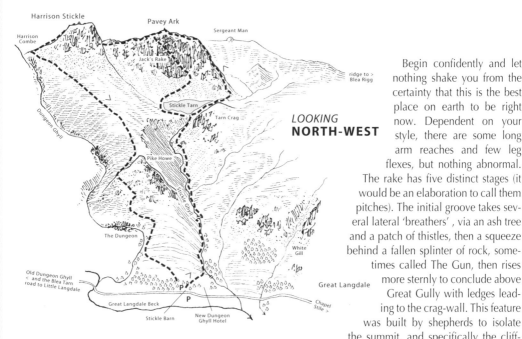

LOOKING
NORTH-WEST

Begin confidently and let nothing shake you from the certainty that this is the best place on earth to be right now. Dependent on your style, there are some long arm reaches and few leg flexes, but nothing abnormal. The rake has five distinct stages (it would be an elaboration to call them pitches). The initial groove takes several lateral 'breathers', via an ash tree and a patch of thistles, then a squeeze behind a fallen splinter of rock, sometimes called The Gun, then rises more sternly to conclude above Great Gully with ledges leading to the crag-wall. This feature was built by shepherds to isolate the summit, and specifically the cliff-edge, from wayward grazing sheep. A simple scramble over coarse boiler-plate rock leads to the summit cairn at 697m/2288ft.

base of the cliff right at its centre, find the first inviting pitch of Jack's Rake. It's hands on rock from the outset. If you can climb a step-ladder then you at least have the basics.

Pavey Ark is a fell apart – its soul and spirit the buttressing crag, the imminent fall from the summit

Pavey Ark and Stickle Tarn on the approach path to Jack's Rake

The impressive profile of Pavey Ark from Harrison Stickle, backed by Sergeant Man with the Helvellyn range beyond

giving a tingling sensation to any visit. The fell top, bereft of a cairn, is composed of an igneous rock displaying intricately confused patterns frozen from the molten state. There is one large perched erratic boulder to the south, and a few pools on the north and west side enhance the rock garden effect. Harrison Stickle dominates the westward view, but beyond the tarn attention focuses upon the Coniston Fells beyond Pike o'Blisco.

Harrison Stickle summit looking east towards Chapel Stile and Lingmoor Fell

Leave the summit, stepping over the wall, and follow the path bound for **Harrison Stickle**, which is in view from the start. The consistent path runs just under the edge, avoids the ridge-top rock tors, and links with the path climbing from the south shore of **Stickle Tarn**. There is scope for good sport in following the ridge-top all the way, though there is no continuous path. The final grassy rise to the summit is quite trouble free.

Being the focal summit of the Langdale Pikes bestows a certain dignity to the place, with an outlook to match. Resting upon a suitable rock plinth, the summit cairn at 736m/2415ft is a grand vantage-point down over Pavey Ark, into Great Langdale

and over Lingmoor Fell. The tilted plateau of bare rock provides several alternative situations to revel in – the views to Helvellyn, Bowfell, Great Gable, Glaramara and elsewhere.

Just make sure that you leave the summit saddle in a northerly direction. There is nothing but peril to the south. Paths are well enough marked by constant use. The easiest line is north, as if to Thunacar Knott, taking a left curving line to the south into the peaty hollow of **Harrison Combe**. The narrow path above the upper gorge of Dungeon Ghyll demands careful footing on the loose gravel path. Beyond, the way is straightforward, heading south-east to round **Pike How** to the right. However, the pimple top itself is worth visiting for its own intimate views over Stickle Ghyll. The path is a common descent route and this has taken its toll, though recent pitching has improved matters somewhat. The path comes down to a wall and keeps right, missing the lower ravine of **Dungeon Ghyll** to reach a high stile. Follow the wall on down the short way by a seat to a hand-gate, where you descend left to regain the wooded environs of the **New Dungeon Ghyll**.

31

Loft Crag and Pike o'Stickle from New Dungeon Ghyll

*F*or as long as man has gazed upon the Langdale Pikes they must have been revered. While each fell is a character in its own right, together they are greater than the sum of their considerable parts. They are truly a special part of our mountain heritage; a scenic catalyst at once captivating and compelling. From that instant adoration comes a desire for a 'must-do' ascent... so why delay? This exhilarating climb goes via Dungeon Ghyll onto Loft Crag, and culminates on the majestic rock stack summit of Pike o'Stickle. It then descends via Martcrag Moor and Langdale Combe to join the Cumbria Way's steep zig-zag descent into Mickleden.

The Start

Either the National Park Authority Great Langdale car park or the National Trust Stickle Ghyll car park GR295064 (both pay and display). As an alternative, during summer months the Langdale Rambler bus service 516 runs the 8 miles between Ambleside and the Old Dungeon Ghyll Hotel.

The Route

From the National Park car park follow the lane leading to, and between, the **New Dungeon Ghyll Hotel** and The Sticklebarn, passing through the gate beyond. Alternatively, from the National Trust car park, start from the interpretative shelter. Follow the confined path through, via a hand-gate, into the small paddock, meeting up with the former path.

↑ *Pike o'Stickle, Gimmer Crag and Harrison Stickle as seen from Wall End*

ROUTE INFORMATION

Distance	9.25km/5¾ miles
Height gain	610m/2000ft
Time	5 hours
Grade	strenuous
Start point	GR295064
Maps	(Harvey Superwalker)
	Lakeland Central
	(Ordnance Survey)
	OL6 South-western area

After-walk refreshment

Stickle Barn, New Dungeon Ghyll and Old Dungeon Ghyll Hotels in Great Langdale

Pass the Trust's **Stickle Ghyll** estate emblem sign, and after going through the coppice gap bear left. The part-pitched path rises quite roughly to a hand-gate at the top of the initial rise, where you go right, beside the wall. As the innocent-looking gill is seen close left, clamber over the tall stile.

Bear abruptly down left to rock-hop over the gill.

Under normal damp conditions this is no hazard. But this tame gill is about to get tough. It's **Dungeon Ghyll** after all, and the dungeon is imminent. You may enter the dark chasm, but a timorous retreat is inevitable for all but the hardened scrambler as there is no way through. A giant chock-stone is a notable feature, as too is a fuming fall, the defile environment a haven for ferns and mosses revelling in the tumultuous permanently shady hydro-sanctuary. Backtrack and step back onto the pitched path, from where the chasm is hidden and only intimated by sprigs of birch and holly. The second phase of Dungeon Ghyll leads to a beautiful waterfall that can be admired from the pitched path.

Walkers with zest can choose to follow the gill rather than the lower section of Mark Gate. For the former, cross the gill, scrambling up the steep bracken bank (almost no path) to follow it into the gill by a rocky shelf path above this fall. There a natural line, involving some boulder hopping, leads to a terminating fall. It is quite the most graceful of the suite of falls associated with this tremendous

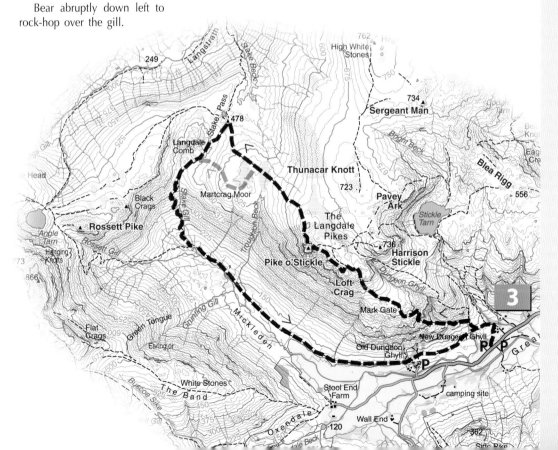

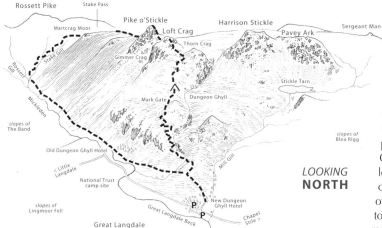

Rossett Pike · Stake Pass · Pike o'Stickle · Loft Crag · Harrison Stickle · Sergeant Man · Martcrag Moor · Thorn Crag · Pavey Ark · Gimmer Crag · Stickle Tarn · Stake Gill · Rossett Gill · Mickleden · Mark Gate · Dungeon Ghyll · slopes of Blea Rigg · slopes of The Band · Old Dungeon Ghyll Hotel · Mill Gill · Little Langdale · National Trust camp site · New Dungeon Ghyll Hotel · slopes of Lingmoor Fell · Great Langdale Beck · Chapel Stile · Great Langdale

LOOKING NORTH

On gaining the alp pasture, Harrison Stickle comes strikingly into view above the upper portion of Dungeon Ghyll. Mark Gate drifts left, passing a small ragged cairn, indicating the start of the climbers' traverse to Gimmer Crag. Pitching resumes, and is well bedded-in in this section, an excellent example of the craft; this locally imported stone is precisely set to encourage walkers to stick resolutely to the path. At last the higher ground is reached overlooking the peat hollow of Harrison Combe. Where the paths fork, keep left.

While a steady path continues on the flank of **Loft Crag** it is more fun to reach the summit, so take to the rake left, with loose stones a minor inconvenience at the start. The 2270ft/692m summit of Loft Crag, marked with a modest cairn, commands a

watercourse, and the sense of being within the bosom of the mountain is most profound. A gully to the left, an apparent baulk to progress, gives an easy scrambling escape onto the broad grassy shelf where the cairns of **Mark Gate** are met. Faithful followers of Mark Gate will find their progress constructively pitch-stepped and cairned, an occasional pause giving the excuse to peer down on the pastures of the curving line of Great Langdale.

↑ *Loft Crag from the west*

Eastern aspect of Pike o'Stickle from Loft Crag →

Pike o'Stickle seen during the descent of Stake Pass

lovely view of Harrison Stickle, the father-figure of the Langdale Pikes. From this spot the most stunning component of Loft Crag, Gimmer Crag, is unseen – the location of some of the sternest and, to the climber, most compelling rock climbs in Lakeland. The best view of the crag is to be had from Pike o'Stickle. But walkers with a head for heights can descend cautiously down the south ridge to reach the col at the top of the crag. This exciting narrow neck between South-east and Junipal Gullies provides a superb vantage for Pike o'Stickle. Clamber back to continue.

Follow the ridge to reach the top of South Screes, the incredible drop towards Mickleden no inducement to scree-running. Indeed, for the protection of the cave part-way down the gully that served as a Neolithic stone-axe factory, this is just as well. Pitched steps guide on to the north side of the striking rock stack, with several late choices for the mild scramble to the 2323ft/708m top. **Pike o'Stickle**, a contraction of the Pike of Harrison Stickle, is a real mountain summit, for all the moorland slopes run away to the north towards Thunacar Knott and High Raise.

The view commands the great amphitheatre at the head of Great Langdale. Pike o'Blisco, backed by the Coniston Fells, Crinkle Crags and Bowfell, can be seen tip to toe. Westwards spot Great Gable and Glaramara, with the summit of Scafell Pike only showing between Bowfell and Esk Pike, while northwards eyes are led to Skiddaw.

Retrace your scramble north to resume your walk – all other directions lead to awful calamity! The path north-north-west leads steadily down the fell, crossing a patch of exposed peat, the erosion eased by stepping stones. As the moorland levels one may bear left and follow a path that zig-zags down the west side of Troughton Beck, but the more natural circuit should include Martcrag Moor and the Stake Pass path.

As the marshy moor swells, break left off the obvious path to thread a way through the pools and marshy ground to reach the distinctive bouldery crest of **Martcrag Moor**. This magical spot commands a grand view down the lower zig-zags of the Stake Pass path to the moraine beneath Rossett Gill, while high above rises Bowfell, with Bowfell Buttress, Cambridge and Flat Crags prominent.

The mingle of large boulders on this scarp edge gives scope for temporary shelter in hostile weather. Walk north either back to the ridge path to accompany it to **Stake Pass**, or better still turn left after some 150m. The thinnest trace of a path descends the pasture slope, largely over grass interspersed with boulders. This joins the Stake Pass path at the lower edge of the pillow moraine of **Langdale Comb**.

On joining the Cumbria Way, an inevitably popular route, go left fording **Stake Gill**. Old and new pitching is evident on the many twists and turns of this steep descent. The cascades of Stake Gill can be exciting to see, though the two are separated in the lower stages. Passing an old fold and a slate sign distinguishing the paths to Esk Hause and Stake Pass, cross the wooden bridge and set forth on the level track, a welcome contrast to the steep ground of recent adventure. **Mickleden**, which means the 'big green valley', is a classic product of glacier erosion, with hanging valleys and extremely steep valley sides.

Eventually walled enclosures come close and a gated gathering fold is passed through, en route to the drove lane that leads to the **Old Dungeon Ghyll Hotel**. Keep left, and above the hotel grounds following the hand-gated walled drove lane to complete the walk.

Bowfell and Rossett Pike
from the Old Dungeon Ghyll

*B*owfell ranks high in many fell-walkers' esteem. It is rooted in Great Langdale, from where its peaked summit has all the air of an emperor's throne, set high above a defending fringe of impressive buttresses and distanced by the long tongue of The Band. The walk sets course up The Band to follow either the rough trail from above Three Tarns or, more ambitiously, the Climbers' Traverse to step onto the thrilling tilted ramp of Flat Crags. The magnificent panoramic summit is a worthy culmination to the day's endeavours.

The route heads on by Ore Gap to join the high dale-connecting trail from Sty Head, and switches east on Tongue Head to pass the outflow of Angle Tarn to either descend Rossett Gill directly or stride handsomely onto Rossett Pike. From there on it follows Mickleden's headwall ridge to Stake Pass. Joining the Cumbria Way through the moraine maze of Langdale Comb the route works down the well-engineered zig-zags into Mickleden – the flat glacial dale an amazing contrast to the soaring fellsides on either flank.

↑ Afternoon sunlight dances across Three Tarns with Mickledore and the Scafells in silhouette   37

ROUTE INFORMATION

Distance	12km/7½ miles
Height gain	854m/2800ft
Time	7 hours
Grade	strenuous
Start point	GR286061
Maps	(Harvey Superwalker)
	Lakeland Central
	(Ordnance Survey)
	OL6 South-western area

After-walk refreshment

Old and New Dungeon Ghyll Hotels and the Stickle Barn, all in the upper portion of Great Langdale, in the immediate shadow of the Langdale Pikes

← Langdale Rambler bus stop at the Old Dungeon Ghyll, backed by Raven Crag and Middlefell Buttress

The Start

From the National Park pay and display car park adjoining the Old Dungeon Ghyll Hotel GR286061 situated in Great Langdale. As an alternative, during summer months the Langdale Rambler bus service 516 runs the 8 miles between Ambleside and the Old Dungeon Ghyll Hotel.

The Route

From the car park either backtrack along the approach road to the bus stop, turning right to the sharp bend, or reach the same point via the old stone bridge, having crossed the paddock via gates. Now embark on the farm-access drive which leads via gates over **Oxendale Beck** and through the busy **Stool End Farm**. Rising beyond to the brow, watch for the breaking path to the right onto The Band ridge.

Pass up to a kissing-gate beside the Hamer memorial seat. The ridge path has received considerable necessary repair work at many stages all the way up.

At the first pronounced step cast a glance down right onto the dense bank of juniper and into Mickleden. Higher the path veers off the natural line of the ridge, taking a side-swipe and missing the actual top of **The Band**. A detour to visit the edge of Earing Crag (eagle's

crag) provides the perfect opportunity to gain a full-on view of Mickleden and the imminent majesty of Bowfell.

From this grassy top re-join the continuing trail. At the shallow depression GR255062, the path forks (see alternative route below). The main right-hand path completes the stony ascent to Three Tarns hause GR248061, though it is rare to see more than two sheets of water. The ridges and gullies of Bowfell Links dominate the view from this point, as too, across the south ridge of Esk Pike, do the twin peaks of Scafell and Scafell Pike on either side of Mickledore. A rough, stony path clambers up the southern flank of Bowfell, reaching the summit by the top of **Flat Crags**.

ROUTE VIA THE CLIMBERS' TRAVERSE

The confident walker, with a head for heights and well-adjusted mountain feet, may wish to consider following the Climbers' Traverse, branching from the main route at the depression GR255062. Rising with the ridge and passing over to the shadowy northern side, the path is consistent but narrow. In some respects it is more exposed than Jack's Rake, so in wet or icy conditions most walkers should give it a miss. The traverse keeps under the banded cliff-end of Flat Crags, and, from the minor col, gains a handsome view of Bowfell Buttress, flanked by runs of scree, across the combe. Coming under the broken wall of Cambridge Crag, the path switches up left, onto the bouldery corner, running up the tilted Great Slab of Flat Crags. If the rock is dry you might find it more comfortable, and certainly more exhilarating, to walk up the open slab itself – just watch your footing on any wet algae. The topmost outcropping exhibits well the banded nature of the volcanic bedrock. The view is consistently exciting, especially back to the Langdale Pikes.

Climbers' Traverse to Bowfell Buttress and access to the great slab of Flat Crags

Flat Crags →

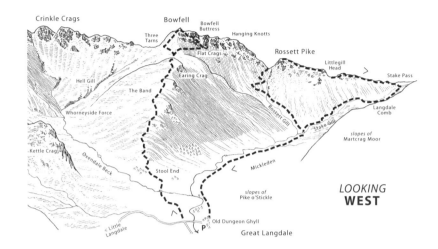

Crinkle Crags · Bowfell · Bowfell Buttress · Hanging Knotts · Three Tarns · Flat Crags · Rossett Pike · Littlegill Head · Stake Pass · Hell Gill · Earing Crag · The Band · Rossett Gill · Whorneyside Force · Langdale Comb · Stake Gill · Kettle Crag · Oxendale Beck · Mickleden · slopes of Martcrag Moor · Stool End · slopes of Pike o'Stickle · Old Dungeon Ghyll · Little Langdale · Great Langdale

LOOKING **WEST**

The final strides to the summit are soon accomplished, though the southern edge above the gullies of Bowfell Links may be visited, in advance, to view the Crinkle Crags ridge. At 903m/2963ft **Bowfell** has a marvellously comprehensive Lakeland panorama. Among the large loose stones composing the summit cairn is one flake inscribed with an Ordnance Survey benchmark, dating from the survey of 1861 – a rare survival in such a loose form. Any visit to the top on a clear day should also include a cautious inspection of the top of Cambridge Crags, some 50m to the north-east, from where there is the most sensational view of the Great Slab of Flat Crags and the prodigious cliff of Bowfell Buttress.

Leave the summit in a northerly direction on a path that latterly drifts stonily down west into

Ore Gap, a name that suggests a shepherds' over-egging of a minor mineral exposure. Turn north under the shadowed walls of Esk Pike to link up with the ancient bridleway on **Tongue Head** curving right, down to ford the outflow of **Angle Tarn**. Miners were of a habit of stocking the fell tarns with fish to supplement their diet, so for all its isolation the name implies a fertile fishing basin. The backdrop of Hanging Knotts casts lovely reflections in the almost perfectly round lake, a popular wild camp site. As the path rises watch for the left-hand fork off the Rossett Gill trail. The main trail down the gill has received major restorative work – hugely necessary as it is used by vast numbers heading, in the main, to and from Scafell Pike. This way goes down to the head of Mickleden, gaining further neck-turning views up to Bowfell Buttress on the way down.

The main route steps onto the emerging ridge which leads onto the neat little top of **Rossett Pike** at 651m/2136ft – a superb spot from which to gaze up at Bowfell's high cliffs, with Flat Crags and Bowfell Buttress prominent. Advance to the east cairn to survey Mickleden and admire the Langdale Pikes, featuring Pike o'Stickle, Harrison Stickle and Gimmer Crag beneath Loft Crag. Turn north with the ridge, which duly dips off **Littlegill Head** through a saddle. A narrow path can be followed down to Stake Gill from this point, but the ridge is worth holding, latterly on an edge-path which leads down by a pool to the large cairn marking the summit of **Stake Pass**. This ancient bridle trail is now a route for Cumbria Way trekkers.

Turn right, with the trail leading down the east side of the moraine-filled hollow **Langdale Comb**. After fording Stake Gill the path takes a series of well-engineered zig-zags, again benefiting

from recent repair. Stake Gill provides some entertainment initially, but gradually the path drifts away from its fuming antics to reach a wooden footbridge where the Rossett Gill bridleway is joined. Cross the bridge and stride out along the turf highway along the floor of **Mickleden**. As you progress, the streaking screes of Pike o'Stickle will turn your eyes up to the soaring stack and later to Gimmer Crag. After a gate the track follows a wall to arrive back at the **Old Dungeon Ghyll**, with Middle Fell Buttress and Raven Crag looming above the conifer copse.

Angle Tarn backed by Hanging Knotts the northern ramparts of Bowfell

Pike o'Blisco and Crinkle Crags from the Old Dungeon Ghyll

*C*rinkle Crags offer a classic Lakeland ridge walk that fully lives up to the expectations its exciting eastern aspect suggests. Undertaken in conjunction with the highly individual peak of Pike
o'Blisco, one has the ingredients for a thoroughly rewarding day on the fell. Keen fell walkers will
eagerly mop up Cold Pike, and on the way round they might include Little Stand. If energies are up,
however, they will be more inclined to bolster their mountain day with the mighty scalp of Bowfell.
The tour concentrates on Oxendale, and brings the drama of Hell Gill and Whorneyside Force into
the equation.

↑ *Bog bean in a pool on Blake Rigg looking to Pike o'Blisco*   43

Distance	13.5km/8½ miles
Height gain	1158m/3800ft
Time	7½ hours
Grade	strenuous
Start point	GR286061
Maps	(Harvey Superwalker)
	Lakeland Central
	(Ordnance Survey)
	OL6 South-western area

After-walk refreshment

Old and New Dungeon Ghyll Hotels and the Stickle Barn, all in the upper portion of Great Langdale, in the immediate shadow of the Langdale Pikes

The Start

The National Park pay and display car park adjoining the Old Dungeon Ghyll Hotel GR286061 situated in Great Langdale. As an alternative, during summer months the Langdale Rambler bus service 516 runs the 8 miles between Ambleside and the Old Dungeon Ghyll Hotel.

The Route

From the car park either backtrack along the approach road to the bus stop, turning right to the sharp bend, or reach the same point via the old stone bridge across the paddock via gates. Follow the Blea Tarn road, passing **Wall End Farm** and 'squeezing' by the roadside barn. After crossing the cattle grid the open road begins a winding ascent – avoid the car fumes as best you can. At the third sharp hairpin bend take leave of the tarmac and set foot on the fell proper, embarking upon the main path up the **Redacre Gill** valley. The path fords three minor gills

The Langdale Pikes from the head of Skull Gill on Pike o'Blisco

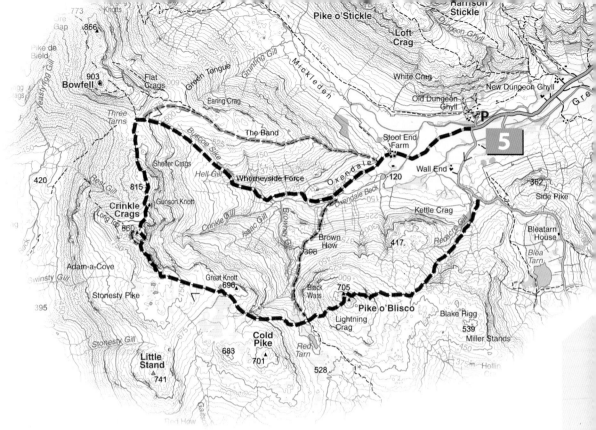

PIKE O'BLISCO

en route to the headstream, where some pitching copes with the gully that rises to the skyline.

Here walkers will notice **Kettle Crag**, a striking feature to the right. The name has nothing to do with boiling kettles, but has its roots in the Old English term 'cetel', meaning 'the valley with a deep inlet'. The name is therefore highly descriptive of Oxendale at the threshold to the valley leading towards Crinkle Crags.

Reaching the open fell ridge with its diverse habitat of heather and bilberries, some walkers may wish to trace the ridge back left. Bejewelled with tiny tarns the ridge rises easily onto the headland of **Blake Rigg**, a marvellous viewpoint over Little Langdale to Wetherlam. Otherwise, keep to a westward rising line passing a massive bare slab, en route to a short scramble through a rock-band shielding the square crown of the fell. The summit of **Pike o'Blisco** has two tops – both have sizeable cairns, though there is no doubt which is the senior partner, the north cairn at 705m/2313ft. From here Crinkle Crags' skyline is seen to perfection, with Bowfell contriving to play second fiddle, in stark contrast to the first impression gained down in the valley where the walk began.

Alfred Wainwright described the fell name as 'swashbuckling', and it certainly rings with a sense of pirates and buccaneers. Time has obscured its original associations, leaving us with 'the pike of the howe of Blisc'. While who or what Blisc was may never be determined, the magic in the name and the joy of the fell top combine to make this a wonderful place to be.

Many walkers arrive on the summit from off the top of Wrynose Pass, passing up by Black Crag. This is a popular summer-evening rock climbing venue – a crag that unusually basks in the last sunlight of the day and, despite its high situation, is comparatively handy for the road.

The pre-1974 Westmorland county mark beat its bounds onto the south top, tracing up from the Three Shire Stone before switching sharply back at a 35 degree angle to the south side of Red Tarn en route to Cold Pike.

And so now to the main event – **Crinkle Crags**. A clear, part-pitched, part-loose-gravel path works its way down the comparatively steep western slopes from between the two summit blocks of Pike o'Blisco. Reaching the depression some hundred metres north of **Red Tarn**, the route crosses straight over the path intersection.

Crinkle Crags and Bowfell from the northern slopes of Pike o'Blisco

The right-hand path, rising from the head of Browney Gill, has some contemporary interest – not only in that you may decide to abort the grand plan here and pass down this way to Oxendale, but in the construction of the **pitched path** itself.

The modern era of path pitching began with the National Trust, who studied the construction of old pitched paths and made every effort to replicate it in their work. The flaw was that they were looking at the paths after they had suffered many decades of often heavy use, so that steps that originally would have been pitched up, were now tilted down.

Once this was recognised, construction was changed, and the transition to the more modern approach occurs part-way down this path. The latest news from the Fix the Fells team is that this older pitching is to be reconstructed to bring it up to the modern spec!

The journey resumes, heading west on a rising path crossing the northern slopes of Cold Pike above the upper ravine of **Browney Gill**. Intrepid walkers will relish leaving the regular path and making onto the adjacent top of **Great Knott**, following the broken edge to Gladstone Knott. Though the crooked pinnacle of Gladstone's Finger

is out of sight, only seen from below, the knott itself provides the most superb view across Great Cove to the two main Crinkles, separated by the gap of Mickle Door. The majority of walkers will be more than content to follow the defined way, higher up being corralled by stones to resist rebroadening the wear. Mount onto the first Crinkle, otherwise nameless, where the **Crinkle Crags ridge** proper begins, as does the fun.

Each crinkle has its own cairn, an understandable circumstance, as each has the bearing of a separate fell. Heading for the first crinkle the path dips through a small grassy depression to meet the only real challenge of the day. The natural ascent works up a scree gully headed with a massive choke of stone, with a three-move scramble up a rib to the right the only recourse. If you cannot face the sequence of moves (inevitably harder in descent) you can bear left at the depression and ascend a grassy rake on an inevitably worn path. Face-saving in every way, both routes come together on the crown of **Long Top** at 860m/2822ft.

The second crinkle may look compact from Gladstone Knott and all points east, but from Eskdale it has the appearance of a flat-topped mountain, in striking contrast to Bowfell's slender peak. The next depression is **Mickle Door**, 'the great gap', and this

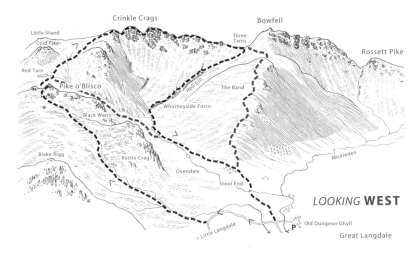

Crinkle Crags
Little Stand
Cold Pike
Red Tarn
Pike o'Blisco
Black Warrs
Blake Rigg
Kettle Crag
Oxendale
Stool End
Bowfell
Three Tarns
Rossett Pike
The Band
Whorneyside Force
Hell Gill
Mickleden
Old Dungeon Ghyll
< Little Langdale
Great Langdale

LOOKING **WEST**

leads on to the third crinkle and then weaves on via crinkles four and five. The last of these, **Gunson Knott**, cradles a large innominate reed-filled tarn. Ahead Bowfell forms an impressive backdrop to the ridge, the peaked summit rising above the gullies of Bowfell Links.

The walk all along the ridge provides an unending chain of delightful changes in outlook and terrain, superb in any measure. Further small tarns are encountered en route to **Shelter Crags**, with further rough dips leading by the final blunt rocky knott short of **Three Tarns**. To complete the trio of tarns one has to include one of a pair of delightful rock-girt pools entangled in the slabs south of the pass depression. To the west see the more famous Mickledore, separating Scafell from Scafell Pike – invariably, by this stage in the walk, the scene is backlit by a

lowering sun sending streaks of golden light across the shallow tarns. On reaching the saddle the impressive Bowfell Links loom, with a steep path mounting for the summit.

However, our route turns east and almost at once bears right, tracing its way down by the emerging stream, **Buscoe Sike**. A definite path emerges along the edge as the sike steepens into a deep ravine, in the process becoming the altogether more treacherous **Hell Gill**. The path steepens, coming down to the foot of the ravine on pitching. There is little or no scope to enter the ravine, and certainly no route up through it. The path continues down to the top of **Whorneyside Force**, a gracious waterfall. The path then carefully negotiates a scoured slope, from where the waterfall is seen at its best. Crossing a footbridge the path enters **Oxendale**, passing on down by gates to **Stool End Farm** and following its approach road to the **Old Dungeon Ghyll Hotel** road-end.

The bad step scramble onto Long Top

Pike o'Blisco from the head of Hell Gill

47

Wetherlam from Coniston

*L*et the crowds congregate on Coniston Old Man, but they who know a good thing will seek out
the many sides of Wetherlam and return for more. Often called the hollow mountain because of
all the mine shafts that pepper its not inconsiderable flanks, the fell has several fine finger ridges and
secret dells to delve into. This walk puts the emphasis on quest rather than pure conquest, gathering
in the Yewdale Fells scarp en route to Tilberthwaite Ghyll and the wonderful climb onto Wetherlam
Edge. It then descends the south ridge from Black Sails via the Thriddle Incline into the Coppermines
Valley and so down beside Church Beck.

The Start
One may arrive at Coniston by Coniston Rambler
bus, or by car, parking in the lower part of village
or even down by the lake. Most convenient to this
expedition is the tree-shaded back lane beside
Yewdale Beck close to Shepherd Bridge, near the
recreation ground and primary school GR304977.

The Route
The walk begins by following the back lane beside
Yewdale Beck and crossing the busy Tilberthwaite

Road into Far End. The subsequent lane leads past
the youth hostel to turn left up the passage by **Far
End** Cottages and reach a hand-gate. Here the route
meets the lateral path from the Coppermines Valley
access track, which runs on right through beautiful bluebell woods below the Yewdale Fells. More
impressive and rewarding is the climb to the top
of that scarp, achieved by embarking upon the
ascent direct from the hand-gate ahead. The climb
is nowhere near as tough as first impressions may
lead one to think, and the views en route back over

↑ *Cottage at Low Tilberthwaite, with spinning gallery*

ROUTE INFORMATION

Distance	13.25km/8¼ miles
Height gain	924m/3030ft
Time	7 hours
Grade	strenuous
Start point	GR304977
Maps	(Harvey Superwalker) Lakeland South West (Ordnance Survey) OL6 South-western area

After-walk refreshment

Black Bull, Ship and Yewdale Inns, Crown and Sun Hotels, together with several tearooms, including the centrally sited Satterthwaite, all in or close to Coniston village

the Coniston vale are hugely satisfying. Small cairns help identify the variably apparent path crossing the headstream of **White Gill**, which has a striking water-slide feature when viewed from Yewdale below. The headland of **Yewdale Crag** may tempt a visit off the path before weaving through the juniper scrub and past the old Penny Rigg slate quarry upon a grassy incline track to reach the road at **Low Tilberthwaite**.

Pass on by the sheepfold created by the artist Andy Goldsworthy to step up the stone steps, left, directly from the car park. Regular paths exist on either side of **Tilberthwaite Gill**, with a through connection by a mid-course scenic footbridge. The path on the south provides an insight into the long dormant slate workings of **Tilberthwaite Quarry**. For much of its life the Coniston/Foxfield Branch Railway served almost exclusively as a means of dispatch for the local slate, which explains why Coniston Old Station Yard is so high in the village.

Wetherlam Edge from Hawk Rigg

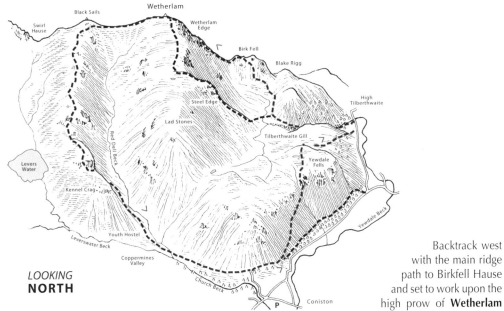

Having crossed the footbridge the path climbs to the lateral path, a mine access way decorated with larch whose picturesque qualities are hard to ignore. Bearing right at the head of the ravine, the path surveys an area of old copper-mine workings. Wetherlam is one of the most complex fells in the district, not so much in terms of surface features, but rather its hidden depths – its holey-ness. Rising above Dry Cove the path climbs stepped pitching onto **Birk Fell**. Once upon the ridge, one may make a right-hand turn to visit a solitary cairn with the most stunning view over Little Langdale.

Backtrack west with the main ridge path to Birkfell Hause and set to work upon the high prow of **Wetherlam Edge**. The climb includes several rocky steps, but nothing extraordinary to halt you in your tracks for long. One gets so involved with the task that, as so often, the summit arrives with a certain disbelief, but no less relief! At 762m/2500ft the ragged cairn marks a point of major scenic delight. The commanding view takes in all the grand surround of the Langdales backed by the Scafells, with Glaramara, Skiddaw, Helvellyn and the High Street ranges, and of course the near neighbours in the Coniston group, all vying for attention.

Wetherlam summit looking north

Follow the ridge path heading west down an early stony slope. Two paths converge to cross peaty ground on the shallow plateau hollow at the head of **Red Dell**. As the clear stony path begins to drift down to Swirl Hawse, make a move left to reach the summit cairn on **Black Sails**. Follow the ridge south. An entertaining, largely grassy ridge with its rockier moments leads down by some wonderfully striated rocks above **Levers Water**, with a handsome view of Raven Tor, the bold shoulder of Brim Fell, looming above the dam. The name 'Levers Water' may derive from the Norse personal name 'Lafhere'.

The oldest copper mine is thought to be Paddy End, situated below Raven Tor. Its massive rift is an eye-catching feature at the head of Boulder Valley, witnessed as you begin the descent, either from the dam down the rough access track, or more satisfyingly (and as described here) from off the **Kennel Crag** ridge. From this point bear left rounding to a grill-gated mine adit at the top of the Thriddle

Water-wheel pit of the Thriddle Incline in the Coppermines Valley, Red Dell Beck

Incline. Follow the incline down by a further adit to the old wheel-pit at the bottom. Here Red Dell Beck is known as the **Coppermines Valley**.

Follow the obvious path traversing the lower slopes of the Lad Stones ridge, witnessing the cascades of Red Dell Beck falling below the **Coppermines Cottages** and **youth hostel** buildings, all active survivals from the copper-mine days. Switch down by Irish Row, an old miners' terrace, to join the valley track. Head down dale, crossing to the far side of Church Beck via **Miners' Bridge** to complete the descent into the village by Dixon Ground and the Sun Hotel. The hotel has its place in Lakeland rock-climbing history, as the Fell and Rock Climbing Club held their inaugural summer meet there in 1907.

Striated rocks on the Black Sails ridge

Dow Crag and Coniston Old Man
from Coniston

*T*he route begins on the Walna Scar Road, rising towards the rock bastion of Dow Crag. Walkers can either stay on the rough track to the top of the pass, climbing onto Brown and Buck Pikes, or – more adventurously – visit The Cove and Goat's Water to scramble up the south rake. Striding down via Goat's Hawse, the walk mounts onto Coniston Old Man, completing the round by descending Little Arrow Moor.

Anyone with time in hand upon reaching the summit of the Walna Scar Road may be tempted to gather up the three tops of the continuing Walna Scar ridge, by bearing left. Walna Scar, plus White Maiden and White Pike, are three grand viewpoints in their own right, with far-ranging views beyond Caw to Duddon Sands. Walkers can then backtrack to climb onto Brown Pike and continue the walk.

↑ *The craggy facade of Dow Crag from Coniston Old Man*

ROUTE INFORMATION

Distance	8.75km/5½ miles
Height gain	742m/2434ft
Time	5 hours
Grade	energetic
Start point	GR289971
Maps	(Harvey Superwalker)
	Lakeland South West
	(Ordnance Survey)
	OL6 South-western area

After-walk refreshment

Black Bull, Ship and Yewdale Inns, Crown and Sun Hotels, together with several tearooms, including the centrally sited Satterthwaite, all in or close to Coniston village

The Start

For all Coniston's handsome position at the threshold of the fells, its car parking has a bias towards lake visitors. In the upper part of the village there is the Old Station car park, left from the Sun Hotel, location of the mountain rescue post. However, for this walk one may just as well drive all the way up the Walna Scar Road

to the fell-gate to use the generous space on the edge of Banishead Common at GR289971 – a springboard with a distinct height saving of some 500ft, being set at 225m/740ft.

Pre-amble

Early climbers were attracted to **Dow Crag's** gullies, horrid places in comparison to the projecting buttresses. The date attributed to the first climb is 1886, though the first properly established route came in 1904. It was here that the Lakeland Fell and Rock Climbing Club was born, the Sun Hotel the setting of its first meet in 1907. Wainwright called Dow Crag 'second only to Scafell Crag in the magnificence of its rock architecture'.

A name synonymous with **Dow Crag** is Harry Griffin, a journalist with a passion for climbing and the great outdoors who supplied *The Guardian* with a 'Country Dairy' column for a staggering 53 years.

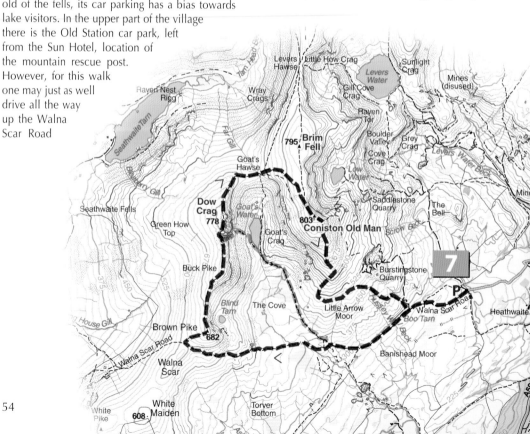

Dow Crag from the South Rake, with the blue mountain rescue MRP stretcher box at its base

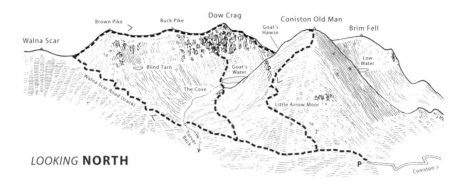

LOOKING **NORTH**

years. Harry coined the terms 'Coniston Tigers' and 'Cragrats' for the fraternity of local climbers, many from his native Barrow-in-Furness, who pioneered routes here. 'Tigers' derives from Nepalese sherpas' name for the adventurous European mountaineers for whom they portered; while 'cragrats' referred to the climbers' instinct for forcing their way up thin cracks and grooves.

John Ruskin, the great Victorian philanthropist and one of the first conservationists, gazed daily upon the **Coniston Fells** from his home of Brantwood on the eastern shores of Coniston Water. With assured wisdom he pronounced that 'mountains were the beginning and end of all natural scenery', and certainly the Coniston Fells always gladden my eyes.

Coniston is the home of the oldest mountain rescue team in Britain, founded in 1947.

The overwhelming majority of fell walkers set their sights on **Coniston Old Man** alone. So to venture further west means that you are less likely to encounter fellow walkers. The significance of this is not conviviality, it is safety – if you get into difficulties you may be more than just lonely in time of need. Winter can bring ice and snow (cornicing on the eastern lip of the ridges), as well as mist, rain and the treachery of wind.

The name **Goat's Water** has a clear allusion to the wild goats that could pick perilous grazing from the cliff. But the word 'goat', like 'cove', might have its roots in pre-Anglian terminology – for, rather like Pen-y-ghent (Yorkshire Three Peaks) and Castell-y-gwynt (Snowdonia), it just might be adapted from these words for wind. The unusual south-facing corrie here has a tendency to generate fierce gusts – winds that can whip the surface of the tarn and

carry walkers, and water, high up towards the cliff … be warned!

The Route

Drive up from **Coniston** via Station Road passing the Sun Hotel. The steep lane eases then bends left, from where there is a more gradual rise to the fellgate, one mile distant from the village (with ample informal car parking). Immediately the tarred road gives way to a rough track heading south-east along the natural line of transition between the Borrowdale volcanic rocks of the Old Man and the lower-lying Silurian shales of Banishead Moor.

Winter gives some chance of locating the Bronze Age stone circle set in the bracken below **Boo Tarn**. The tarn, nothing more than rushes, comes just after the barred access track climbing right to Burstingstone Quarry, which is at the foot of our ultimate descent from the Old Man. Pass through two rock cuttings: quarrymen from the slate quarry above Blind Tarn enlarged the ancient cross-ridge way. A large cairn, where the path up from Torver via Banishead Quarry crosses, marks the point of decision – whether to take the main route to Dow Crag via Brown and Buck Pikes or (more adventurously) to go via The Cove and Goat's Water then make a simple scramble up the south rake. (Note: avoid the alternative route in mist or bad weather.)

The **main route** continues upon the track, crossing Cove Bridge and winding up the zig-zagging way to the top of the pass, passing near the top a stone alcove shelter (replica of the tiny booths beside Small Water in the Far Eastern Fells). Switch right, climbing the rather loose path to the first summit cairn of the day, **Brown Pike**, at 682m/2238ft. The view into the bowl of Blind Tarn will be keenly anticipated, and the mystery of its outflow not resolved should you venture to the tarn itself, there being nothing more than a surreptitious soak away, though the crystal-clear waters will delight. Small populations of char and trout, established by quarrymen for sustenance and recreation, linger in the tarn.

Follow the natural ridge, making a second step up to the cairn on **Buck Pike**. Now the scarp edge becomes all the more enthralling and, at the point at which the south rake path arrives (alternative route: see below), you gain a superb profiled view of the famous cliff. The main cliff of **Dow Crag**, pronounced as you would 'doe' (as in deer), is composed of five projecting buttresses and six gullies – Easy Gully, to the left of Great Gully, being in the realm of rock climbers.

Ordnance Survey pillar on Coniston Old Man looking to the Scafells

ALTERNATIVE ROUTE

The alternative approach begins back down at the large cairn off the Walna Scar Road. The path, well used, being pitched at various points, rises up the open bowl of The Cove. A rock band intervenes, though easily overcome, and the path strides on towards the outflow of Goat's Water. The main path keeps to the eastern shore, mounting beyond the tarn to Goat's Hawse. However, our intent is the south rake.

Walkers with red blood racing through their veins will enjoy this more challenging route, but in mischievous mist or if the elements are bitter, steer clear. Ford the outflow and follow one of the inevitably loose, steep scree paths from the shelter boulders to the blue mountain-rescue first-aid box. From there trend left along the base of the cliffs to ascend south rake, a name coined by Wainwright. It's a superb simple scramble, gaining an intimate perspective on this magnificent climbing ground.

The two routes join here. On reaching the ridge go right. The ridge path comes up over a broken wall, in former days set up to steer sheep away from the cliff. It is not uncommon to spot the odd ewe and/ or lamb nibbling along tiny ledges, mindless of their peril. The path scrambles onto **Dow Crag's** rock-castle summit – a cairn is superfluous. This is among the top tier of Lakeland fell tops. Having witnessed Dow Crag from below, standing at its apex is a sensation quite without rival. If the rocks are the least bit icy, tread warily. Coniston Old Man looks nothing from this side; the Duddon and the distant Scafells amply compensate, but the main focus of attention will be the cliff's edge ... and rightly so!

The ridge path steps cautiously down then proceeds more easily, curving to cross straight over **Goat's Hawse**, dialect variant spelling of 'hause', meaning 'a pass'. As the path forks, keep to the right-hand edge, curving from east to south en route to Coniston Old Man. Higher up, the view back to Dow Crag is ever more impressive. The edge arrives, allowing a fabulous view down into the corrie cradling Low Water and beyond into the Coppermines Valley. Reminiscent of Scafell Pike, the summit of **Coniston Old Man** (803m/2635ft) has an Ordnance Survey pillar and a ravaged squat slate tower; many would rate this the better viewpoint. Certainly it is easier to reach, and the imminent fall of the slopes gives a wonderful sense of spaciousness. It is the scene of many a picnic and therefore many a ravenous raven.

Leave the summit in a south-south-east direction. Note that this is not the popular and very steep path leading down to **Low Water**. Cairns come to your aid on this path less travelled. It runs across the south ridge on **Little Arrow Moor**, curving to the edge overlooking The Cove before bearing left and stepping down via ledges to ultimately come onto the **Walna Scar Road**.

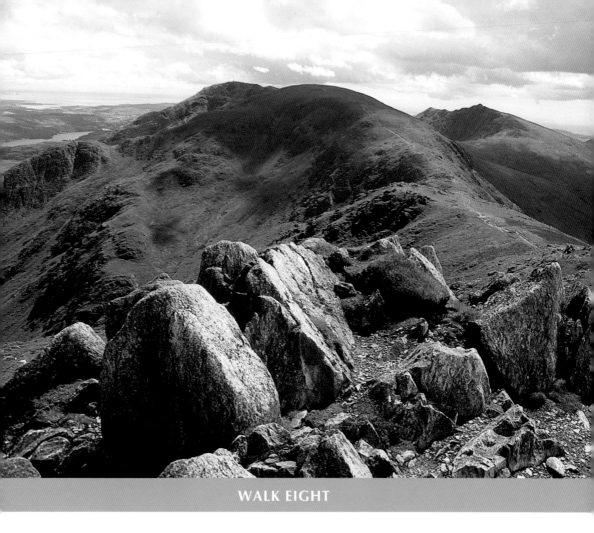

Dow Crag, Brim Fell, Swirl How and Grey Friar from Seathwaite

*T*he Duddon is a scenic treasure, less crowded than counterpart dales in the central Lakes. The valley road is perennially popular with drivers who delight in travelling its length, pitching out over Hard Knott or Wrynose Passes, or traversing the adjacent moorland roads of Birker and Corney Fells, or tripping over into the diminutive Dunnerdale, all renowned for their wonderful mountain outlooks. The tiny community of Seathwaite lies at the Duddon valley's heart, and from here the best walking begins. The route follows the age-old Walna Scar Road to climb onto the airy perch of Dow Crag, before tracing the skyline ridge over Brim Fell to Swirl How and cutting back onto Grey Friar. It then descends by Seathwaite Tarn to thread through the impressive wooded Wallowbarrow Gorge.

↑ *Coniston Old Man, Brim Fell and Dow Crag from Great How Crags*

ROUTE INFORMATION

Distance	18km/11¼ miles
Height gain	1030m/3380ft
Time	8 hours
Grade	strenuous
Start point	GR229960
Maps	(Harvey Superwalker)
	Lakeland South West
	(Ordnance Survey)
	OL6 South-western area

After-walk refreshment
The Newfield Inn at Seathwaite

The Start
Roadside parking in the hamlet of Seathwaite, north of the Newfield Inn, GR229960.

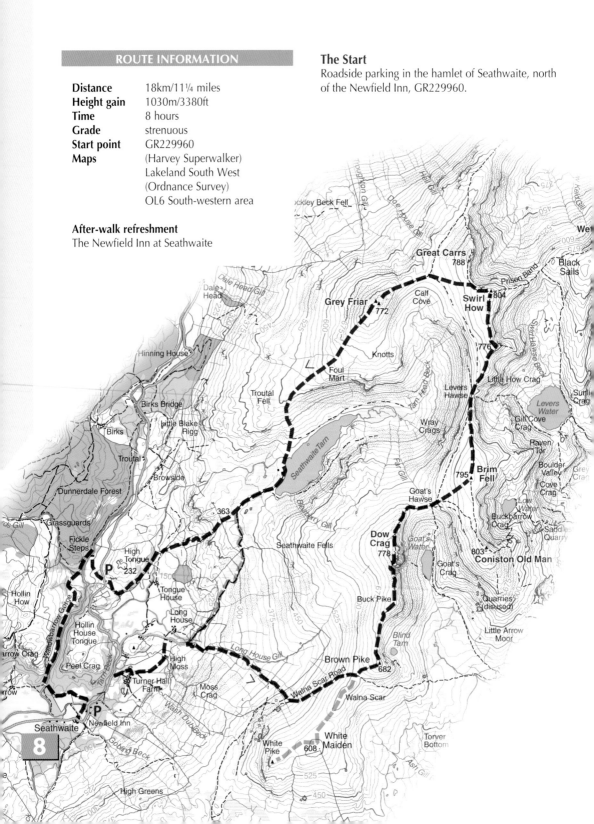

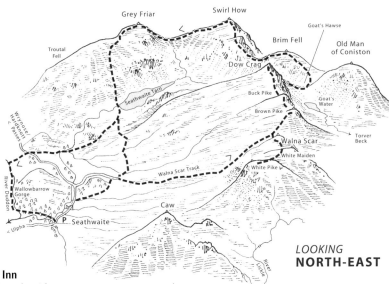

LOOKING
NORTH-EAST

The Route

From the **Newfield Inn** follow the valley road north, either tracking right with the footpath passing **Turner Hall Farm** and leading via gates by **High Moss** (Rucksack Club Hut) onto the fell road; or continuing on the road then turning right after Undercrag. By either means gain the foot of the **Walna Scar Road**. At the first gate the road reverts to a rough track. Ascend via a further gate, the 'road' now blessedly relieved of 4x4 vehicular (ab)use. See the massive slate tips high to the right, gathered by the huge quarried hollows under White Pike. The distinctive banded flag floors in the Newfield Inn are hewn from this source. The steady plod achieves the shallow saddle, from where you branch off left (north), climbing simply onto **Brown Pike**.

After savouring this rewarding moment, from the cairn gaze back into the Duddon and down the upper Torver Beck valley, with the basin of Blind Tarn tucked in under the eastern scarp, its crystal waters cradled as if in suspension. The ridge path heads on over **Buck Pike**, coming above the top of Easy Gully, from where the massive **Dow Crag** (pronounced as a female deer, 'doe') is seen in sharp profile. The final feet onto the fell top at 778m/2553ft bring hands into play as the summit is a rocky bastion befitting the majestic cliff.

One senses every inch of **Dow Crag's** height, and the impressive gulf beneath one's feet will ensure that there is no 'laekin aboot' (Cumbrian dialect for 'playing about'). Dow derives its name from the Celtic for dark, *dubh* – the crag casting a mighty shadow over the chaos of boulders running down to Goat's Water. There is no cairn here, just naturally sculpted rock.

Clamber off north, naturally following the scarp-edge path down to **Goat's Hawse**. The name is thought to be a variant on the modern 'Windy Gap'. For all that goats would have colonised the cliffs, the name appears to have older origins and is rather like

Swirl How summit, a place to relax and gain refreshment after the long climb   61

'ghent', as in Pen-y-Ghent, one of the Yorkshire Three Peaks, and Goat's Fell on Arran, which mean 'the pass of strong gusts'. Heed the implicit warning.

The path forks on the rise from the pass. Ignore the strong leftward path unless you wish to avoid Brim Fell and aim directly to Levers Hawse. Instead keep straight on up the grassy slope to reach the summit cairn of **Brim Fell** at 795m/2608ft. The flaked slate cairn crowns a featureless dome. What the view lacks in drama it compensates for in the extent and detail of its full panorama – this is, after all, right at the centre of the Coniston Fells, with much of mountain Lakeland spread out within a wide northern arc from west to the north-east.

Head north, the ridge narrowing and permitting westward views down towards Seathwaite Tarn (reservoir). Crossing **Levers Hawse** (decidedly not an east–west pass, though there is a regular path right leading steeply down to Levers Water) the path mounts by **Little** and **Great How Crags** (the latter a fine viewpoint worth visiting off the strict line of the ridge path) to reach the summit cairn of **Swirl How**. At 804m/2638ft this actually is a metre superior to Coniston Old Man, and was the highest point in Lancashire prior to the boundary reorganisation in 1974. Swirl meant 'neck', like Swirral Edge on Helvellyn, and describes a handsome culmination of ridges.

Descend west, bearing off the regular path which hugs the rim to Great Carrs. There is little hint of a path on the grassy slope leading down to the broad prairie depression, known appropriately as Fairfield. Paths converge, one from off the northern slopes of Great Carrs and the other a contouring path from Levers Hause. Ascend south-west onto the wide top of **Grey Friar**. Pass the Matterhorn rock, and continue to the northernmost of two separate summit cairns. The rockier north top commands a cracking view north to the Scafells.

Leave the summit in a south-westerly direction with cairns guiding down onto **Troutal Fell**, seeking the easier slopes leading down to **Seathwaite Tarn's** concrete dam. Crossing the outflow bridge join the reservoir track. In this vicinity recent archaeological research has identified a cluster of Bronze Age settlement ring cairns.

One has two options to finish the walk. Either follow the track simply down to the foot of the Walna Scar Road, retracing your outward march, or alternatively, and quite to be preferred, visit the Wallowbarrow Gorge, as described here. Follow the reservoir track for 300m, and as it begins a leftward curve dip into the shallow valley on a path which leads through a gate beside a sheepfold. The path zig-zags down the rough Tongue House Close. Two further gates lead to an opportunity to cross a small footbridge spanning Tarn Beck. Continue, passing Thrang Cottage and its sheltering oakwood and slipping over the ridge via stiles onto the common and the open road below **High Tongue**. Cross the road directly descending to cross **Fickle Steps** – stepping stones assisted with a taut wire (if the Duddon is running high then the river will be unfordable – fickle indeed).

Once safely over the stepping stones follow the path left, crossing Grassguards Gill footbridge, to enter the beautiful wooded **Wallowbarrow Gorge**. The intimate surroundings provide a wonderful contrast to the rest of the route, and make a perfect ending to a high mountain day. Cross the Memorial Bridge and follow the ensuing path straight ahead, duly crossing Tarn Beck footbridge. A stile and a small meadow lead to a gate onto the road opposite the **Newfield Inn**.

Black Combe
from the Whicham Valley

*S*outh Cumbrian fell walkers have an abiding affection for this great whale-back hill. I have even been told, in no uncertain terms by a teenager from Millom, that it was the highest 'mountain' in England, such is the impact it has on local life. Yet clearly Black Combe is a modest massif, with many of the characteristics typical of the Howgills. It makes an honourable appearance in this guide by dint of its presence and the perspectives it provides.

Appearing to project into the Irish Sea, the fell has a real maritime feel. A good half of the summit view takes in a mighty sweep of ocean, the flat horizon broken only by the floating skyline of the Isle of Man, some 50 miles distant. Yet it is into the heart of Lakeland that most eyes will be trained, a magical compression of familiar fell tops. With the view from here you could start to build a wish-list of fells to climb from this guide!

Traditionally ascents begin from Whicham church, following a green carpet right to the top, popular with local dog walkers and gangly runners – few days pass when someone is not seen on this steady track. But the more mountain-like approach sets its sights on the subsidiary ridge of White Combe to view the main mass of the fell at its most dramatic, above the great hollow of Black Combe itself. For, like Helvellyn, this is a fell named after the hollow in its mighty lap.

↑ *Black Combe from White Combe*

ROUTE INFORMATION

Distance	11km/8 miles
Height gain	600m/1960ft
Time	5½ hours
Grade	energetic
Start point	GR153846
Maps	(Harvey Superwalker)
	Lakeland South West
	(Ordnance Survey)
	OL6 South-western area

After-walk refreshment

King Billie (William) at Kirksanton, Punch Bowl at The Green and High Cross at Broughton-in-Furness

The Start

From Broughton-in-Furness follow the A595 via Duddon Bridge to locate the roadside lay-by at Beckside Farm GR153846, 2.4km/1½ miles west of the Hallthwaites fork in the road to Millom.

The Route

From the lay-by take an immediate turn away from the fell by following the field-path heading east, using hand-gates, via Cross Bank, thus minimising the vergeless A595 road. Regaining the road, find a footpath sign above Fox & Goose Cottages directing through a gate into a confined hedged lane. Where the lane emerges at a gate onto the bracken-clothed slopes of **White Hall Knott**, bear up left then slant

9

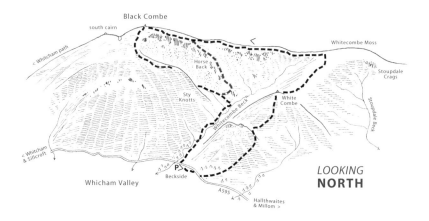

Black Combe

south cairn

< Whitcham path

Whitecombe Moss

Horse Back

Stoupdale Crags

Sty Knotts

White Combe

Whitecombe Beck

Stoupdale Beck

< Whitcham & Silecroft

P

Beckside

Whicham Valley

A595

Hallthwaites & Millom >

LOOKING **NORTH**

right on a clear grooved track, climbing diagonally across the slope to the northern shoulder. The short ridge of White Hall Knott may tempt as a first viewpoint of both the Whicham valley and the impressive bulk of Sty Knotts ridge of Black Combe.

The drove-way slices through stunted gorse and bracken, but watch carefully in order to bear off left (pathless) to gain the cairn on **White Combe**.

The tumulus cairn makes a good place to really appreciate the great scoured hillsides of Black and Whitecombe Screes. The albino name quite simply implies sunlit white grass slopes in contrast with the shadowed dark side of Black Combe to the west.

A modest ridge path leads north-west, only to fade as it approaches the valley-head. Join the well-marked path climbing out of the **Whitecombe Beck**

Black Combe from the Giant's Grave standing stones, Kirksanton

valley, and curve from north-west to south-west on the long, steady rise to the summit. The eastern scarp is always the object of attention, though the path tends to keep well onto the broad pasture ridge. Make a point, if the wind is not too fierce, to find and follow the craggy rim before reaching **Black Combe** summit at 600m/1970ft.

BLACK COMBE

The extensive domed summit of Black Combe would be featureless but for the shaggy shelter cairn and old triangulation column. The majority of such pillars have now been rendered redundant, but this spot still serves cartographers, being a strategic point in the network of the global positioning system. As you come upon the shallow domed table-top, with the wind whistling off the ocean, the crude wind shelter has a greater than usual value. One may wonder who gathered the stones and over what period, though you'll be more grateful than quizzical.

The nature of the hill means that its summit is seldom perceived from afar, but 'afar' is certainly perceived from it! Skiddaw, Great Gable, Scafell Pike, Helvellyn and much else of Lakeland, too, crowd into view. The vista extends from St Bees to the Howgills, with Ingleborough, the Bowland Fells and even Blackpool Tower, bless its heart, completing the extensive prospect south-east. All too commonly cloud hangs on this fell top, when most other fells are clear. Here's hoping you'll not be missing the view by viewing the mist!

There is also a second meritable viewpoint, the south cairn (587m). Its plump form can just be seen from the summit – make a bee-line south, dipping by a pool and crossing stony ground to reach this prime location. Seen from the south, notably Kirksanton, this portly cairn pricks the skyline as a sham summit, the convex slope hiding

← *White Combe from Black Combe*

Sunkenkirk stone circle, Swinside, just north of the area covered by the walk

the true top. Millom and Barrow claim most attention from this splendid landmark, as too from the wind-farm at Haverigg ('the ridge where oats were grown'), whose whooshing turbines are no doubt the bane of inmates' lives at the adjacent prison!

The descent can be taken via one of two ridges. For the first route, step back to the pool and bear directly east, descending the broad grassy ridge, glancing into the adjacent dark combe drained by Blackcombe Beck. As the ground steepens on **Sty Knotts** choose a natural line left down to the beck. Ford and join a clear path through the bracken which dips to join the valley track close to the confluence with **Whitecombe Beck**.

The more excitingly rugged alternative is to continue north beyond the pool and regain the summit. Press on north-east, keeping the broken scarp at a comfortable distance to the right. The northern rim of **Blackcombe Screes** acts as guide, and a narrow path becomes apparent, stepping down the **Horse Back** ridge in steady stages. At the low saddle pass a small fenced enclosure, where you keep right to join the path through bracken down to the main Whitecombe Beck track. Follow the track down the narrow valley via a footbridge and gate, passing the secluded **Whicham Mill** and then the old farmstead of **Rallis**, following the continuing gated lane back to the valley road at **Beckside**.

Harter Fell and Hard Knott
from Brotherilkeld

*T*he walk reveals the natural harmony of Harter Fell, part of the Southern Fells group, and Hard Knott, belonging to the Mid-Western Fells. From the start, this walk scenically excels, climbing across the flanks of Harter Fell on the Eskdale/Duddon bridle path, then diverting up the steep western slope to visit the triple mock rock-castle summit. It then descends north-east to reach the Hardknott Pass. You can then either descend by Hardknott Castle Roman fort or, far better, climb onto the Border End headland, with its classic view of the Scafells, before venturing to view The Steeple (Eskdale Needle) and cross the fell summit of Hard Knott. The walk then traces the declining ridge north towards the valley of Lingcove Beck and joins the valley path, leading impressively down the confined dale by Lingcove Bridge.

↑ *The arc of mountains forming the head of Eskdale from Harter Fell*

ROUTE INFORMATION

Distance	11.25km/7 miles
Height gain	732m/2400ft
Time	6 hours
Grade	strenuous
Start point	GR214012
Maps	(Harvey Superwalker) Lakeland West and South West (Ordnance Survey) OL6 South-western area

After-walk refreshment
The Woolpack Inn near Boot

The Start

The head of motorable Eskdale, situated at the foot of the Hardknott Pass, close to the cattle grid and Jubilee Bridge GR214012.

The Route

Start by crossing **Jubilee Bridge**, the little stone footbridge spanning Hardknott Gill. It was erected in the Queen's silver jubilee year, 1977, by Malcolm Guyatt, for 30 years National Park ranger for this area, with a special interest and talent for stylish foot-bridges, a classic being the Hollow Gill/Groove Gill double footbridge above Wasdale Head Hall. Pass through a succession of kissing gates, quickly taking the more obvious 'peat road' forking left to begin a steady ascent, flanked – but not inhibited – by dense bracken. This bridle path, with the appearance of a miners' incline, provides excellent views of upper Eskdale. A grand girdle of Lakeland's mightiest mountains

conclusively rims the horizon, an outlook that holds its fascination throughout the walk. Climb on by two hand-gates.

As the path from Boot, via Penny Hill, merges from the right, take your leave of the notoriously marshy path, which is bound for Grassguards and

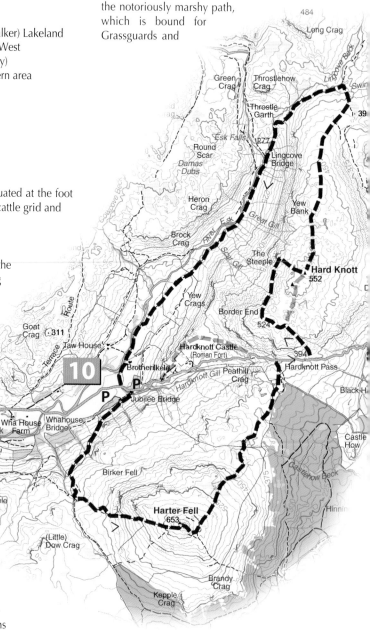

70

Upper Eskdale emerging during the ascent from Jubilee Bridge →

the Duddon, now running on beside the moorland flanking fence. The clear ascending path, left, now takes precedence. If you miss this left turn, continue to the forest-edge gate, but do not go through. Instead bear up left, initially following the rising fence, to reconnect with the popular path high up, beneath a classic contorted volcanic outcrop. There are some newly pitched sections to ease erosion on the steep slope advancing to the gap between the summit battlements. Bear up left to gain the Ordnance Survey pillar and then, if you are so inclined, scramble onto the ultimate rock tower citadel, one of only a handful of Lakeland summits of naked rock. Quite a place to linger.

The three principal 'castle' eminences on **Harter Fell** summit deserve a visit in turn to enjoy outlooks around the compass. The peerless view north to the Scafells spies down on Hardknott Castle – its original Roman (Latin) name is not known. In spite of all the hype that Housesteads (Vercovicium) on Hadrian's Wall receives, Hardknott fort was – and remains – the most impressively sited of all permanent Roman camps in Britain.

A prominent path leaves the eastern edge of the summit. It begins east-south-east (bound for Birks and the Duddon), but soon watch for a path veering northeast bound for the Hardknott Pass. Descend through

Border End from the Roman bath-house

the gullied head of **Castlehow Beck** into heather. After crossing a fence stile veer right over marshy ground, aiming closer to the top fringe of forestry in undulating terrain. Cross a fence stile to join the old Blackhall bridle path (thought to have been the original Roman road) to reach the public road.

Here you have two choices. At this point you may feel content just to have gathered in Harter Fell and opt to descend promptly west down the **Hard Knott road** and back to the start. But do not feel obliged to tussle with the tarmac and fuming traffic – make a point of bearing right onto the signed footpath at the very first tight hair-pin bend. This turf trail leads through the bracken by the Roman parade ground and down the handsome edge beside the Roman fort, a fine excuse to reflect on the prospect of the Scafells enjoyed by the legions.

With so few pre-Norse names left in the Lakes, one must wonder what descriptive name the Romans used to identify the Scafell massif, it being such a profound part of their daily outlook. The name of the fort, which pre-dates Hadrian's Wall, is also an enigma.

If you don't go down past the fort at the road, continue to follow the main route, which turns right upon meeting the road and crosses the cattle grid. Pass the cairn marking the summit of **Hardknott Pass** to reach a lay-by. A path rises directly left, currently accompanying an electric hefting fence. This fence was installed directly after the 2001 Foot and Mouth Disease wiped out the National Trust's Duddon estate Herdwick flock. Cross a stile to reach a boggy

ridge-top hollow, then another stile is encountered with paths going to the right and left.

To visit **Border End**, in all honestly a must, go left. Pass on a further 150m from the cairned top to reach a final cairn which provides a memorable outlook. Harter Fell is seen in all its majesty tip to toe; the verdant strath of Eskdale too. The majestic mountain sanctuary of upper Eskdale excites and uplifts eyes and hearts.

Then you have another choice. To continue on the main route, backtrack to the stile and cross the boggy hollow weaving along the fell ridge, negotiating two marshy hollows and stiles en route to the **Hard Knott** summit knoll. But you're in it for the adventure so why miss out on The Steeple (Eskdale Needle)? This can be reached, with nothing more than the occasional sheep track for surety, by dipping north off Border End. Grassy ground can easily be found as one drifts slightly down and across the upper slope of the fell. Keep an eye out for the handsome pinnacle, and thread up behind to observe it from both sides. **The Steeple** makes a superb foreground for a photograph of the Scafells. Aim directly uphill from the pinnacle to cross the heaf fence, as you find convenient, to make it to the **Hard Knott** summit cairn. Again the view is dominated by the amphitheatre of upper Eskdale, a magical mountain scene.

HARDKNOTT ROMAN FORT

Sometimes shown on maps as Hardknott Castle, the Ordnance Survey for long gave the fort the Latin name Mediobogdum. This scholarly attribution was based on surviving references to listed forts. However, less than a decade ago it was realised that this name actually refers to a fort at Watercrook, near Kendal. The clue lies in the name – for Mediobogdum translates as 'middle of the bow'. Hardknott fort's Roman name remains a mystery.

The fort's construction was contemporaneous with the early phase of Hadrian's Wall, the fort being an outpost garrison on the wild west–east mountain road linking the port of Glanoventa (Ravenglass) and Galava (Ambleside). The fort was part of an early Celt-calming communication network, and coin-finds suggest it was occupied AD120–138 and again AD160–197. An inscribed stone, discovered in 1964 near the south-east gate, recorded that the fort was erected 'for the Emperor Caesar Trajan Hadrian Augustus' by the Fourth Cohort of Dalmatians.

On site, the outline reconstructions of the playing-card-shaped perimeter wall and externally sited bathhouse show the fort's magnificent situation. The parade ground and command platform are evident to the east. Quite what the soldiers thought of their posting one can but muse.

A ridge path leads north, flirting with the heaf fence (used to keep the sheep within their grazing ground, a process also achieved through 'heafing' or 'hefting' – using the instinctive sense some breeds have of their home territory). The fence crosses two stiles and a considerable marshy hollow, trending down to the head of Mosedale and the connection with the Lingcove Beck valley path. Turn left, taking opportunities to view the beck's increasing gorge. Pass, but do not cross, **Lingcove Bridge**. This quite elegant single-span footbridge provides a fine excuse to pause, though you may venture across expressly to view the fine waterfall upstream. Immediately downstream the Esk conflues, below which you will find Tongue Pot, a popular attraction for skinny dippers in high summer.

The path is now consumed by the confined nature of the dale. After fording **Great Gill** look up right to Heron Crag (the name associated with the former range of the sea-eagle) – The Steeple high to the left seems ultra-remote. The valley track reaches the intake wall gate from where footpaths fork. The less-trod path forks left, in effect straight on, though invisible on the ground, via three ladder stiles. The more obvious path keeps upon the open track right and leads via a further gate, and then at a hand-gate is held tight alongside the River Esk by a fence. On reaching **Brotherilkeld Farm**, pronounced 'butter-ill-ket', complete the walk along the farm approach track.

Hard Knott summit backed by the Scafells across the head of Eskdale

Scafell Pike and Esk Pike
from Brotherilkeld

A fell walk writ large with high adventure, this is Lakeland's answer to a Scottish Highland glen. Preferably choose settled weather and the long daylight hours of summer to undertake this walk. The walk ventures into the wildest upper reaches of Eskdale to catch Scafell Pike unawares. Climbing via Cam Spout and Mickledore to reach the summit, it then sets course across the boulders to Esk Hause to capture Esk Pike, from where the long south ridge is traced back down into the Esk gorge at Throstle Garth.

The Start

The head of motorable Eskdale, situated at the foot of the Hardknott Pass, close to the cattle grid and Jubilee Bridge lay-by GR214012, or the lay-by west of the Brotherilkeld Farm road-end telephone kiosk.

The Route

Follow the gated track approach to **Brotherilkeld Farm**. Keep left short of the farmyard and join a permissive path which hugs the tree-shaded riverbank from a hand-gate confined by a fence. Ignore the

↑ Esk Buttress, backed by Scafell Pike, Little Narrowcove and Ill Crag from Yeastyrigg Crags

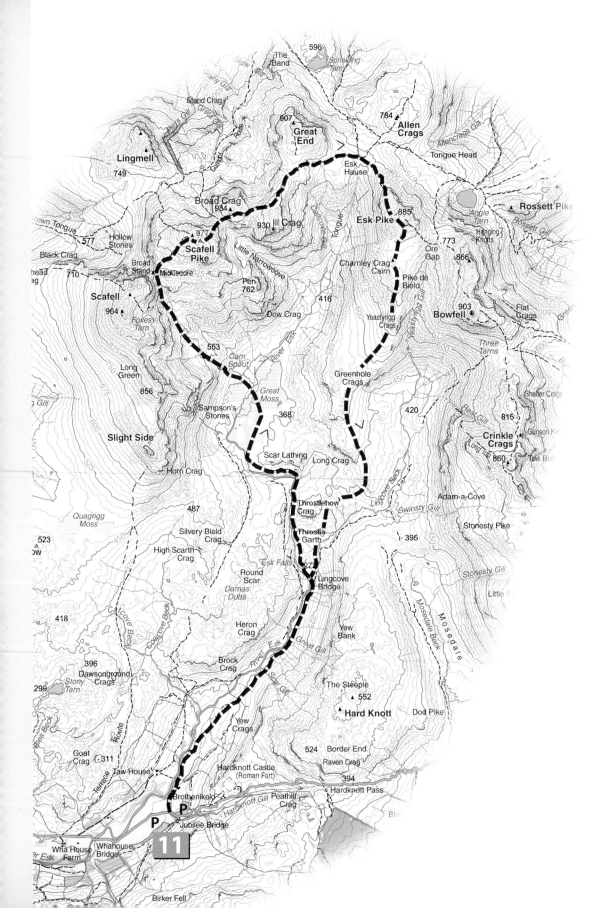

ROUTE INFORMATION

Distance	19.75km/12½ miles
Height gain	1146m/3760ft
Time	10 hours
Grade	arduous
Start point	GR214012
Maps	(Harvey Superwalker)
	Lakeland West
	(Ordnance Survey)
	OL6 South-western area

After-walk refreshment
The Woolpack, Burnmoor and Brook House inns at Boot

footbridge (path to Taw House) and continue until a second hand-gate releases the path into the pastures. An open track leads on, via a gate in a wall, and continues to a ladder stile beside a gate and small fold.

The gorge of the Esk is entered, with three great cliffs catching the eye – Yew Crag up to the right on Hard Knott, with Brock and Heron Crags up to the left, the latter with a large free face. Quickly The Steeple (Eskdale Needle) is visible up to the right as **Scar Gill** is forded. The undulating path varies from rough to even during the approach to the sheep-wash fold and elegant single-span **Lingcove Bridge**. From here The Steeple takes on the appearance of a Roman 'thumbs up'. Close to the bridge is quite the most excited passage in the Esk's beautiful career. Deep plunge pools and falls abound, making it a place to linger briefly.

Cross the bridge and follow the path up **Throstle Garth**, passing too high to catch a glimpse of Esk Falls. These are known intimately only from the infrequently followed and infinitely rougher west side path. As the mass of Throstlehow Crag is left behind the river takes wide meandering sweeps through a landscape reminiscent of a remote glen, with the peak of Scafell Pike looming on the horizon ahead. The path keeps close company under **Scar Lathing**, and as the vast amphitheatre surrounding **Great Moss** takes centre-stage, see a turf-topped wall close right. This is the remnants of a medieval deer compound built by the monks of Furness Abbey. Wet marsh is unavoidable, but

once the Esk shallows are forded the sponge is less of a problem and the route trends north-west to the foot of **Cam Spout**, the most handsome of pencil-thin waterfalls.

The real rigours of the day are about to begin. The path climbs steeply upon naked slabs close to the falls – two tails of water spilling down the gully, intermingled with a few smaller spills. The path ascends the increasingly rough combe, passing up beneath Scafell's massive East Buttress. The combe has no name; though, to correspond with Little Narrowcove, this might be considered the Great Narrowcove. There is a path all the way to the saddle of **Mickledore**, though it is increasingly loose near the top. Bear right, mounting north-east onto **Scafell Pike's** stony summit.

SCAFELL PIKE

The thousands of visitors to this summit find no Shangri La of beauty. Indeed, on many occasions they find they are obliged to queue for the honour of standing upon the shambolic walled memorial crowning this rooftop of the realm. As a matter of English pride, periodically this pile gets a facelift, and is presently sorely due a spot of robust restructuring. The resident ravens take their pick of residual refreshment. Adjacent stands a stone-built OS pillar together with several wind-shelter cairns, mostly quite sorry sights, excepting the Victorian roofless shelter just down to the east – be warned this may have the odour of a loo!

Scafell Pike summit, bereft of people,
a rare moment on a gorgeous day

Esk Pike and Bowfell from Ill Crag

By contrast the view is uplifting and richly rewarding. The best outlooks inevitably are found nearer the plateau's edge, notably the north-western above Dropping Crag, a view that features Lingmell and Great Gable. Westwards the Irish Sea glistens beyond Wastwater, and it may be possible to see the far-off outline of the Isle of Man, 60 miles away, looking like a giant in repose – the island's highest point, Snaefell, suggesting his head to the north.

The energy that got you this far will yet be tested, so give yourself a good break before heading off north down the very loose path into the narrow gap of **Broadcrag col**. The saddle provides a particularly wild view down into Little Narrowcove to the right, and no less inviting is the view left towards the Corridor Route, scree ensuring that anyone venturing either way has to concentrate intently on their footing, but that's for another day.

The next phase is notoriously difficult under foot, the route being more a process of boulder hopping to traverse the upper shoulder of **Broad Crag**, with the occasional random cairn the only apparent hint

of a way. Then slip through the succeeding and far easier depression.

Over to the right the rock tor of **Ill Crag** merits a diversion for its view into upper Eskdale. The near view is stunning down into Little Narrowcove, revealing the top of Dow Crag (Esk Buttress) peaking on The Pen, and the upper rim of crags forming a castellated rampart to Scafell Pike's summit.

Cairns plot a north-easterly course that duly leaves the rough plateau descending into Calf Cove. In Victorian days the ascent of Scafell Pike was conducted saddleback by local guides. The rings where the ponies were tethered still exist, and from here the intrepid tourists were obliged to trek the final stretch on foot, the plateau boulders being quite beyond equine hooves. Continue to the true **Esk Hause** ('true' because the common way from Great Langdale to Sty Head crosses a transverse pass just below, which is frequently wrongly described as Esk Hause).

Leave the popular path, which heads down by the cross-wall. Instead mount the well-marked path clambering up the north-west ridge onto **Esk Pike**.

Esk Pike from the head of Calf Cove →

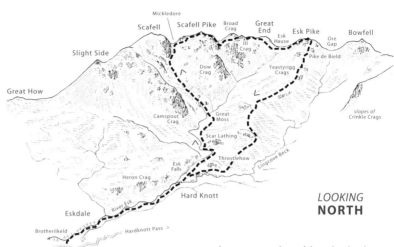

Mickledore
Scafell Pike · Broad Crag · Great End · Esk Pike · Bowfell
Scafell
Slight Side
Esk Hause
Ill Crag
Ore Gap
Pike de Bield
Dow Crag
Yeastyrigg Crags
Great How
Camspout Crag
Great Moss
slopes of Crinkle Crags
Scar Lathing
Throstlehow
Lingcove Beck
Esk Falls
Heron Crag
Hard Knott
River Esk
Eskdale
Brotherilkeld
Hardknott Pass >
< Boot   P

LOOKING
NORTH

There are two tops – the south predominantly rock, the north a loose affiliation surmounted with a more concerted cairn. The chalky appearance of the higher rocks prevalent on the south side presents a curious pale, flaky surface. The views are superb north to Glaramara and south-east to Bowfell.

The walk now turns purposefully south, aiming for another prize viewpoint – that of **Pike de Bield**, the cairn providing a lovely prospect towards the Scafells

over the upper reaches of the Esk. The three-mile journey from Esk Pike down to Throstle Garth is wonderfully secluded – this is fell walking right off the beaten track. There is a path which avoids the sequence of rocky headlands and keeps predominantly to grass. Descend via **Yeastyrigg Crags** and along the edge of Pike de Bield Moss, slipping by **Long Crag** and Pianet Knott to cross the low vestigal wall that enclosed Throstlehow Crag – hence **Throstle Garth**. Run on above the heather-fringed Lingcove Beck to once again reach **Lingcove Bridge**. Two miles of familiar valley walking complete the walk.

Scafell and Slight Side
from Wha House

*P*assengers on the enchanting miniature railway La'al Ratty reach Dalegarth Station to be assailed with notices proudly proclaiming a view of Scafell Pike, the highest mountain in England. Well, what they actually see is Scafell, no less handsome an object of admiration. The best way to the top from Eskdale begins a little further up the valley beyond Boot and the Woolpack Inn. The walk heads for the Cowcove zig-zags, where it takes a wild moorland course to reconnect with the River Esk under Cam Spout Crag, climbing directly to the foot of Scafell's East Buttress. Here it enters a tight gully leading to Foxes Tarn and makes the final push to the high saddle, visiting the top of Deep Gill and the brink above Broad Stand before reaching the actual summit. It then heads south down the ridge by Long Green and the superb summit of Slight Side to complete the round upon the Terrace Route.

↑ *The Esk takes an exaggerated sweep beneath Scar Lathing with the peak of Scafell Pike beyond*

ROUTE INFORMATION

Distance	13.5km/8½ miles
Height gain	908m/2980ft
Time	7 hours
Grade	strenuous
Start point	GR200009
Maps	(Harvey Superwalker)
	Lakeland West
	(Ordnance Survey)
	OL6 South-western area

After-walk refreshment

The Woolpack, Burnmoor and Brook House inns in Boot

The Start

Park in the small car park opposite Wha House Farm, GR200009, situated 1km east of the Woolpack Inn in Eskdale.

The Route

Follow the valley road east branching onto the inviting farm access track to **Taw House**. On reaching the farm, note a permissive path option signed left, via a gate (avoiding the farmyard). This leads to a wall on a rough track, wet at the start, that leads to a ladder stile. However, to be frank, this is better reached through the farmyard. In which case, continue through the farmyard to leave by the gate at its northern end and follow the lane to a gate. Thereafter follow an open track, via two gateways, to a gate/ladder stile below the aforementioned ladder stile at a sheepfold. A clear track continues to **Scale Bridge**, crossing the shaded cascades of Scale Gill.

The footpath is signed further along the track, though an intermediary path takes a cavalier direct diagonal line up to the zig-zags from the bridge. The footpath track becomes the lesser-used west-side valley route, rougher than the parallel path to Lingcove Bridge, particularly above Esk Falls, but nonetheless fascinating to tramp. If keeping to the strict line of the Cowcove zig-zag footpath, watch for the acute turn left up through the bracken – the path is clear enough. Higher, the zig-zags afford a view into the **Cowcove Beck** ravine, laced with birch and rowan, before entering the first of two marshy hollows. Keep to the dry western edge, crossing a plank over **Damas Dubs**, the natural drainage for the two apparently separate hollows.

The path, well evidenced underfoot, leads into the Esk catchment and meets up indistinctly with the west-side valley path. The combined path leads through what could be mistaken for a remote deserted farmstead, but in reality is a multi-penned sheepfold. The path curves round a low spur, littered with huge erratics known as **Sampson's Stones**, set beneath the massive cliff of Camspout Crag. Keeping to the fringe of **Great Moss** marsh, the path now bears up half-left to reach the foot of **Cam Spout**, the most handsome of pencil-thin waterfalls.

Ascend the slabs to the right of the falls leading by How Beck, and a clear path gains height into

Lingcove Bridge, a packhorse turned backpacker's bridge at the Esk's confluence with Lingcove Beck

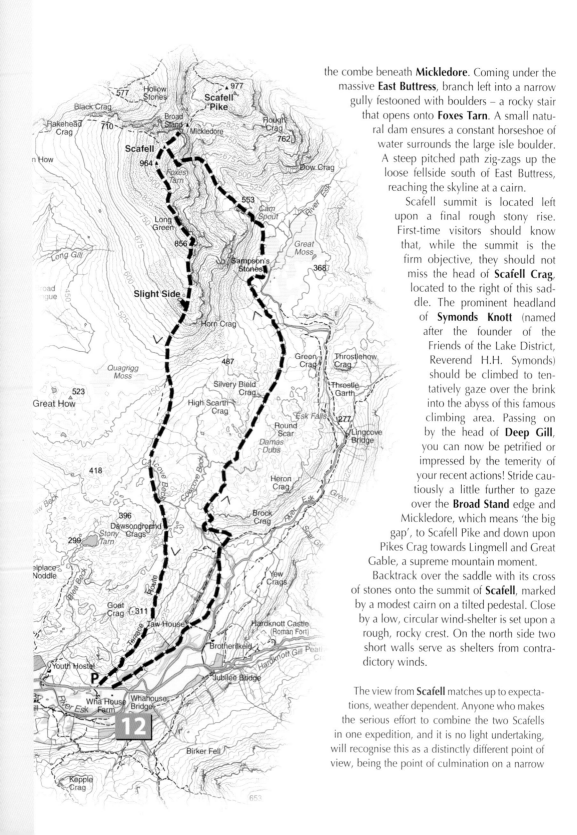

the combe beneath **Mickledore**. Coming under the massive **East Buttress**, branch left into a narrow gully festooned with boulders – a rocky stair that opens onto **Foxes Tarn**. A small natural dam ensures a constant horseshoe of water surrounds the large isle boulder. A steep pitched path zig-zags up the loose fellside south of East Buttress, reaching the skyline at a cairn.

Scafell summit is located left upon a final rough stony rise. First-time visitors should know that, while the summit is the firm objective, they should not miss the head of **Scafell Crag**, located to the right of this saddle. The prominent headland of **Symonds Knott** (named after the founder of the Friends of the Lake District, Reverend H.H. Symonds) should be climbed to tentatively gaze over the brink into the abyss of this famous climbing area. Passing on by the head of **Deep Gill**, you can now be petrified or impressed by the temerity of your recent actions! Stride cautiously a little further to gaze over the **Broad Stand** edge and Mickledore, which means 'the big gap', to Scafell Pike and down upon Pikes Crag towards Lingmell and Great Gable, a supreme mountain moment.

Backtrack over the saddle with its cross of stones onto the summit of **Scafell**, marked by a modest cairn on a tilted pedestal. Close by a low, circular wind-shelter is set upon a rough, rocky crest. On the north side two short walls serve as shelters from contradictory winds.

The view from **Scafell** matches up to expectations, weather dependent. Anyone who makes the serious effort to combine the two Scafells in one expedition, and it is no light undertaking, will recognise this as a distinctly different point of view, being the point of culmination on a narrow

LOOKING
NORTH

The homeward journey begins by descending the bouldery stepped south-south-east ridge to the shapely summit of **Long Green**, the culmination of the Camspout Crag ridge. A simple path, if occasionally loose underfoot, leads south, and the fell

ridge, and sufficiently set apart to give perspective on Scafell Pike and upper Eskdale. The Western Fells about Wastwater and Mosedale are well displayed, as too are Burnmoor Tarn and Miterdale, with the Isle of Man on the far maritime horizon.

The Mosedale fells from the head of Deep Ghyll

83

levels before the final easy scramble onto **Slight Side** – a perfect termination of the high massif. There is nothing slight about it, its fortress summit exhibiting the same white-flecked tone of Esk Pike. The view extends from Bowfell via the Coniston Fells down to Black Combe, the seaward sector of the view made special when evening light sparkles in the ocean with golden hues.

There is but one way down, making life simple. Leave the summit, rounding the eastern end of the main outcrop and taking an initial south-west line. The scree soon relents and the path descends uneventfully. A small cairn marks the point where the Boot path veers half-right. Ignore this and keep to the main path that runs south down the west side of **Cow Cove** and briefly accompanies **Catcove Beck**. Thereafter keep to the natural shelf, hence **Terrace Route**, which comes by a wall and, via a hand-gate through a fold, finally descends to the fence stile into the car park where you began.

Slight Side from the Terrace Route at Catcove Beck

Illgill Head and Whin Rigg
from Wasdale Head

Wastwater is not only the deepest lake in the district but has the most prodigious backdrop of rock and scree of any sheet of Lakeland water. An astonishing facade, captivating at any time of day or season, the famous Screes tumble at a ferocious angle from an otherwise modest fell ridge. This ridge has a wide saddle connecting the summits of Illgill Head and Whin Rigg with southern slopes that just could not be more plain, falling into secretive Miterdale.

The walk climbs onto Illgill Head and, dependent on one's appetite, follows either the open ridge or the sheep trod along the exciting rim, both routes crossing the saddle onto Whin Rigg. As the route descends beside Greathall Gill it switches right upstream with the River Irt to the lake's outflow, and then sets to work engaging with the unique challenges of the shoreline path. Here, one particularly huge fan of monster boulder scree brings its own, not insuperable, demands, with the worst section occurring early on.

↑ *Red Pike, Pillar and Yewbarrow from Illgill Head*

ROUTE INFORMATION

Distance	14.75km/9¼ miles
Height gain	609m/2000ft
Time	6¾ hours
Grade	strenuous
Start point	GR183074
Maps	(Harvey Superwalker)
	Lakeland West
	(Ordnance Survey)
	OL6 South-western area

After-walk refreshment
Wasdale Head Inn and The Screes at Nether Wasdale

The Start
The dedicated and discreet parking adjacent to the National Trust's Wasdale Campsite, GR183074, a small tree-shaded area perfectly situated for the purposes of this walk.

The Route
Follow the farm track left, crossing the cattle grid and subsequent bridge spanning **Lingmell Gill**. Bear left, flanked by gorse, following the gill upstream to a fork below **Brackenclose** – the Lakeland Fell and Rock Climbing Club Hut. Follow the path right, signposted 'Eskdale'. The track passes through three gates, rising via a quaint **double-arched footbridge** where Hollow and Groove Gills converge. Pass a group of ruined

18th-century peat store huts. Shortly after the conifers of Fence Wood end, the path forks, with cairns indicating the old corpse road up to the saddle. These trackways were used to transport coffins from remote communities to the nearest consecrated burial ground.

However, keep right to ford **Straighthead Gill** and begin the grassy climb in earnest. Soon the wall draws close to the path, left. Higher up, the main path crosses the wall and continues unshackled. One may choose to keep by the wall in misty conditions, but its ultimate fate is the top of a crag, not the summit of the Illgill Head! Hence by this variant it is necessary to bear off left to reconnect with the, by now, strongly evident ascending path. Nearing the prominent shoulder the principal path splits again. Hold to the more regular path which takes the ridge head on by a cairn and leads irrevocably to the wind shelter cairn on Illgill Head's east top. While not the true summit of Illgill Head, this point does provide a priceless view of the head of Wastwater. The actual summit of **Illgill Head** (609m/1998ft) lies on the next swelling of the plateau south-west, the small summit cairn set only 30m from the escarpment brink. This is a breath-taking moment when clear – and heart-stopping moment when swirling mist envelops the fell top. So be warned.

Here you have a choice between the main ridge path and the sheep trod close to the rim. The ridge path heads on, falling steadily westward into the wide depression. There is every good reason to follow the lead of sheep and adopt their narrow trod along the very brink of **The Screes** escarpment. To

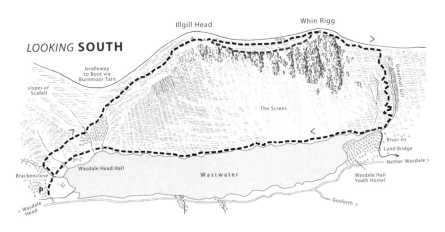

← Whin Rigg and The Screes bathed in evening light reflected in Wastwater

do so, trend right, off the common ridge path, to reach the obvious edge.

Excitement as you walk along the edge of the escarpment must be tempered by the severity of the fall and attention given to its nuances. There are sections where the continuing process of slippage is revealed in fracture slumps; note how even the sheep show due caution and keep to the firmer ground.

There are several places where arêtes permit one to venture onto spurs, allowing a more dramatic involvement in the majestic declivity and offering views of the dark depths of Wastwater from on high. The main ridge path, which has two winding variants, passes a pairs of tarns before ascending to the shelter cairn on the more certain summit knoll of **Whin Rigg** at 536m/1759ft.

This is a splendid spot, on the north side of the path, the ultimate ground of a mighty cliff. Gingerly walk the few paces further north to look down Great Gully towards Wasdale Hall Youth Hostel, backed by the lonely Western Fells, Buckbarrow, Middle Fell and Seatallan. The continuing path leads west at a gentle downward angle; watch for the prominent cairn marking the top of the

Path steps onto the chaos of boulder scree, seen pitching steeply into Wastwater

Greathall Gill path. This well-used path runs down the very steep grass slope to the east of the massive ravine. Its popularity ensures that lower down, during the zig-zags, it is untroubled by the otherwise dense bracken growth. Crossing a stile continue down with the gill to join the path beside the River Irt at the outflow of **Wastwater**.

Turn right passing the pumping house, emitting a steady hum. It is time to focus on the rigours ahead. Rigours? You've climbed the fell – what rigours can there be walking along the shore of a lake? Well, the path dwindles to a narrow trace and weaves through

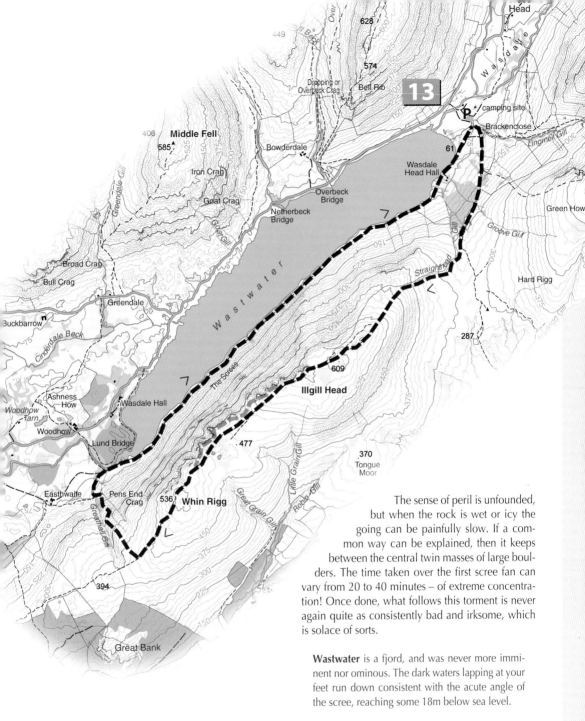

The sense of peril is unfounded, but when the rock is wet or icy the going can be painfully slow. If a common way can be explained, then it keeps between the central twin masses of large boulders. The time taken over the first scree fan can vary from 20 to 40 minutes – of extreme concentration! Once done, what follows this torment is never again quite as consistently bad and irksome, which is solace of sorts.

Wastwater is a fjord, and was never more imminent nor ominous. The dark waters lapping at your feet run down consistent with the acute angle of the scree, reaching some 18m below sea level.

an area of light tree growth to face, as face you must, the most awful tilt of boulders nature bequeathed a Lakeland path. Not even Broad Crag on a bad hair day can match the sheer mind-boggling maze of minor boulder problems, which seem to accumulate one after another, constantly raising the question as to whether the path is this way or that, up or down. There can be no true or constant path.

As the scree recedes and the bracken takes over, the beauties of Wasdale Head fill the senses with anticipation of a majestic mountain landscape. A field-gate heralds the advent of in-bye pasture (good quality land close to the farmstead), passing **Wasdale Head Hall**. Cross a stile and join the farm access lane leading back to base. Good job done – though for a 400 lateral metres, hard won.

← *Outflow of Wastwater from Greathall Gill*

Great End, Scafell Pike and Lingmell from Wasdale Head

*T*he majority of walkers attack Scafell Pike on long there-and-back expeditions from Borrowdale, Great Langdale and even Eskdale. However, the Scafells naturally belong to the company of Wasdale, a harmony revealed on this compact round trip. From Wastwater, Great Gable and Scafell command attention; from Wasdale Head all eyes rest upon Great Gable. Rough, tough and aloof, Scafell Pike resists valley admiration, and has to be climbed to be understood and known – Great Gable may be standing by, but this is the metaphorical roof of England.

The walk follows Lingmell Beck and the old pony route to Sty Head Pass and quickly steps onto The Band, mounting impressively up the north ridge of Great End. The broad stony plateau leads via Ill Crag into Broadcrag col and the final uncomfortable pull to the top of the Pike. The walk then descends north-west via Lingmell col to claim arguably the day's best moment, the view of Great Gable from Lingmell. Certainly by this moment you will be thoroughly relaxed, as the hard work of the day is all but done, and you can engage in the beauty of the view, especially if drenched in the warm evening sun.

↑ *Seathwaite Fell and Sprinkling Tarn from Great End*

ROUTE INFORMATION

Distance	13.5km/8½ miles
Height gain	1051m/3450ft
Time	8 hours
Grade	strenuous
Start point	GR183074
Maps	(Harvey Superwalker)
	Lakeland West
	(Ordnance Survey)
	OL6 South-western area

After-walk refreshment

The Wasdale Head Inn at Wasdale Head, The Screes or Strands Hotel at Nether Wasdale some 4 miles down the valley, and the Bridge Inn, a further 2 miles at Santon Bridge

The Start

The dedicated and discreet parking adjacent to the National Trust's Wasdale Campsite, GR183074.

The Route

Walk through the **Wasdale Campsite**, either by way of the main entrance, passing the reception/shop, or by following the farm track left via the gates. The ensuing bridleway fords the pebble beach of Lingmell Beck, proof positive of the violence of storm waters gathered from the highest ground in England. Note that at times of flood using the ford is impractical, and the valley road should be followed instead. Gorse as high as an elephant's eye ushers the track through via gates into pasture, with the track eventually emerging onto the valley road. Follow the road right and bear off right at the Millennium Village Green stone – on high summer weekends passing serried ranks of parked vehicles – to enter the walled lane at Lingmell House.

Pass the little yew-shaded church of St Olaf, patron saint of Norway, affirming the strong Viking link with this valley. The mass of gathered beck-stone accumulated in thick walls are a feature of

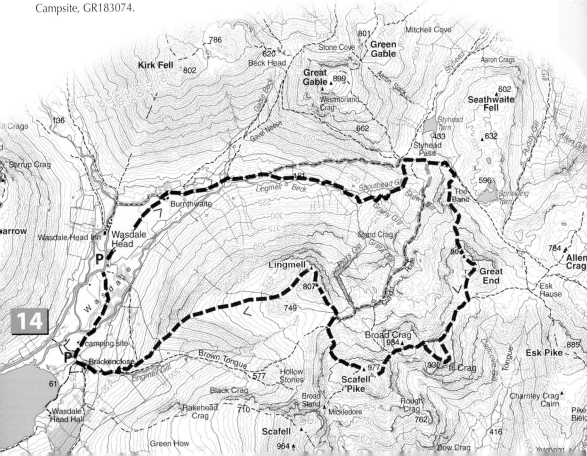

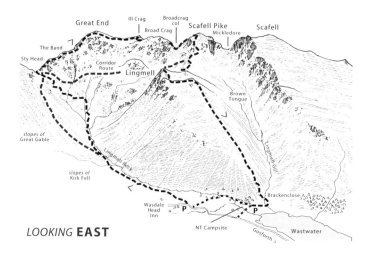

LOOKING **EAST**

the valley enclosures. Before the walls were built the valley floor must have been strewn with them, matching the confusion of boulders in **Lingmell Beck**. The bridleway is guided left between the barns at **Burnthwaite Farm**. From the gate go right. The lane balloons then constricts to a further gate and widens again on course to a footbridge over Gable Beck. There is a choice of paths to Styhead Pass. One may either stick with the common trail climbing across the apron strings of Great Gable or, as here preferred, turn to the historic course of the old pony route. As the path begins to rise a clear path forks right, shortly accompanying the beck-side wall to a hand-gate. Pass on through and keep close company with Lingmell Beck, crossing the stony feeder gills, with the bristling crags of Great Napes high to the left. Passing the confluence with **Piers Gill** find an appropriate ford some hundred metres further on, the pony path winding on up the grassy rigg initially close to Spouthead Gill.

Crossing the debris of **Skew Gill** bear up the fell left to reach the stretcher box at **Sty Head Pass**, where paths intersect. Turn right (east) and cross the stepping stones over the broad marshy depression upon the heavily used path (bound for Esk Hause). Ignore the obvious path right at a large cairn – this is the Corridor Route, a securely pitched and popular path leading to the head of Piers Gill. At that point the Corridor Route provides two options – the horrid scree path direct to Broadcrag col, left, or the route ahead via Lingmell col that joins the Brown Tongue route to the summit of Scafell Pike.

But the preferred option of the day heads east, and once the craggy end of **The Band** is passed and the first good stretch of pitching complete, veer off right ascending the grassy fellside to gain the skyline at your earliest convenience. There is no path to this point. At a shallow nick in the ridge a path draws in from the left (the more regular approach), but that first section of the ridge was certainly worth visiting. The ridge mounts easily, providing numerous gilt-edged excuses to pause and peer over the brink right towards Lingmell, with the head of Skew Gill a classic moment.

The ridge path now steepens, tackling a short, easy scramble that leads onto easier but nonetheless steep ground, with superb views down onto Sprinkling Tarn. Above a branch gully, a boulder slope spells the approach of the plateau. The second gully is worth gazing down. This is Cust's Gully, distinguished by a massive chock-stone.

Visit the western top of **Great End** before tracing the northern scarp to the stunning cliff-rimmed view of the Langdale Pikes and reaching the eastern top. The western top has the better situation, though the rockier eastern top is the highest point by a whisker at 909m/2982ft. All told the fell top is one of the most satisfying viewpoints in Lakeland. It is ignored by the majority of walkers, who unwittingly pass it by on the Calfcove path from Esk Hause, a mere inconvenience with Scafell Pike their singular intent.

Head south, keeping to the middle of the broad plateau for the easiest going as the route heads down to the junction with the Calfcove path, with

Lingmell Beck looking to Great End →

Lingmell and Great Gable from Scafell Pike

views east to Esk Pike. The popular path boulder hops onto the next narrower ridge before descending into the dip between Ill and Broad Crag. The scenic virtues of **Ill Crag** make it a worthy addition, the moss- and stone-mingled ground easily crossed. There are two rock castles to visit, both providing magnificent views into Eskdale. The higher commands a fine view over Little Narrowcove to Pen and, of course, the wildest, craggiest facade of Scafell Pike.

Regain the main thoroughfare and rise onto another travail of boulders before descending to the small gap of **Broadcrag col**. The path rising south-west from this point is in a horrid state – pity those who are forced to ascend and descend it. **Scafell Pike**, the roof of England, duly arrives at 977m/ 3206ft.

SCAFELL PIKE

From 11 till 4 on any normally welcoming day the summit is invariably as crowded as a city street, which promptly brings to mind William Blake's lines 'Great things are done when men and mountains meet/That are not done whilst jostling in the street'. In bitter conditions choose to harbour in the sturdy square Victorian 'open to the sky' shelter to the east; at other times the more solitary will wander off to the near outcrops to the east or west.

However, most will bide their time queuing to step up onto the summit rostrum. It is not the viewpoint one might have hoped for; Scafell trumps it. But then there is satisfaction in arrival, and on this particular walk a better viewpoint awaits at Lingmell. There is also solace in the knowledge that there is far less tough walking to contend with en route back to your valley base than most other visitors will have in store.

A chain of cairns guides west, the characteristic stony ground sustained. The path is never excessively steep, though it tilts down a slab at one point. Watch for the point where the **Corridor Route** branches right. Follow this, but immediately it shapes to descend, bear off left through outcrops. Cross the broken wall in the Lingmell col depression and ascend the largely grassy slope north-west. Make a point of keeping a right-hand bias as height is gained to revel in the stunning view down the vertical gully into **Piers Gill**, the portal pinnacles making fine photographic subjects framing Great Gable. **Lingmell's** rotund summit cairn, set upon a fine outcrop, very soon arrives at 807m/2649ft.

After the congregations at Scafell Pike the solitude is exquisite. The view of Great Gable is matchless, the impressive facade of crags, the Great Napes, seemingly spilling screes vertically to Lingmell Beck far below. Looking back south, Pikes and Scafell Crags form a magnificent focus above Hollow Stones. Invariably the day will be waning, and the softer light of early evening playing on the fell sides gives the scene a magical air. Evidence of heather has long since departed this fell, for all the implications in its name. Follow the edge naturally down in small steps to reach a spindly cairn marking the *piece de resistance*, a scenic viewpoint of Great Gable, with the fells girdling Mosedale, Kirk Fell, Pillar and Red Pike prominent. What a triumphant spot to conclude your mountain day.

Leave the cairn half-left, south-west, aiming across the slope to the high ground and crossing a broken wall to join a clear path which now embarks on a long descent of Lingmell's west ridge. As the slope steepens an initial set of stone steps flatter to deceive, for they are followed by unrestored loose gravel, and if you've avoided using walking poles hitherto, then they'll now prove their worth. The grassy slope is joined with much relief (one suspects that shortly after this guide is published the Fix the Fells project will have stabilised this path). The view left up Brown Tongue to Scafell Crag is spellbinding. Continue down via a ladder stile, crossing a transverse path with sporadic bushes and trees. As a fence is neared bear left to the kissing-gate on the Brown Tongue path. Continue on naturally via a stile and footbridge to pass **Brackenclose**, a club hut of Lakeland's elite Fell and Rock Climbing Club. Join the **Wasdale Head Hall** farm track, and cross a bridge and grid to complete the walk.

Broad Crag from Lingmell

Pillar, Scoat Fell,
Red Pike and Yewbarrow
from Wasdale Head

A natural skyline tour of the Mosedale Beck valley, otherwise known as the Mosedale Horseshoe. The ridge is gained at Black Sail Pass, rising by two stages to reach the high-domed summit of Pillar. Descending to Wind Gap the ridge path clambers onto the stony prow of Black Crag, from where walkers can either climb onto Scoat Fell, taking a spur route to capture the Steeple, or contour from the depression to rise more naturally onto the striking escarpment of Red Pike. A stepped descent to Dore Head brings a final decision to either take the easier line down the Over Beck valley or add the undoubted rough, tough spice of Yewbarrow to a stunning fell encounter.

The Start

Many drivers use the village green at Wasdale Head, but more appropriate parking lies close to the National Trust Wasdale Campsite, GR183074, at the head of Wastwater. This small tree-shaded area is respectful of the valley.

The Route

Walk through the **Wasdale Campsite** either via the main entrance, passing the reception/shop, or by following the farm track left via gates. The ensuing bridleway fords the amazing pebble beach of Lingmell Beck. Note that at times of flood using the ford is

↑ *Remarkably long-arched footbridge close to Wasdale Head Inn*

Distance	17.5km/11 miles
Height gain	1117m/3665ft
Time	8½ hours
Grade	arduous
Start point	GR183074
Maps	(Harvey Superwalker Map)
	Lakeland West
	(Ordnance Survey)
	OL6 South-western area and
	OL7 North-western area

After-walk refreshment

The Wasdale Head Inn

impractical, and the valley road should be followed instead. Ranks of gorse usher the track through via gates into pasture, with the track eventually emerging onto the valley road at a stile. Follow the road right, passing the village green to reach **Wasdale Head Inn**, and bear left in front of the Barn Door Shop, via a gate, turning right. Cross a stile, resisting the temptation to cross the beautifully simple stone bridge. Instead, follow the beck upstream, bearing left at the fork and rising through a gate and its left-hand successor.

The clear bridle path follows the wall above the well-hidden **Ritson Force** to a gate. Thereafter the path runs free of the wall, with the profound mountain bowl of Mosedale ahead. Bearing uphill to a gate, climb steadily, with a fine view back to Stirrup Crag and the screes running down from Dore Head. Ford the beck and zig-zag onto **Gatherstone Head**, continuing up the combe more steeply to reach the grassy saddle of **Black Sail Pass** at 542m/1778ft.

Leave the bridleway (bound for the Black Sail Youth Hostel in upper Ennerdale), bearing left from the large cairn, following the line of old metal boundary stakes and mounting onto **Looking Stead**. Immediately before the next steeper step in the ridge spot a small cairn above **Green Cove**, marking the start of the Climbers' Traverse to Pillar Rock (see below). However, it is a strenuous route and will not be within everyone's capacity. If in doubt, better save your energies for later in the day when you might contemplate the rigours of Yewbarrow, the last golden nail in the boot.

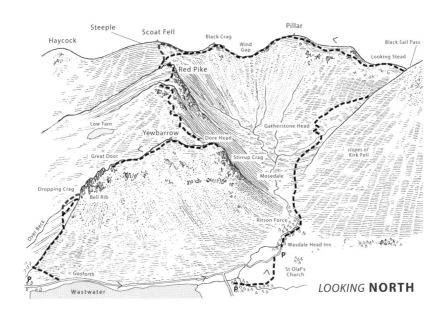

LOOKING **NORTH**

EXTENSION:
THE CLIMBERS' TRAVERSE TO PILLAR ROCK

Sure-footed walkers with the energy might consider following this intimate route. A very narrow path hugging the craggy northern escarpment rises and falls in staccato waves through Hind Cove to reach Robinson's Cairn, above Pillar Cove. At this point bear up the cove to the obvious, if loose, Shamrock Traverse rake, to the base of Pisgah.

From here the subsequent loose scree gully to the plateau is a fair scrambling tussle. During this adventure Pillar Rock is discovered and then appreciated in its magnificent whole.

The main route sticks to the ridge path and takes in a steep, rough section, the reward being stunning views of Robinson's Cairn far below and across Ennerdale to the High Stile ridge. Later still, steep gullies

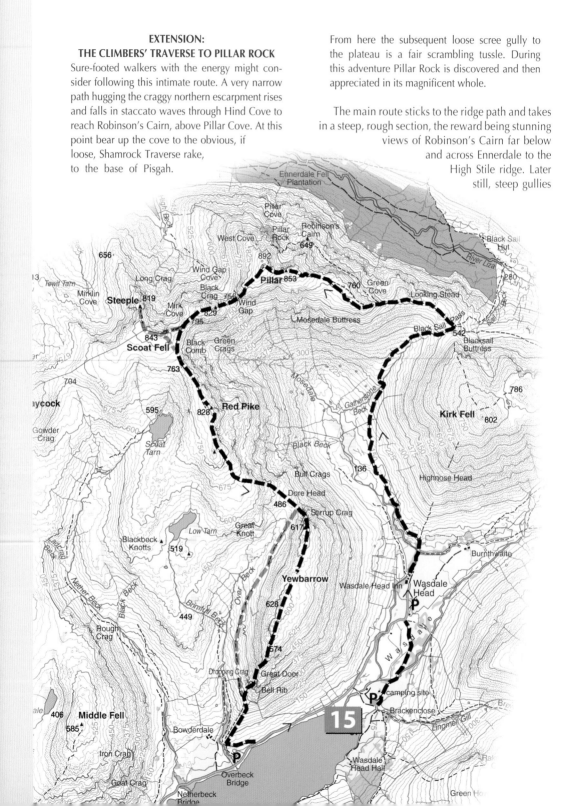

offer stirring views down into Pillar Cove, ahead of the final rise to the summit of **Pillar** at 892m/2926ft. This is one of the most compete fell viewpoints in Lakeland, a place to idle and visually absorb the layout of the greater fells. The wind-shelter and stone-built cairn appear fractionally lower than the cairn to the north, which marks the way to the brink high above Pillar Rock, with Pisgah and High Man only in view.

From the Ordnance Survey column turn southwest, with cairns a sure guide in mist. The slope steepens, with a fine view across Wind Gap to Black Crag. Rock steps lead to the saddle, with Windgap Cove right and the huge hollow of Mosedale left. Clamber onto **Black Crag**, latterly working over boulders to this intermediate summit. From the next top the Steeple is well seen across Mirk Cove.

There are two alternatives here. One may ascend the ridge to the wall-end amongst the boulders, continuing beside the wall on **Scoat Fell** 843m/2766ft (the wall occupying the summit) to make the enticing spur north onto **Steeple** (819m/2687ft), the top more a blunt rapier on a steep ridge rising out of Ennerdale. Having done so backtrack to the wall-end and descend south. The more natural course is

Wind-shelter on the summit of Pillar

to follow the contouring path which bears left just above the depression, crossing easy ground with a superb view of the magnificent scarp of Red Pike.

After reaching the depression south of Scoat Fell the climb south onto **Red Pike** (828m/2717ft) is simply achieved. The sensation of the abyss beneath one's feet is very much on a par with Dow Crag. The high ground holds awhile to a south-top cairn then falls. Keep to the ridge left of broken ground, with the path angling south-east to **Dore Head**.

Dore Head and Stirrup Crag

Appraise your strength and desire. The simple course of action is to bear right on the south side of the **Over Beck** valley to follow naturally beneath the steep slopes of Yewbarrow, passing beneath Dropping Crag to unite with the Yewbarrow route. However, if you have the stamina and agility Yewbarrow is a must, but consider your state of readiness carefully!

If you choose this more challenging option, cross Dore Head and follow the path up to the foot of **Stirrup Crag**. Until you actually reach this point the route appears to be for brave hearts only, but a large block hides a short gully weakness, and once underway the sequence of short scrambly pulls is easy to unravel, though would be a horrid winter descent. Beyond the large cairn is an easy ridge-top sheep pasture. **Yewbarrow** summit, a little further south, has a less substantial cairn at 628m/2060ft. This is a unique station commanding wonderful outlooks upon Great Gable, the Scafells and Wastwater – the unique preserve of Yewbarrow's private gallery.

Continuing south by steps and stages the ridge narrows down to **Great Door**. For walkers the ridge terminates here, and after glancing down the gully, left, to Wasdale Head Hall make the definite turn right. Steep ground leads to an old wall along the nape of **Dropping Crag**. Walking poles come to your rescue as the loose gully gives untidy footing. Scout to the left-hand side for the best going, more evident lower down, and you will eventually gain the salvation of firmer ground. The path goes left to cross a ladder stile, well below the fearsome peak of **Bell Rib**. Follow the wall down to where a stile crosses from the right-hand side. Here bear left, traversing the pasture to a stile in the fence. Resist attempting to join the road through the dense gorse, and follow the fence those few extra metres left. Within a mile the turning to the **Wasdale Campsite** is made.

Summit of Yewbarrow backed by Kirk Fell and Great Gable

Kirk Fell and Great Gable from Wasdale Head

*S*tanding in the open space of the Wasdale Head village green the fells seem to zoom up quickly on all fronts, shielding their finer qualities behind walls of bracken and scree. Only Great Gable is seen in true perspective, its distinctive 'gable' form flattering the eye, demanding attention. This walk sets its sights on Great Gable, but not in isolation, however splendid this may seem, for Kirk Fell is a true companion in arms. Perhaps the most profound mass of fell at hand, Kirk Fell rises a magnificent 722m/2370ft in one fell swoop immediately to the north of the Wasdale Head Inn.

Yet who in their right mind would think of tackling Highnose Head after breakfast? Well, having eyed it for many a long year and taken side swipes via Black Sail Pass and Beck Head, I fixed my mind on doing it, not just for the sheer hell of it, but because I felt it may very well prove a richly rewarding experience. I have to say I loved it. Accepted, it has a certain perverse purgatory written all over it, but by climbing and resting, climbing and resting, any ordinarily fit person can undertake the ascent and be heartily chuffed they did.

The option of heading for Black Sail Pass remains for other mortals to consider; the height gained over a greater distance ensures moderation. At Beck Head there is another choice – one may either stride over the top of Gable or delight in the South Traverse to Sty Head. Great stuff.

ROUTE INFORMATION

Distance	11.25km/7 miles
Height gain	1012m/3320ft
Time	6½ hours
Grade	strenuous
Start point	GR186085
Maps	(Harvey Superwalker) Lakeland West (Ordnance Survey) OL6 South-western area

After-walk refreshment
The Wasdale Head Inn

The Start
Park on the Wasdale Head village green, GR186085.

The Route
Follow the lane to the **Wasdale Head Inn**, bearing left in front of the Barn Door Shop. If it's a hot day, a bottle or two of water from the shop's chiller will be appreciated later. Pass through the gate and go right, crossing the stile but not the inviting single-arch stone footbridge. Continue upstream beside Mosedale Beck, taking the left-hand fork to begin the ascent.

At the top of the short bank a fence plugs the gap where the walls widen. Here you can choose the alternative, less strenuous route to Kirk Fell via Black Sail Pass. Take the left-hand gate and follow the bridle path to **Black Sail Pass**, en route fording **Gatherstone Beck** to ultimately reach the grassy pass. Here follow the line of the old fence right, clambering, and occasionally stumbling, to the **Kirk Fell** plateau.

Black Sail and Kirk Fell seen from Looking Stead on Pillar

The main route takes the right-hand gate in the short connecting fence. While you will expect a path to mount ahead, you'll also suspect it to be a small path, and sure enough it is! Nonetheless, it beats back the bracken on the turf bank, and a moment's rock-step is perhaps the first point where you'll stop for a breather. Climb on, mounting to a pronounced lip on **Highnose Head**, where you can take a longer pause and look appreciatively into Mosedale, measuring up Stirrup Crag on Yewbarrow and the great rough east face of Red Pike, invariably cast in dark shadow.

Turning again to the task all seems well – just a steep grass trod and the occasional pause to relish the increasingly heady view back down Wastwater to the famous flanking wall of The Screes. But after what seems an interminable time, scree intervenes and matters do worsen. Keep slightly to the right and walk on the undisturbed boulders, taking care to avoid the loose stuff – the product of over-enthusiastic athletes one suspects. Be heartened – it is only a matter of time before the loose gravel is surmounted.

A narrow grassy neck with eroded tufts of turf leads onto the coarse but easier header slopes leading over natural dykes to the **Kirk Fell** summit cairn.

KIRK FELL

Wow, that was invigorating and, it has to be conceded, a bit tiring too! The shelter cairn at 802m/ 2631ft is a place for a well-deserved rest – phew! The fell walkers who pass this way are, by and large, from the dedicated tier of the genre. They know a good place to visit right in the midst of mountain Lakeland, off the mule trails of the multitude.

Obviously Great Gable claims a lion's share of the visual attention, and rightly so – it is Kirk Fell's noble companion. The Scafells pitch in too, but don't pull rank, though they obscure the Coniston fells. While Pillar shows only its blank facade, elsewhere are riches and tantalising fell detail that will give the tired-limbed walker a good excuse to linger a little longer and absorb a sumptuous view.

The path angles down east-north-east, passing through the midst of **Kirkfell Tarns**, and climbs onto the adjacent rocky headland, which has more the air of a summit than the actual top. The old metal fence-line continues to the eastern brink and commands a superb view over Beck Head to Great Gable, an aspect that looks uncompromisingly rough. Thankfully, this is deceptive, and the imminent descent through the outcropping is on a well-evidenced path. **Beck Head** has two summer-dry tarns.

After Beck Head is a point of decision. Verve may seek to pull you irresistibly over the top of Great Gable, but you are not obliged to fall prey to this instinct and can circumvent the summit by taking the South Traverse path.

SOUTH TRAVERSE PATH

One of the fell's special delights is its girdle path, which evolved to provide access to the fell's famous climbing grounds. The south traverse is the main route giving access to, and enticing views of, the stirring detail of the Great Napes, mingled with easy tussles with boulders and Hell Gate screes.

The route begins down to the right, before the slope of Gable Beck falls away. From a cairn a contouring path works across the boulder scree due south, crossing the head of the Gavel Neese ridge, then angles east over Little Hell Gate. By one modest rock-step it sets course under the famous Great Napes cliffs, glimpsing Napes Needle and, later, a backward view up to the Sphinx Rock. Such places may be reached by competent scramblers. But the traverse itself drifts down over Great Hell Gate and, via the huge boulders beneath Kern Knotts, contours over the near edge to arrive at the stretcher box at Sty Head.

In spite of the attractions of the South Traverse route, from Beck Head the summit of Great Gable remains the principal destination. The ascending path begins upon loose gravel, crossing the course of **Moses Trod**. It climbs the rocky north-west ridge, with only the briefest moments when hands to rock may be needed among the large blocks as the ridge steepens; but there is nothing to impede. Cairns lead away from the northern edge to **Great Gable's** summit rocks at 899m/2949ft.

Great Napes from the Lingmell Beck bridle path

SUMMIT OF GREAT GABLE

A plaque records the acquisition of the near sur-round of high fells in memory of those members of the Fell and Rock Climbing Club who gave their lives in the two world wars. This is the scene of an annual Remembrance Sunday service, per-haps the most poignant occasion that occurs on the Lakeland fells. It is now open to all fell walkers, who attended, almost regardless of the weather, in large numbers at the heart of moun-tain Lakeland, celebrating the liberty so won.

First-time visitors to the summit will adore the all-round panorama, in spite of the assem-bled crowds. For personal peace visit the Westmorland Cairn, situated a matter of 130m to the south-west. The view of the Scafells and Wasdale is peerless.

Leave the summit in a south-easterly direction. The path begins at an easy angle and never really worsens. In fact, so much remedial work has been done on the path, especially solidly stepped pitch-ing, that one drifts down almost at ease.

Arriving at the stretcher box marking the **Sty Head Pass** intersection (the alternative route via the South Traverse joins the main route here), simply turn right the main path, step-ping down over Toad How to angle steadily down across the lower scree-streaked slopes of Great Gable. After a gate the part-pitched path evolves into a grass path leading over a

*Fell and Rock memorial on the summit of Great Gable
(photo: Peter Burgess)*

footbridge spanning Gable Beck. It then continues via two gates, passing through **Burnthwaite Farm** and along its approach lane to complete a thor-oughly rewarding mountain day.

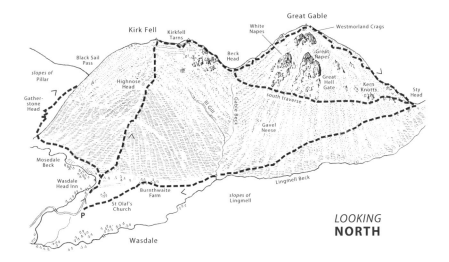

LOOKING
NORTH

Buckbarrow,
Seatallan and Middle Fell
from Nether Wasdale

A natural fell circuit at the entrance to Wasdale proper. The route embraces the rugged scarp facade of Buckbarrow (approx. 427m/1400ft), takes in the great leg-stretching march over Nether Wasdale Common onto the whale-backed Seatallan (693m/2274ft), and turns back over the deceptively simple ridge of Middle Fell 585m/1919ft. The latter part of the walk enjoys superb perspectives towards the magnificent screes of Illgill Head and Whin Rigg, which appear above stately oakwoods.

In haste most fell walkers actually choose to start from the open road at Greendale rather than Nether Wasdale, perhaps oblivious of the virtues of the longer approach – the lower woods and pastures giving truth to the descriptive 'green dale'. Nether Wasdale is exemplary as a community – whilst forfeiting nothing to its setting, it serves the needs of the visitor with two hotels, a pub with B&B, a sensitively cared for camping ground and even a beautifully positioned camping barn at Murt Farm.

　　　　　↑ Buckbarrow from Gill

ROUTE INFORMATION

Distance	13.5km/8½ miles
Height gain	808m/2650ft
Time	6 hours
Grade	energetic
Start point	GR125041
Maps	(Harvey Superwalker)
	Lakeland West
	(Ordnance Survey)
	OL6 North-western area

After-walk refreshment

The Screes or Strands Hotel, not forgetting (up the hill) the Low Wood Hotel, all located within the tiny community of Nether Wasdale

The Start

Park either in the car parks of the Strands Hotel or The Screes (seek proprietor's permission), or on the green in front of the little parish church of St Michael and All Angels at Nether Wasdale, GR125041.

The Route

Follow the footpath signed 'Gill and Buckbarrow' that leads via the farmhouse and sheep-handling pens at **Church Stile Farm**. The track leads on by the farm holiday park. The site fully merits the Gold Conservation Award posted at the entrance. The waymarked footpath bears right onto a green track leading beside an oakwood to a ladder stile. A more confined path rises through gorse to reach a further ladder stile and duckboards, then the pasture footpath heads on via gates, with Buckbarrow a striking feature ahead. Enter an outrake lane (the traditional term for a passage leading to common grazing) at a gate. This leads via a ford and footbridge, and on passing **Gill Farm** it becomes a gravelled farm access lane. Rising by a cottage, cross the cattle grid then bear right to join the open road.

Almost at once step off the road and ascend to the right of **Gill Beck**, with the rising wall close right. The wall is soon lost on the obvious ascending path through the depleting bracken. The path draws right on the steady climb with every excuse to stop and look back over the diminutive **Tosh Tarn** and the wood-dappled vale. Ford the upper gill, rising with the ridge, and either scramble up the steep slab

Rock-band and steep ramp scramble to the summit of Buckbarrow   107

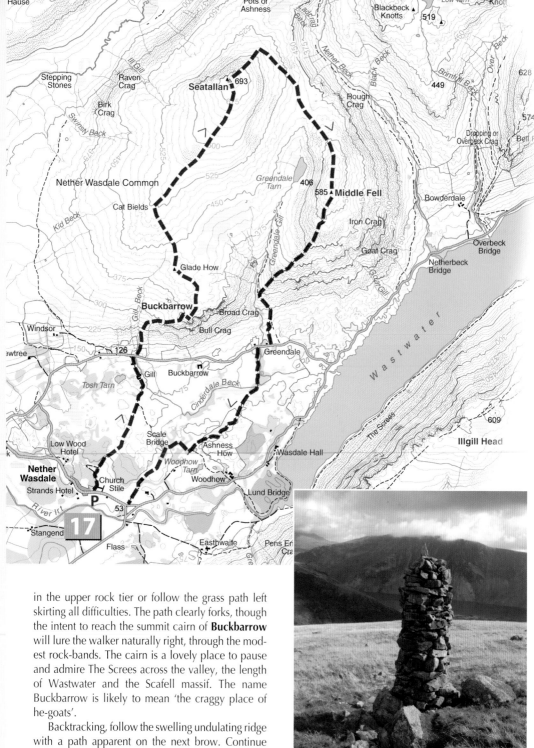

Map labels:

Hause · Pots of Ashness · Blackbeck Knotts · 519 · Low Tarn · Knott

Stepping Stones · Raven Crag · Seatallan 693 · Rough Crag · 449 · 628

Birk Crag · Swinsy Beck · Ill Gill · 574 · Dropping or Overbeck Crag · Bell B

Nether Wasdale Common · Greendale Tarn · 406 · 585 Middle Fell · Bowderdale

Cat Bields · Kid Beck · Greendale Gill · Iron Crag · Overbeck Bridge

Glade How · Goat Crag · Netherbeck Bridge

Gill Beck · Buckbarrow · Broad Crag · Wastwater

Windsor · Bull Crag · Greendale

wtree · 126 · Gill · Buckbarrow · The Screes · 609

Tosh Tarn · Cinderdale Beck · Illgill Head

Scale Bridge · Ashness How · Wasdale Hall

Low Wood Hotel · Woodhow Tarn · Woodhow · Lund Bridge

Nether Wasdale · Church Stile · Strands Hotel · P · 53

Stangend · **17**

Flass · Easthwaite · Pens En Cra · River Irt

in the upper rock tier or follow the grass path left skirting all difficulties. The path clearly forks, though the intent to reach the summit cairn of **Buckbarrow** will lure the walker naturally right, through the modest rock-bands. The cairn is a lovely place to pause and admire The Screes across the valley, the length of Wastwater and the Scafell massif. The name Buckbarrow is likely to mean 'the craggy place of he-goats'.

Backtracking, follow the swelling undulating ridge with a path apparent on the next brow. Continue north-east to the old shepherd's cairn on **Glade How**, which translates as 'the mound of the red kite'. The open pasture loses its rocky ribs on the steady rise to the isolated cairn on **Cat Bields**, evidently once frequented by wild cats. To the west the towers and turrets of Sellafield are a reminder of 20th-century

Joss Naylor's cairn on Buckbarrow

Yewbarrow backed by Great Gable from Seatallan

technology, a stark contrast with this bare upland which is almost devoid of man-made distractions – intervening clear-felled conifers in the upper Bleng valley apart. A narrow path winds easily on along the broad ridge in a confident north-easterly direction, rising onto **Seatallan's** gently domed top.

SEATALLAN

Seatallan stands at arm's length from the best of Wasdale, but provides an impressive perspective on it all, with the summit tumulus suggesting an ancient landmark significance, adapted into a wind-shelter. A matter of 20m west stands a stone-built Ordnance Survey column; otherwise the summit is barren.

Enjoy the spacious views: Haycock seems perhaps more distant than one might have expected; Scoat Fell and Red Pike are in simple profile; while Great Gable and the Scafells beyond Yewbarrow sit grand and aloof.

The name Seatallan means 'high land belonging to Ailene', a old Irish-Norse personal name, also apparently evidenced in the fell name Starling Dodd.

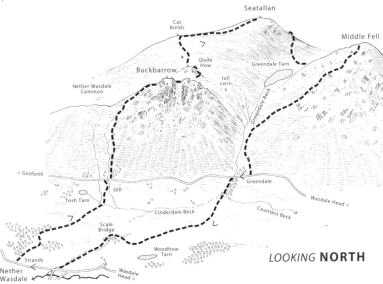

LOOKING **NORTH**

From the summit a small cairn gives guidance for the easy, progressively steepening descent from the north-east brow. As the ridge starts to ease, with the deep hollow of the **Pots of Ashness** below, break right, guided by a prominent cairn on a rock. Pass under the rocky bluff of Winscale Hows along a definite shoulder to reach the broad rushy saddle at the head of Greendale. In misty conditions take care to avoid being drawn down into the deeply entrenched Nether Beck valley. From the saddle **Greendale Tarn** can be espied down-dale, the upland bowl within which it rests is less than emerald. The intention is to keep to the emerging ridge leading south via prominent and avoidable rock outcrops onto **Middle Fell**.

The cairn is a further place to stop and enjoy the Wasdale scene, the Scafells especially revealed in grand perspective. The name Middle Fell described the high fell between the two 'barrows' – Buckbarrow and Yewbarrow – where the term 'barrow' signifies a rocky mountain eminence. From the open road, running close to the shores of Wastwater, Middle Fell looks uninviting, with no hint of a break in the irregular craggy wall. However, a clear path, free of obstacles, runs over the top leading down the south-south-west ridge to join the Greendale Tarn path. The Wasdale Screes command attention as the path sweeps down through the bracken to reach the open space next to **Greendale House** (alternative parking at GR145056 for this walk).

Go right along the road and, crossing **Greendale Bridge**, take the footpath left at the gate, signed 'Galesyke'. The clear path leading down through Roan Wood emerges into pasture at a gate, and a green track ensues. After the second gate, ignore the signed path to the lake and advance to a third gate by the attractive rocky eminence of Ashness How. Ignore the fenced lane at the next gate. Turn immediately right at the stile, follow the green track via a gate and bear left upon meeting a wall in open woodland, crossing the gated **Scale Bridge**. Go half-left, and continue the short distance to pass through the gate and wall squeeze-stile. Joining the green bridleway go left, with the wall close left, to a gate at Mill Place. Pass the cottages, following the access lane to the road, and turn right to complete this grand little fell round to **The Strands**.

Newly weaned Herdwick lambs backed by Illgill Head and Whin Rigg

Crag Fell,
Caw Fell and Haycock
from Ennerdale Bridge

*E*ntering into the spirit of Wild Ennerdale, this expedition ventures onto the high southern skyline ridge of the valley to claim the comparatively remote summit of Haycock. In the process it gets close up to the curious curtain of rock known as Crag Fell Pinnacles, striding beside the well-constructed ridge wall over Iron Crag and visiting four very different summits – each with notable viewpoints to savour. The latter stages of the walk run down through the heather and along the bowered southern shore of Ennerdale Water in the company of the Coast to Coast Walk and scramble over the craggy base of Anglers' Crag.

The Start
Drive to the village of Ennerdale Bridge, turn east at the primary school and fork right at the Broadmoor Forest Enterprise sign to reach a naturally well-screened car park at Bleach Green Cottages, GR086154.

The Route
Leave the cosy environs of the car park, via the hand-gate, strolling close to the meandering **River Ehen** as the path leads smartly to the outflow of the great lake, a place of congregation for families and friends. Ahead across the lake rises Great Borne backed by

↑ Crag Fell across Ennerdale Water, a glorious blending of heather and bracken tones　　　111

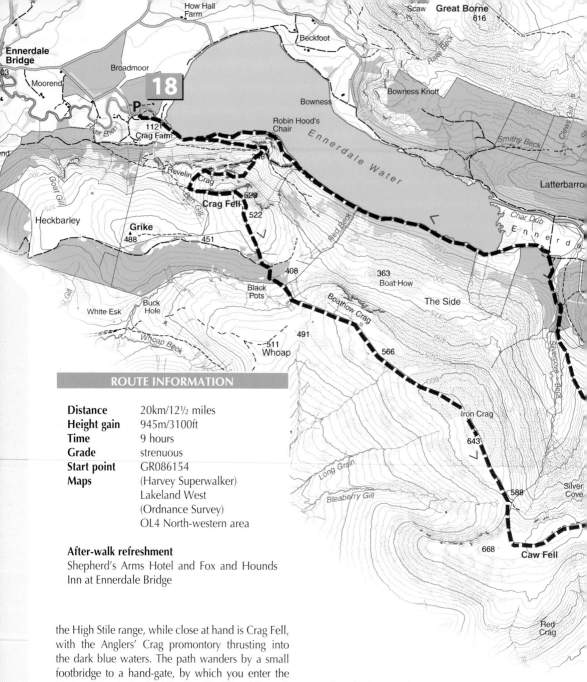

ROUTE INFORMATION

Distance	20km/12½ miles
Height gain	945m/3100ft
Time	9 hours
Grade	strenuous
Start point	GR086154
Maps	(Harvey Superwalker)
	Lakeland West
	(Ordnance Survey)
	OL4 North-western area

After-walk refreshment

Shepherd's Arms Hotel and Fox and Hounds
Inn at Ennerdale Bridge

the High Stile range, while close at hand is Crag Fell,
with the Anglers' Crag promontory thrusting into
the dark blue waters. The path wanders by a small
footbridge to a hand-gate, by which you enter the
National Trust's Anglers' Crag land holding. The path
continues at lake level, though be watchful for the
indistinct fork in the way, midway towards the headland. Here, take the rising path moving easily up to
the saddle of the **Anglers' Crag** headland. Visit the
craggy headland's crown, which is quite a viewpoint,
commanding Ennerdale Water. Notice the mid-lake
shallow isle and, beyond, see the afforested slopes
of Bowness Knott before Great Borne's scree-scarred
slopes. Ennerdale's majestic flanking fells are well
seen, with Pillar an eye-catching object of attention.

Step back onto the
saddle and branch south.
With the objective of a close
inspection of the **Crag Fell Pinnacles**, your choice
of path is critical. Quickly the path forks. The more
obvious right-hand path leads securely under the pinnacles, but once beyond you will have to clamber up
the rough bilberry bank and backtrack over the brow
to get that all-important close-up view. Alternatively,
the preferred route takes the less likely left-hand fork
straight uphill, which looks little more than a sheep

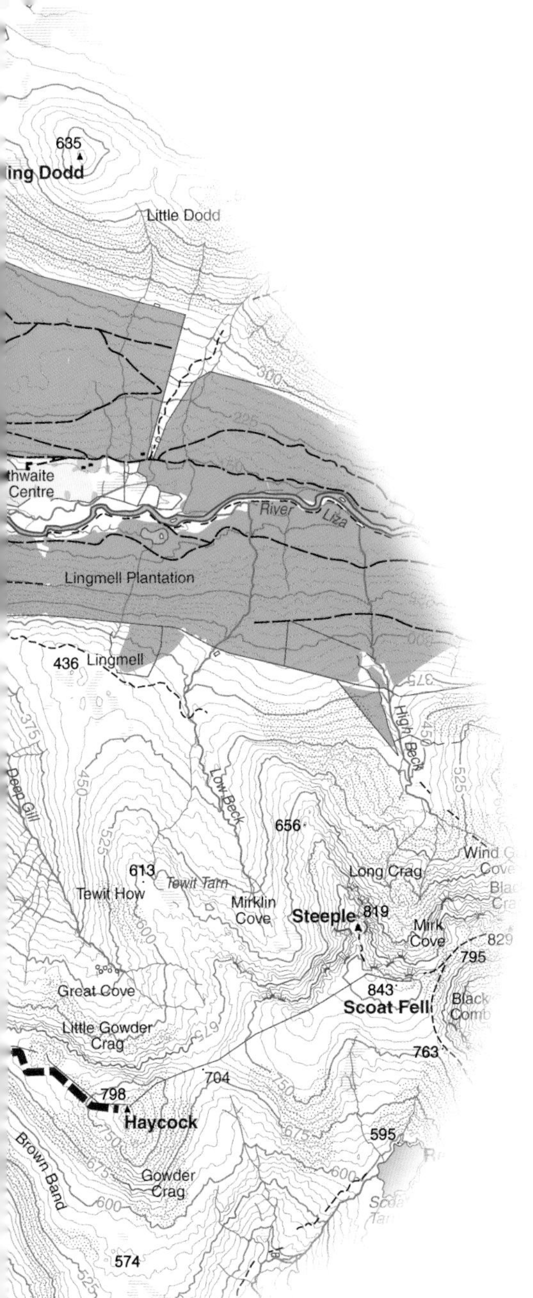

The map labels (read as on the map):

635
ing Dodd
Little Dodd
thwaite Centre
River Liza
Lingmell Plantation
436 Lingmell
High Beck
Low Beck
656
613 Tewit Tarn
Tewit How
Mirklin Cove
Steeple 819
Long Crag
Mirk Cove
Wind
Cov
Bla
Cra
829
795
Great Cove
843
Scoat Fell
Black Comb
763
Little Gowder Crag
704
798
Haycock
595
Gowder Crag
574

The exiting path, to the west, basically contours round to the plain fell edge, meeting a rising path over a curious grassy rampart. Switch up the edge passing an old metal strainer post to wander along the lip of the escarpment. Revel in **Revelin's** outlook high across the mighty lake to the ever more impressively displayed mountains surrounding and compressing Ennerdale proper. Revelin is an intriguing name; Sheffield climbers will recognise the name from their own Revelin Edge north-west of the city.

A suitably large cairn marks the summit of **Crag Fell** 523m/1716ft. Achieving of the first summit of the day is always a satisfying moment, especially one so well favoured, the situation confirming one is at the portals of a great valley. Back to the near west the plain-featured fell Grike is seen crowned with a considerable cairn. While the low country to the north-west leads the eye to coastal Cumbria with the potential to see the Scottish hills beyond, notably Criffel near Dumfries. Wander onto the second top – a mere metre lower, but no less scenically endowed.

path. Skirt the fans of scree into a shallow rake, from where one may clamber up close above the Crag Fell Pinnacles.

The name 'pinnacles' is a trifle over-egging the matter, though the end rock tower of this curtain of slumped rock certainly meets the criteria or critical mass. The area behind, in the shadow of the Revelin Crag edge, is fun to explore, and various creative camera angles on the shapely rocks can be found to encourage an indulgent few minutes.

Haycock from the Croasdale road in winter

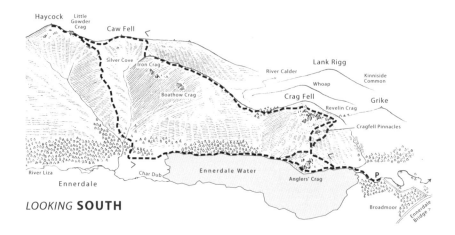

LOOKING **SOUTH**

Attention now turns to the inviting ridge of Iron Crag, rising some distance away beyond a finger of forestry in the depression to the south-east. The path leaves Crag Fell summit approximately south. There is a regular path, which drifts easily and naturally south-east after some 300m, heading down to a light fence stile at the leading corner of a plantation. Traverse the heather clearing, passing wind-blown conifers to join a track at a cairn. No sooner have you set foot on the track than you are impelled to strike right down a damp, shaded forest break. As this forks keep left on a rough path that leads to a fence stile beside a fixed gate. Freedom again.

A steady ascent begins, with the handsome dry-stone wall climbing the ridge for company. The construction should impress – great craftsmanship deserves admiration. This pasture is part of the vast **Kinniside Common**, the impoverished white grass, with little else, indicative of a tradition of heavy sheep stocking. Contrast the dense blanket of

Pillar and Steeple from Iron Crag

Steeple and Scoat Fell from Haycock

Haycock from the foot of Deep Gill

heather and bilberry rampant over the wall. The wall first climbs above the unseen **Boathow Crag** then, with a ruckle of rock, mounts onto Iron Crag's crest, again the named crag lies out of sight on the east side of the ridge.

During the ascent the lonely, single gill-scarred slope of Lank Rigg (which meant 'long ridge') is seen across Worm Gill. The term 'worm' probably suggests a traditional haunt of adders. There are three hand-gates in the wall that may be used to venture through the third gate, gaining access to **Iron Crag's** summit cairn at 640m/2100ft. A further cairn stands beyond the habitat-monitoring enclosure, and on the southern edge there is a fine viewpoint across the head of Silver Cove to Haycock. The enclosure proves that the grazing regime over the whole of the Iron Crag ridge is in balance, there being negligible difference between the vegetation within and that without.

Continue on the Kinniside Common side of the wall, descending through the depression to mount the blunt north ridge onto Caw Fell. Reaching the wall corner one might bear right to pass the shallow wind shelter and visit the western brink cairn, with the towers of Sellafield seen dead ahead and, down below, Stockdale Moor, with its evidence of ancient settlement. The more likely course is to turn left with the broken wall and new fence to the summit cairn of **Caw Fell**, reached via a fence stile. The fence has been installed while the wall is being rebuilt to nurture these high sub-alpine meadows.

Step back over the stile, continuing on the south side of the wall to either climb the broken outcrop of **Little Gowder Crag** or skirt to the right, avoiding all trace of rock. The ridge wall leads unerringly to the marvellous top of **Haycock**. There are two cairns of equal height on either side of the broken wall; the shelter cairn on the north side the better viewpoint by a whisker. The most arresting point of interest is Scafell Crag and, to a lesser degree, Seatallan, the latter best viewed from the outcrop to the south, above Gowder Crag.

The trail now turns tail, backtracking beyond Little Gowder Crag to cross the first stile, right, and angle across the slope, passing over the top of the prominent outcrop to join the path descending Caw Fell's north ridge. This eventually leads down through heather to a fence stile and continues into light woodland, branching left at the foot to cross a footbridge spanning **Silvercove Beck**. Starling Dodd becomes a prominent subject above the conifers to the north. Galloway cattle graze in this partially felled enclosure.

The path leads to a track junction, where you keep right to reach the forest exit gate. Go through, but turn immediately left, via the kissing-gate, and in so doing join the Coast to Coast Walk. Follow this in pasture via a stile and a succession of hand-gates, coming in alongside the southern shore of **Ennerdale Water**, beautifully fringed with native woodland and pitched to cope with long-distance trekkers. The path eventually rises, above the steep scree tilting into the lake, onto **Robin Hood's Chair**, beneath **Anglers' Crag**. Hands may be called into play as you work over this minor rock obstacle. Thereafter the path dips back to shore level and reconnects with the out-walk leading to the lake outflow.

Steeple, Scoat Fell and Pillar
from Bowness Knott

*T*he re-wilding of Ennerdale, known as the Wild Ennerdale project, is a laudable attempt to restore nature's balance in a valley that has been ill served in the last hundred years, particularly with the imposition of alien conifers. Progressively the pines and firs are being felled and the valley given a new lease of life, restoring it to a more natural state. With vision and patience, time is the great healer.

This is a long walk, and the mountain experience is well worth the effort. The route follows the main valley track to the head of Ennerdale Water and branches over the river above Char Dub to climb through the plantations onto the dense heather moor and high onto Steeple. Quickly and easily connecting with Scoat Fell, the walk follows the skyline over Black Crag to Pillar and down the stepped ridge by Looking Stead to Black Sail Pass. Here it takes leave of the ridge and follows the old bridle path from Wasdale Head that leads down into upper Ennerdale. After passing the remote Black Sail Youth Hostel, the walk concludes some 5 miles down-dale, largely in the company of Coast to Coast walkers.

↑ *Mountain backdrop to Ennerdale Water in winter*

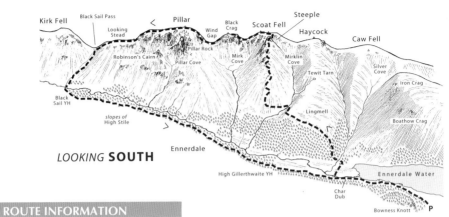

LOOKING **SOUTH**

ROUTE INFORMATION

Distance	21km/13 miles
Height gain	914m/3000ft
Time	9 hours
Grade	arduous
Start point	GR109153
Maps	(Harvey Superwalker)
	Lakeland West
	(Ordnance Survey)
	OL4 North-western area

After-walk refreshment

The Shepherds Arms Hotel and Fox and Hounds Inn at Ennerdale Bridge, and the Lamplugh Tip Inn at Lamplugh

The Start

Park in the Forest Enterprise Bowness Knott car park, GR109153. In the best of modern traditions this facility is lost among the trees at the formal road-end from Croasdale. There is no public vehicular access beyond the car park, for all the appearance of the roadway leading on to High Gillerthwaite. Youth hostellers are the one exception, as they can legitimately drive to their accommodation.

The Route

Embark upon the forest track which soon reverts back to metalling. Attention early on is captured by Anglers' Crag projecting into the lake from beneath Crag Fell, yet, on turning a corner, eyes are drawn by the distant prospect of Pillar. The track crosses **Smithy Beck**, with its attendant trails, and passes a picnic spot on a short promontory, the end of many a casual family stroll. The River Liza feeding into the

lake is known as **Char Dub**, and the road runs beside this to an obvious T-junction. Turn right, crossing the ford-bridge, with a fenced track leading to a gate into the thinned plantation, where a small herd of docile Galloway cattle may be encountered. Bear left, crossing the concrete ford-bridge over Woundell Beck to locate a rising break right.

Leave the level track, with little early evidence of a regular path, and ascend via a fence stile and oddly located bench in the midst of **Lingmell Plantation**. Higher, go through a gate climb with an evident path up a rough tapering fenced passage. The backward views feature the full length of Ennerdale Water. As the heather moor is gained bear up left to cross a fence stile and, keeping close to the left-hand fence-line, traverse **Lingmell**. Passing a large erratic, the path veers away from the fence en route to a ford in **Low Beck** at the foot of Mirklin Cove.

The path subsequently contours a further erratic 150m before drifting uphill with a rather lackadaisical and vague commitment to climbing Steeple. The path is steady but sure, with the sense of climbing a peak little appreciated. The higher you go, the better the outlook, and the route is surprisingly devoid of hazard. Progressively one is aware of coming onto a narrowing ridge, and the senses are excited as the great hollow of **Mirk Cove** grows beneath one's feet. Peering eastward the crags spilling from Black Crag captivate, though the famous Pillar Rock is poorly viewed at this stage of the journey. The final rocky ground on **Steeple** gives way to the neatest of summits at 819m/2687ft, quite the fulfilment of one's fell-climbing dreams. If the link with Scoat Fell were greater, with a correspondingly deeper gap, it would be one of the premier fells in Lakeland. But that is not the case – and the connection is simply traversed.

The parent fell, Scoat, appears to derive its name from the Scandinavian describing 'sharply projecting ground' (in parallel to Kinder Scout). One must assume this to be a reference to Steeple. The ridge has a substantial wall running along its spine, and takes in its stride the actual summit of **Scoat Fell** at 843m/2766ft. At the eastern end slip down through the boulders, via a shallow depression, rising gently onto the top of **Black Crag**, 829m/2720ft.

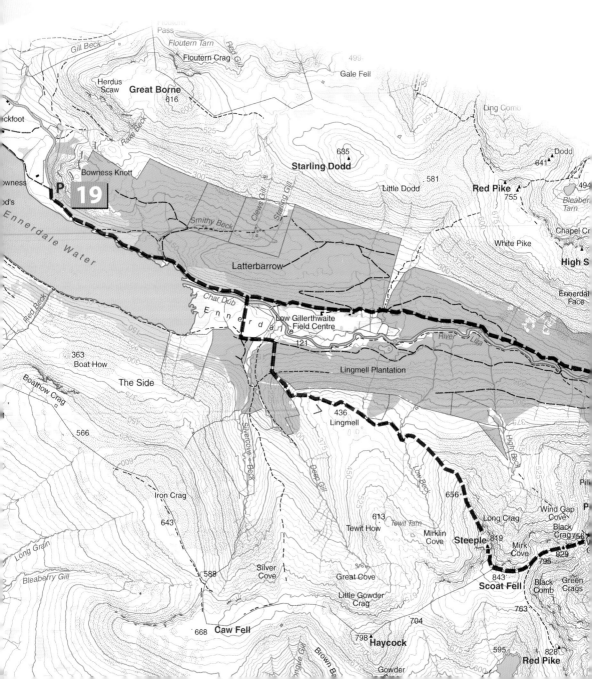

A group of walkers congregate on the summit of Steeple as seen across Mirk Cove from Black Crag

The **view** back from the northern edge of Black Crag to Steeple above Mirk Cove is hugely impressive – wild Ennerdale exists in these hanging valleys. Down to the right the vast hollow of Mosedale leads the eye to the Scafells and Great Gable above Wasdale Head.

From the cairn on Black Crag the path again encounters large boulders, but the way soon eases on the way down to **Wind Gap**, a narrow saddle. Next comes one of those messy, scrambly climbs that must always defy the best efforts of the Fix the Fells squad. The one solace is that it's easier in ascent. The roughest terrain soon overcome, the path leads unerringly to the summit of **Pillar** at 853m/2799ft. The wind shelter and stone-built OS column seem a shade lower than a further cairn 50m to the north, marking the high ground above Pillar Rock.

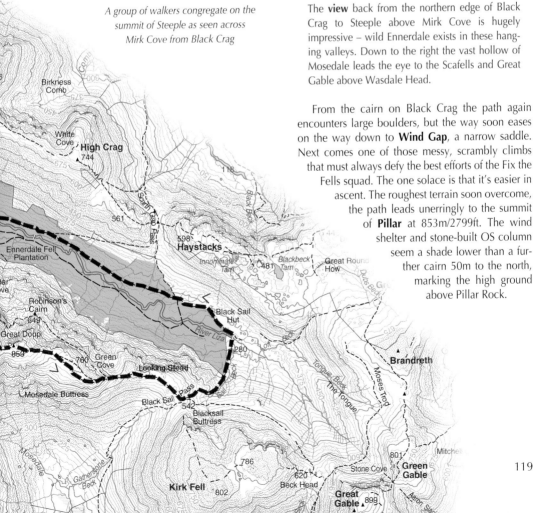

PILLAR ROCK

If you are feeling like a spring chicken then you might fancy a closer look at the magnificent Pillar Rock, as a spur. Descend the north-west ridge, where a handsome aspect can be gained, then climb back to continue.

This is no place to recommend venturing down to the Shamrock Traverse, gained by a more direct descent over steep and hostile ground towards the Rock. The ordinarily competent walker can follow it, but then it is better taken during an ascent out of Pillar Cove off the Climbers' Traverse from Robinson's Cairn.

While Pillar Rock may be tempting, this current long expedition needs no hold-up, so it is recommended that the natural ridge path is followed eastwards, with cairns confirming the way in mist. The ridge comes above northern gullies with views down into Hind Cove, from where Robinson's Cairn

Plaque on Robinson Cairn beside the climbers' traverse in Pillar Cove

may be spotted far below, with the plain south slopes of the High Stile ridge beyond across the deep trough of Ennerdale. The path drifts slightly right off the strict top of the ridge, stepping down rough ground coming left above **Green Cove**, where the Climbers' Traverse begins at a coy cairn. Ignore this, and keep to the ridge path running over **Looking Stead** to join the broken line of an old metal boundary fence down to **Black Sail Pass**.

By comparison with the rough terrain elsewhere, this broad grassy saddle comes as welcome relief. The popular bridle path is now joined at a cairn. Turn left to begin a steep but untroubled descent into upper Ennerdale, coming by **Sail Beck** and a wall bounding the extent of formerly afforested fell.

Cross the new footbridge and bear left, the path striding on past **Black Sail Youth Hostel**. Here it becomes a track that continues without further incident for 5 miles down-dale to the car park. After all that rough ground the simplicity of the track will be greatly enjoyed, as too the camaraderie shared with Coast to Coast walkers, who by-and-large walk eastbound, up the valley.

← *Pillar Rock, western aspect*   ↑ *Pillar Cove from High Crag*

Mellbreak from Lanthwaite Wood

*F*rom Kirkstile, Mellbreak rises like some colossus, a great gable if ever there was one. Fear not the climb – it's a steady pull despite the loose shards and lack of pitching. With the north top underfoot the hard work is largely done, but the scenic delights roll on and on. The route crosses the broad heather-clad saddle to reach the higher south summit, then descends towards Scale Beck to visit Scale Force before heading north-east to follow the lakeshore path beside Crummock Water to its outflow, thus completing a most rewarding fell/lake encounter.

The Start

The Loweswater locality is not well supplied with car parking. In the vicinity of the Kirkstile Inn there is room for half-a-dozen orderly parked cars at Church Bridge (GR139203), with a couple more on the verge below the Inn and at the road junction by the phone box to the east. The only formal car park in the vicinity lies at Lanthwaite Wood, a National Trust access point to the foot of Crummock Water (GR148215), so this is the start of the walk.

The Route

From Lanthwaite Wood car park turn left. Cross Scalehill Bridge, following the road, and take the second left, at the telephone kiosk, advancing below St Bartholomew's Church and the Kirkstile Inn, the most densely inhabited part of the rural parish of Loweswater.

Follow on, with the road signed 'No through road', crossing Church Bridge and swinging from west to south as you rise past **Kirkgate Farm** and

↑ *Buttermere from the southern end of Mellbreak*

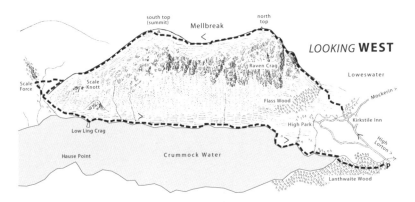

LOOKING **WEST**

ROUTE INFORMATION

Distance	11.5km/7¼ miles
Height gain	686m/2250ft
Time	4½ hours
Grade	energetic
Start point	GR148215
Maps	(Harvey Superwalker) Lakeland West (Ordnance Survey) OL4 North-western area

After-walk refreshment
The Kirkstile Inn at Loweswater

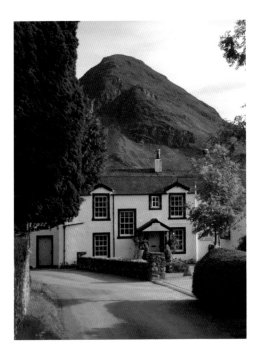

Kirkstile Inn backed by Mellbreak

the modern house after it. The bridle lane rises, and soon becomes flanked by sturdy walls, winding attractively through pastures mingled with cattle and sheep. The lane leads up to and through a gate. Now leave the bridle track and head straight up through the break in the plantation strip onto the fell pasture. The popular path climbs up through the bracken, so keep to the rising line, ignoring the faint right-fork trod into Mosedale – frequently used on a shorter return descent from the saddle of Mellbreak.

The path drifts half-left and steps into a trail of loose shards. The going inevitably slows as you concentrate on each step. The path zig-zags, with no evidence of modern pitching, although some is needed on this inevitably much used and enjoyed fell ascent. The view back to Carling Knott, Loweswater and Low Fell will give rise to frequent stops, the prospect enhanced in late summer when the heather becomes a foreground delight. Viewed from below, the scree- and crag-dominated northern aspect of the fell looks problematic, but the path proves no more difficult than any steady plod. Indeed, for all the discomfort of climbing what can feel like a quarry path, situations are soon encountered that lift the whole experience, as intermediate shelves are attained giving thrilling views steeply down on Flass Wood and High and Low Park.

The path mounts by two prominent bluffs – the first gives an exciting view down a deep gully, while the second gives views running across **Dropping Crag** to Crummock Water. Watch for the next surprise, a short leftward traverse to a sneaky corner with a view over Rannerdale Knotts to Robinson, Fleetwith Pike and Buttermere. The climb might be steep, and the path less than firm in places, but there is a certain infectious fun in it all, and too soon one arrives on Mellbreak's **north top**.

123

Grasmoor from the western edge

Mellbreak has two summits – the south top is higher by 3m, but is inferior as a viewpoint. Two cairns grace the north top, the one to the west being the higher by a whisker at 509m/1670ft. When viewed from the road on the eastern shores of the lake, Mellbreak is dominated by its dark eastern scarp. While it is possible to walk along this edge, the rank heather gives tough going, with little more than the occasional narrow sheep track for encouragement. Better to stay resolutely to the main summit ridge path.

The 1km journey across the saddle, treading through wonderful heather, that links the north to south summits may come as a surprise; it is as though they are separate fells. The **south top** is marked by a very modest cairn, appropriate for a modest summit, but at 512m/1680ft it can hardly be all that modest, for the scenic setting has everything to commend it. For the best views head south-east as the ground breaks away and enjoy the fantastic view over the head of Crummock Water, with Buttermere and its spellbinding surround of fells causing you to linger pleasurably, with Fleetwith Pike, High Stile and Red Pike strong elements in the view.

Backtrack across the southern top to rejoin the ridge path, now beginning its steady, unflustered descent. There are no hazards, and the path takes its own confident line down a mainly grassy slope, drifting right over the shoulder of the knoll to meet a light fence. Many walkers step over and drop directly down to Black Beck, while others, more thoughtfully, bear right beside the fence to a gate, on the line of the **Mosedale bridleway**. This descends by a fence to quickly meet the old **Floutern Pass bridle route**, linking Buttermere with Ennerdale Water.

Ahead, unseen, lies **Scale Force**, a slender freefall of 40m, the tallest fall in the Lakes, tucked into the dark, wooded ravine. To visit go through the adjacent gate, descend to ford Black Beck, and clamber up the bank beyond to join the traversing path leading left to the foot of the falls. Having furtively peered at the chasm, follow the path leading straight down to the Scale Beck footbridge, amid the chaos of flood boulders, to reconnect with the bridleway.

The clear path leads through rank bracken and passes a large fold to meet up with a well-used track emerging from a gate on the right. The path now swings left (north), and there is much evidence of solid path maintenance that ensures a firm footing over intermittently damp ground. The shores of **Crummock Water** come close and soon, too, the **Low Ling Crag** peninsula, which inevitably invites a visit. Perhaps you too will share the low rocky knob with gulls and waders. The contrast of being sky high at one moment and then looking straight across a sheet of reflective water the next is an amazing sensation. The fells actually look lower from lake level.

Follow the obvious path along the shore, passing the lonesome Iron Stone, sitting a few yards into the lake. Continue via a kissing-gate, rounding two bays and passing to the left of the circular pump house. Go through a hand-gate and cross a footbridge spanning Park Beck, whose peaty waters stem from Loweswater. A further pair of footbridges span Crummock Water's outflow, the River Cocker, and the weir is equipped with a salmon ladder. The view all along this final shoreline concentrates on the majestic surround of fells, with the soaring pyramid of Grasmoor imperious above Lanthwaite Wood. Follow the obvious track, left, leading back through the National Trust woodland to the car park.

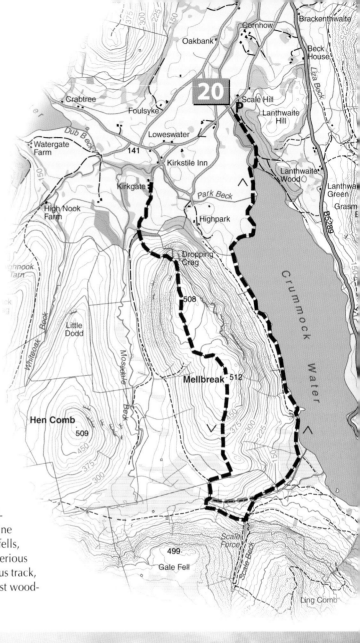

Whiteside, Hopegill Head, Grasmoor, Wandope, Whiteless Pike and Rannerdale Knotts from Lanthwaite Green

*T*he North-Western Fells are walkers' territory par excellence, and sleek lines predominate. Grasmoor has such a presence over Crummock Water, yet modestly contrives to play second fiddle in most views of the group.

The walk leaves the open common and makes swiftly onto the steep heather-clad slopes of Whiteside. The connecting ridge to Hopegill Head merits plaudits; it is just a pity that the outlook east is hemmed in by Grasmoor's bulky presence. The summit of Hopegill Head is more like a real peak.

An easy descent to Coledale Hause presages a steady climb up the edge leading to Dove Crags and the summit of Grasmoor. Switching back to the col at the head of Rannerdale Beck, the walk heads for the eastern brink top, Wandope, before tracing the ridge down via Thirdgill Head Man to climb the mini-mountain Whiteless Pike.

Following the popular path towards Buttermere village the route turns right at the minor col, holding to the switchback ridge of Rannerdale Knotts, a brilliant final 'lookout point' for Crummock Water and Grasmoor's sleek massif.

ROUTE INFORMATION

Distance	18.25km/11½ miles
Height gain	1120m/3675ft
Time	8 hours
Grade	strenuous
Start point	GR158207
Maps	(Harvey Superwalker)
	Lakeland West
	(Ordnance Survey)
	OL4 North-western area

After-walk refreshment
The Kirkstile Inn at Loweswater

The Start
The Lanthwaite Green car park, GR158207, is situated on the B5289 on the open common section, 3 miles south of High Lorton.

The Route
Cross straight over from the car park onto the common, where a broad path sweeps easily through the bracken to a footbridge over Gasgale Gill. Climb direct – there is some restorative work apparent on this steep route up and over the heather-rich **Whin Ben**. The term 'whin' identifies an area of excessive gorse growth. Thankfully today only a few straggling bushes are encountered at the very foot of the slope, but the name implies the plant was once in far greater evidence. The path climbs irresistibly to the ridge crest of Whiteside. Nearing the craggy brink pause to admire a stunning scene along the ridge to Hopegill Head, set off by a foreground of splintered outcropping. Lacking a cairn and clearly not the highest point, this is the summit of **Whiteside**, 707m/2320ft.

As you progress along the ridge, crossing higher ground, the scenery will put a smile on your face – this is a classic ridge walk, not quite like walking along the crest of a roof, but comfortably comparable. Looking south down the ribbed slope of Gasgale Crags admire the bulk of Grasmoor and the high combe backed by Dove Crags, quite a contrast with the northern outlook to Lorton Vale and, 6 miles away, the market town of Cockermouth. The ridge draws handsomely up to the tilted slab peak of **Hopegill Head**, again bereft of a distinguishing cairn.

The Whiteside ridge from Hopegill Head

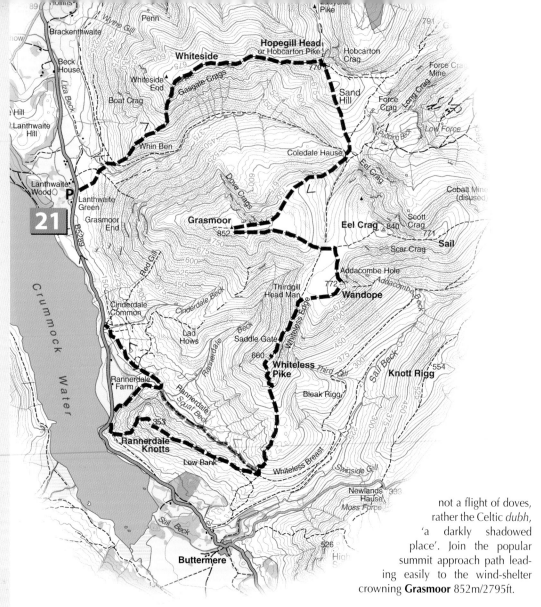

not a flight of doves, rather the Celtic *dubh*, 'a darkly shadowed place'. Join the popular summit approach path leading easily to the wind-shelter crowning **Grasmoor** 852m/2795ft.

This is a wonderful perch from which to enjoy views north-east over Hobcarton Crag and the Hobcarton valley to Grisedale Pike, and west over Ladyside Pike to Whinlatter.

Turn south following the open ridge over **Sand Hill**, the descending path to **Coledale Hause** treading angular scree shards. Traverse the broad depression, taking the right-hand rising path off the main newly made path – that is, unless you are content to omit Grasmoor and choose instead to head direct to Wandope. However, sticking resolutely to the chosen way, ford Gasgale Gill and climb the obvious north-eastern edge. A thin path ascends onto the plateau, via the impressive rim of **Dove Crags**, a place to savour in its own right. The implication here is

Grasmoor summit is another of those magic viewing stations, providing an unrivalled view down on Buttermere. To the south the High Stile range is beautifully complemented by the shapely edge of Fleetwith Pike, with Haystacks backed by Great Gable and, beyond that, the Scafells – a magnificent mountain prospect to savour. A small alcove cairn provides the perfect spot to take it all in sits on the very brink of the abyss. Walkers who are tempted by the easy angle of the west ridge to drift that way will be rudely awoken by its almost sheer termination on Grasmoor End.

Turn tail from the summit following the ridge-top path east. One may opt to follow the Lad Hows ridge south irresistibly down onto Cinderdale Common,

Thirdgillhead and Whiteless Pike from Rannerdale Knotts →

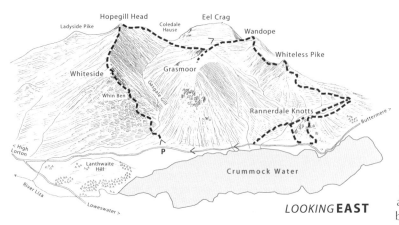

Hopegill Head
Ladyside Pike
Coledale Hause
Eel Crag
Wandope
Whiteless Pike
Whiteside
Grasmoor
Whin Ben
Gasgale Gill
Rannerdale Knotts
Buttermere >
< High Lorton
P
Lanthwaite Hill
Crummock Water
River Liza
Loweswater >

LOOKING **EAST**

the craggy west slope to join a bridleway at an old hause, leading down right to the lakeside road.

Go right, bearing off the road at the lay-by recess and following the signed footpath via a handgate. This leads, via a second gate, round beneath the craggy end of Rannerdale Knotts – in late spring a gorgeous carpet of bluebells tells of a former rich woodland habitat.

but that would be to miss the considerable pleasures of Whiteless Edge and Rannerdale Knotts. The path dips to a path intersection. Ascend with the newly restored path east (towards Eel Crag) a matter of 50m, then bear off south on little more than a sheep path that leads gently onto the edge to the top of **Wandope** at 772m/2533ft. The outlook south-east towards the Scafells is yet again superb, and there is an intriguing view down into the little hanging valley of Addacombe Hole.

Follow the ridge path south-westwards onto **Thirdgillhead Man** and down the razor-sharp **Whiteless Edge** to the descriptive **Saddle Gate**, before climbing abruptly onto **Whiteless Pike** at 660m/2165ft. This provides an exquisite viewpoint both down on Buttermere and beyond to its magical backdrop of fells centred on Great Gable and the Scafells, with the High Stile range ever more majestic.

The popular path steps down to the south, with some pitching, to gain the grass slope leading to the head of Rannerdale. At this point branch from the path, evidently bound for Buttermere village, and either turn right onto the Rannerdale valley path itself or (scenically more impressively) follow the emerging switchback ridge to the rocky summit of **Rannerdale Knotts** 353m/1158ft. For all the modest height the prospects are superb – south over Crummock Water to High Stile and Mellbreak, and north over Rannerdale to Grasmoor. Continue with the clearly etched path which now pitches down

Rannerdale has its place in local legend, being the reputed site of a late 11th-century battle of resistance. Here the Anglo-Norse hillmen under Earl Boethar defended their mountain sanctuary against Norman militia under Ranulf Meschin, the latter being ambushed in the dale's upper confines.

Cross a wooden footbridge over **Rannerdale Beck**. Now upon a green track heading north-west, pass on via a gate to join the open road at a casual car park. Follow the road verge along **Cinderdale Common**, rising to **Lanthwaite Green**.

The appearance of the term 'cinder' is a further indication of old woodland, for it describes an area of slag associated with iron-smelting bloomeries and, thus, coppicing.

Grasmoor from Rannerdale Knotts

High Crag,
High Stile and Red Pike
from Buttermere

*O*ne of the truly classic high-fell rounds, comprehended at a glance. High Stile is the centre-piece of a magnificent fell massif abruptly looming over Buttermere – brazen with all the finest qualities of the Lakeland mountain form, and yet quite unique. The route includes three delectable summits and a procession of uplifting views. It initially runs through the forestry on the southern shore of Buttermere, a charming interlude to get you into full stride. The walk then mounts steadily up to Scarth Gap, the pass impressively flanked by Haystacks. It clambers onto the emerging ridge to the right, crossing the minor ridge-top height Seat to tackle the more stern climb onto High Crag. Thereafter, the ridge-top walking is sublime, via High Stile and Red Pike, from where the walk slips down to Bleaberry Tarn and the well-pitched path down to the lake's foot, with stunning views too.

↑ *High Stile range from Fleetwith Pike* 131

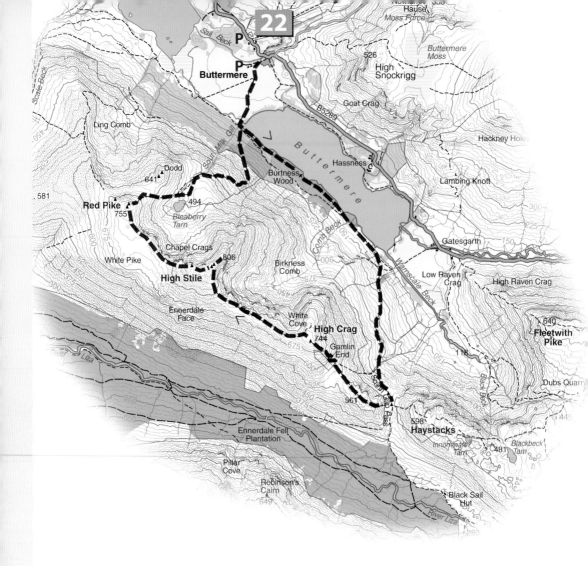

ROUTE INFORMATION

Distance	8.75km/5½ miles
Height gain	793m/2600ft
Time	6 hours
Grade	strenuous
Start point	GR174169
Maps	(Harvey Superwalker)
	Lakeland West
	(Ordnance Survey)
	OL4 North-western area

After-walk refreshment

The Fish and Bridge Hotels, plus two scrumptious farm-based tearooms, one with its own delectable ice-cream in Buttermere village

The Start

There are two formal car parks within the village of Buttermere: the National Park Authority facility beyond the Fish Hotel, GR174169, and the National Trust enclosure on the west side at GR174172. Too many motorists litter the verge above St James' Church. Parking for free has a cost – it spoils the view for everyone.

The Route

Follow the lane leading left from the **Fish Hotel**, signed to the lake – don't take the lane to the right, as it leads to Crummock Water. The lane bends and forks, and you keep left again, continuing to a gate that is frequently the location of a National Trust recruitment vehicle. Who would not wish to support the Trust when one knows they nurture this heavenly place? Bear right beside the hedge to cross a footbridge spanning Buttermere Dubs, the outflow of the

Heading for the hills from Buttermere

lake. Pass through a hand-gate and bear left following the lakeside trail, the surface graded for all-comers. Keep to the lower line to take fullest benefit of the outlook across the lake to the rocky ribs of Goat Crag on High Snockrigg, the wood-shielded house Hassness, and the glorious soaring ridge of Fleetwith Pike at the head of the lake. The maturing conifers of **Burtness Wood** form a petticoat fringe hiding the craggy wall of High Stile above.

Exit at a hand-gate and proceed via a footbridge over **Comb Beck**, tumbling from Birkness Comb, to where the path forks. Let the climbing begin! Fork

right, rising to the conifer copse and meeting the path from Gatesgarth. Continue ascending, and note that the path's popularity has brought the Fix the Fells team into action with necessary pitching work. The path runs through a broken wall after Wax Knott, fording a pair of gills to gaze at the big stack of Haystacks ahead, and duly arriving in the broad 'door' of **Scarth Gap**. Resist the temptation to break off earlier to climb beside the wall on the north side of Seat – this is an awful travail of loose stones.

Step right, onto the ridge at the top of the pass. A secure path winds up onto **Seat** 561m/ 1841ft. Seat falls short of separate fell status, though it has qualities that means it might make it into some pernickety 'lists'. Its summit certainly merits a visit, though the popular path ignores it. The views to Pillar Rock and Great Gable, lording over the head of wild Ennerdale, are worthy outlooks to savour. With the rigours of Gamlin End to face, savour the moment's pause. Passing a marshy hollow, the path drifts slightly left to embark on the stern climb. Matters are infinitely better since the Fix the Fells team met the challenge of pitching the path.

Warnscale Head and Haystacks from Seat

Red Pike and Bleaberry Tarn from Chapel Crags

Steep it may be, but a measured ascending stride is achievable most of the way. The final pull to the top is a moment of great elation, with **High Crag's** summit cairn the immediate reward at 744m/2441ft.

Inevitably walkers pause at **High Crag** summit, reach into their packs for refreshment... and invariably do not stop again, though they should. There are a succession of excellent viewing stations to investigate as the ridge progresses. For the present the panorama from High Crag will be gleefully enjoyed, with most eyes falling upon Haystacks and the magnificent parade of fells surrounding the head of Ennerdale, with the Scafells peering over Kirk Fell.

The ridge walk begins, and immediately the contrast is noticeable between the plain southern slopes and the deeply entrenched, crag-bound hanging valley of Birkness Comb to the north. The ridge undulates, and after crossing the top of Eagle Crag climbs easily onto **High Stile**, with the remains of an old metal fence leading to the top. Striding naturally to the first cairn you may ponder if it is the ultimate point, for the highest ground has several claimants. Covering all bases, and because the view deserves it, wander north-east, where the next cairn is considered the highest point at 807m/2648ft. Then step onto the top of Grey Crag overlooking **Birkness Comb**. Keen photographers, who think nothing of losing height that has to be retraced, will relish continuing down the north-east ridge to a cairn immediately short of the great plunge towards Buttermere, a stunning stance from which to point the lens.

Returning, head on west to the next rocky headland, which would appear to have the most credibility as the summit, though Ordnance Survey data shows it to be 806m/2646ft. It crowns the great cliffs of **Chapel Crags** that overbear upon Bleaberry Comb, and is a fine spot to linger and peruse the brink view. The ridge path descends simply enough, providing fine side views of Chapel Crags from the top of a gaping gully and into the deep bowl cradling the tiny **Bleaberry Tarn**.

Climb again to the less pretentious summit of **Red Pike** at 755m/ 2477ft. The usual cairn, partially fashioned into a wind-shelter, provides a good place for a final halt. The view concentrates most emphatically on Grasmoor and the North-Western Fells, with a marvellous exhibition of lakes – Crummock Water and Buttermere dominate. The way down starts from a cairn on the eastern edge. The upper section of eroded red-soiled scree (hence the fell name) has long been a *bête noire* of fell walkers as they progress down to the saddle short of the subsidiary top **Dodd**. Take care, especially if it is icy.

The path angles down to ford the outflow of Bleaberry Tarn. This stream, known as **Sour Milk Gill**, in its latter stages turbulently tumbles down as a series of cataracts fully meriting the description,

though the path makes no contact with it. Red Pike has another fine waterfall, the 40m-high Scale Force, the tallest in Lakeland, though this lies hidden to the north-west beyond Lincomb Edge, visited on Walk 19 during the tour of Mellbreak. The engineered path, with much new pitching, provides an assured descent. Take time to absorb the view periodically, for the beauty of the scene never fails to please. The firm stepped way leads down to a fence stile into the coniferous woodland, and continues to the hand-gate and subsequent footbridge over **Buttermere Dubs**, with its lovely view up the lake to Fleetwith Pike, a fine finale of a view to hold in your mind.

High Crag from High Stile

Haystacks from Buttermere

*C*ombining a shoreline circuit of Buttermere (lake), the ascent of Warnscale Head and the magi-cal crossing of Haystacks itself, this expedition ranks as one of Cumbria's truly great little moun-tain extravaganzas. The walk may begin from Gatesgarth, if you simply want to climb Haystacks, but when begun from Buttermere this is the complete 'great mountain day'.

The Start

Buttermere village has a choice of car parks – the National Park enclosure beyond the Fish Hotel, GR173169, and the National Trust enclosure at GR173172 (both with pay meters). Alternatively, start the walk from Gatesgarth, GR195150, making a shorter round trip omitting the lake (farm car-park pay meter).

Pre-amble

The Buttermere valley, commonly accepted as running from High Lorton to Honister, has a gracious mountain beauty of wide renown. From Buttermere's tiny village, set at the edge of the green strath between Crummock Water and Buttermere's lake, you can witness the most exquisite scenic cre-scendo. Stand on the verge above St James' Church to fully comprehend the grand parade of woods, crags, combs and fells encircling the valley, perfectly complementing the serene waters of the lake – peer-less, spirit-lifting, restorative.

Spoilt for choice when it comes to which fell to climb, most walking visitors, even those who might claim to have only the vaguest knowledge

↑ Haystacks and High Crag from Buttermere

ROUTE INFORMATION

Distance	13km/8¼ miles
Height gain	518m/1700ft
Time	6 hours
Grade	energetic
Start point	GR174169
Maps	(Harvey Superwalker)
	Lakeland West
	(Ordnance Survey)
	OL4 North-western area

After-walk refreshment

In Buttermere village the Fish and Bridge Hotels and two farm cafés at Sykes and Croft

of Lakeland, would probably think of Haystacks. Situated at the head of the lake, like a corner-cupboard between the soaring ridge of Fleetwith Pike and the mighty High Stile range, its dark armour of cliffs suggests a certain impregnability. Observed from neighbouring heights the fell appears to promise nothing special, and it may have retained its shy secrets but for one man.

Haystacks will forever be associated with Alfred Wainwright. It was without question his favourite haunt... his ashes were strewn along the shores of Innominate Tarn, fulfilling his wishes. AW's influence persists, and his many pilgrims, clinging on to his *Western Fells* or *Coast to Coast Walk*, traverse the fell in strict procession, tremulous to stray. Yet it was AW's favourite place to stray, and here his fell-wandering spirit finds eternal liberty.

Just before you begin, perhaps you might visit the little church of St James, as much as anything to view the small plaque set into the south window by the door. This reads:

'Pause and remember
Alfred Wainwright
Fellwalker, guide book author
And illustrator
Who loved this valley
Lift your eyes to Haystacks
His favourite place
1907–1991'

The Route

Leave the road in **Buttermere** village above the Bridge Hotel and below the church, through the yard of Syke House Farm.

You may encounter the herd of Ayrshire cows, pacing from pasture to parlour to provide the cream-base for ice cream – to be savoured with relish at the farm tearoom at the end of the walk. What more appropriate continuity for this place, as the place-name Buttermere would appear to mean the 'mere by the butter-enriching meadows'.

Walk on through the yard via gates. The ensuing open track leads across the pasture to a gated passage down a rock exposure, then via further

Wainwright memorial window looking to 137
Haystacks in St James', Buttermere

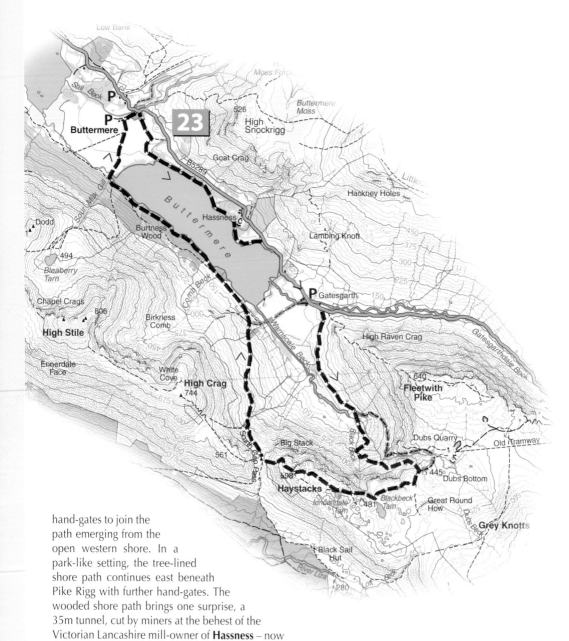

hand-gates to join the path emerging from the open western shore. In a park-like setting, the tree-lined shore path continues east beneath Pike Rigg with further hand-gates. The wooded shore path brings one surprise, a 35m tunnel, cut by miners at the behest of the Victorian Lancashire mill-owner of **Hassness** – now a holiday haven, then a private mountain retreat known to few. Anyone over 6ft tall must duck!

Curve around a bay, and pass stately pines with a marvellous command of the dale-head. Shapely Fleetwith Pike and sturdy Haystacks vie with the soaring mountain mass of High Stile and its compatriot shoulders, High Crag and Red Pike. The high corries of Burtness and Bleaberry Combs respectively spill fuming cascades of water via Comb and

Sourmilk Gills. The path curves left, drawing awkwardly under the road and, eventually, onto the road, passing the secretive Low Gatesgarth.

There are few verge concessions to walkers along the road to embowered **Gatesgarth Farm**, which in summer is the site of a refreshment caravan. Pass by the farmer-provided car park and the cottage; the hens and a cockerel play Russian roulette with Honister-bound traffic. The name Gatesgarth meant

Slate quarryman's track ascending Warnscale, backed by Fleetwith Pike →

'goat enclosure', probably referring to the ancient enclosure of goats in Gatesgarthdale valley, leading up to Honister Pass.

Leave the shelter of trees, and bear right onto the open bridle track which leads beneath Low Raven Crag at the foot of Fleetwith Pike. Stride purposefully towards the **Warnscale Bottom** valley, with the dark cliffs of Haystacks ahead. Drawing approximately beneath the Big Stack, fork right off the main track on a grass path leading to a wooden footbridge over **Warnscale Beck**.

The ascent effectively begins. Cross the stony bed of Black Beck en route to a zig-zagging quarryman's path, with some loose stony stretches – but far fewer than those encountered on the main bridle path to Dubs Quarry that you recently left. The impressive water slides and cascades of Warnscale Beck catch the eye, though the path never gets really intimate as it mounts to pass below the well-hidden stone bothy at **Warnscale Head**.

Originally a slate-quarrymen's lodging, this modern **bothy** is kept in good order as a welcome, if draughty, sanctuary by the sterling efforts of volunteers from the Mountain Bothies Association. Within the last year a new roof has been constructed and respectful over-night visitors are welcomed – mindful that camping about Haystacks is not encouraged. It is no more than a stone tent, yet performs a distinct service. The nearby Dubs Hut, another stone tent, is adopted and cared for by the Galloping Horse Mountaineering Club of Workington.

High Crag and Haystacks summit tarn

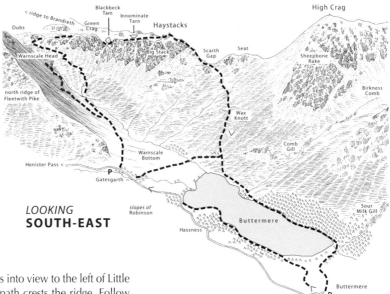

LOOKING
SOUTH-EAST

The Dubs Hut comes into view to the left of Little Round How, once the path crests the ridge. Follow the path right, weaving around the back of **Green Crag**. Spot the silhouette of a boulder perched near the south-western edge, well removed from the path underfoot. Passing close to the outflow of **Blackbeck Tarn**, enjoy the sneaky view down the Black Beck ravine as it breaks through the cliffs.

Here you have a choice. The common way, which is easy to follow, passes the beautifully irregular shores of **Innominate Tarn** and rises by rocky knolls to the bare summit ridge. Alternatively, the wandering spirit may perhaps follow my footsteps by visiting the top of **Green Crag**, breaking off at Blackbeck Tarn to visit the perched boulder through the rank heather. The route weaves back from the ridge fence via the shores of Innominate Tarn to regain the northern cliff edge, making for the top of Big Stack, before stepping onto the summit ridge – placing hardly a stride on the popular path. Big Stack is a special place, and its forward position gives it a privileged view down on Buttermere – the top knot a tight concave fold of lava emphasising the extra hardness and erosion resistance of the rock.

Innominate Tarn has a shy beauty all its own. It is not the biggest of its kind, nor perhaps the most attractive, though Great Gable at the very head of Ennerdale does make a stunning backdrop. However, thanks to Wainwright this tarn now has a special place in many a fell-walker's heart.

The north/south summit ridge has cairns at either end. The northern end is frequently taken as the true summit, at 597m/1959ft, and has a small tarn to its west. Take your time explore the summit of **Haystacks** and nearby edge, and perhaps you too will spot the tiny memorial to a certain Dennis Hobbs on the western scarp brink – a heavenly outlook into eternity.

The early westward descent reveals more attractive folded rock beds. The path is partially pitched, though there are some inhibiting loose stones on the quite abrupt descent to the broad **Scarth Gap**. Scarth meant 'notch', so the name Scarth Gap is a tautology. The pass is marked by a large cairn near a fence-end, which arises out of Ennerdale from the remotely sited Black Sail Youth Hostel. Walkers with boundless energy and the time will accept the challenge of the High Stile range, climbing via Seat and High Crag, now a well-pitched trail.

Well pitched where needed, the popular descent from Scarth Gap to Buttermere provides lovely views back to the towering stacks of Haystacks. If opting for the abbreviated walk option, turn right on passing a conifer spinney, down to a gate and a fenced lane leading back across the meadows to the road at Gatesgarth Farm.

The route to Buttermere village has the joyful stroll along the southern shore in store. So bear left to meet and merge with the lower path, passing on via a footbridge spanning **Comb Gill**. Note the old bridleway splits at this point: the walkers' way keeping right and passing through a hand-gate to enter the conifer plantation of **Burtness Wood**. On reaching another fork, either stay on the broader path or bear right, keeping close to the shore – enjoy those fine views across to Fleetwith Pike and Hassness backed by the rocky ribs of Goat Crag on High Snockrigg. A further hand-gate, short of **Sour Milk Gill**, leads to a footbridge over the lake's out-flowing stream.

Buttermere Dubs is the connecting stream between Buttermere and Crummock Water. The term 'dubs' is Celtic for dark or black. (You may remember that it crops up in the old nursery rhyme 'Rub a dub dub, three men in a tub'.) No doubt here it refers to the stream's function as a sheep wash.

In summer the western shore beyond the foot-bridge leading to Pike Rigg is thronged with families and couples, a National Trust recruiting Land Rover being set nearby. The lake has belonged to the Trust since 1930 and is sensitively cared for – fishing is permitted, but no boats, other than for angling.

The path soon enters a lane leading easily back into the village, passing the **Fish Inn**, once a farm and home to Mary Robinson, 'The Beauty of Buttermere'. The story of her marriage at Brigham, and the death by hanging of her bigamous husband, John Hatfield, at Carlisle in 1803, were the inspiration for Melvyn Bragg's book *The Maid of Buttermere*.

Contorted strata during the descent to Scarth Gap

Fleetwith Pike, Dale Head, Hindscarth and Robinson from Buttermere

*T*he grand show of rugged and majestic fells commanding attention on the south side of the Buttermere valley may be a delight to casual traveller along the dale road, but for best effect one needs elevation. This walk provides just that, and begins in reflective mood by strolling along the shore of Buttermere before pitching up the magnificent razor ridge of Fleetwith Pike. On reaching the mitre-top the feeling is that of soaring above the wild pass, with the spacious view back over the Buttermere and Crummock Water vale a heady cocktail for the senses. From the crest of Honister Crag the route draws down by the old slate quarry incline (the quarry now very much in active service) to the road pass and mine shop. From here it sets course for Dale Head, followed by Hindscarth and Robinson, and completes the ridge trail by plunging from the scarp brink of High Snockrigg and bowling back down into the village.

↑ *Fleetwith Pike summit looking to Great Gable and Kirk Fell*   143

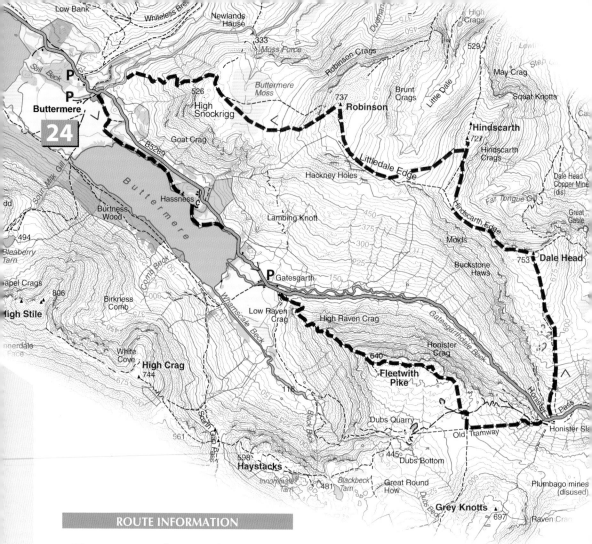

ROUTE INFORMATION

Distance	16.5km/10¼ miles
Height gain	1188m/3900ft
Time	7½ hours
Grade	strenuous
Start point	GR174169
Maps	(Harvey Superwalker)
	Lakeland West
	(Ordnance Survey)
	OL4 North-western area

After-walk refreshment
In Buttermere village the Fish and Bridge Hotels
and two farm cafés at Sykes and Croft

The Start
There are two formal car parks within the village
of Buttermere: the National Park Authority facility
beyond the Fish Hotel, GR174169, and the National
Trust enclosure on the west side at GR174172.

Should you wish to savour the lakeside stroll
at walk's end, getting to grips with the ascent of
Fleetwith Pike at the outset, then use the small car
park sheltered by a copse of pines at Gatesgarth Farm
(pay meter), GR194150. It is located on the west
side of Honister Pass at the foot of Gatesgarthdale.
In high summer the farmer opens a meadow for the
inevitable increase in demand.

The Route
Leave the road in **Buttermere** village above the
Bridge Hotel and below the church, passing through
the yard of Syke House Farm via gates. The ensuing open track leads across the pasture to a gated
passage down a rock exposure, then via further
hand-gates to join the path emerging from the open
western shore. In a park-like setting, the tree-lined

View down the Fleetwith Pike ridge to Buttermere ➔

shore path continues east beneath Pike Rigg with further hand-gates. The wooded shore path brings one surprise, a 35m tunnel, a folly cut by miners at the behest of the Victorian Lancashire mill-owner of **Hassness** – now a holiday haven. Watch your head.

Curve around a bay, and pass stately pines with a marvellous command of the dale-head. Shapely Fleetwith Pike and sturdy Haystacks vie with the soaring mountain mass of High Stile and its compatriot shoulders, High Crag and Red Pike. The high corries of Burtness and Bleaberry Combs respectively spill fuming cascades of water via Comb and Sourmilk Gills. The path curves left, drawing awkwardly under the road and, eventually, onto the road, passing the secretive Low Gatesgarth. There are few verges for walkers to use along the road to **Gatesgarth Farm**, which in summer is the site of a refreshment caravan.

Pass by Gatesgarth Cottage. The name Gatesgarth meant 'goat enclosure', probably referring to the ancient enclosure of goats in the natural amphitheatre of Gatesgarthdale leading up to Honister Pass. As the open fell is met, bear off right where a bridle track begins. However, ignore the track, instead following the signed footpath which heads purposefully towards the base of Fleetwith Pike's west ridge.

A part-pitched path zig-zags up **Low Raven Crag**, passing below the white cross memorial erected in memory of Fanny Mercer, who died in a mishap during a descent of the ridge in 1887. The ascent provides a multitude of opportunities to peer down upon the winding road as it climbs the bare glacial valley of Gatesgarthdale to the summit of Honister Pass. This first rocky obstacle surmounted, a grassy ridge path leads invitingly on from a small cairn. The craggy backdrop of Warnscale with the stack-like cliffs of Haystacks feature prominently to the right, as soon bilberry and then heather mingle with the rocky ridge path, ever more sternly rising. Take frequent pauses to admire the backward view of Buttermere and the High Stile range – the latter only improves with height. The ridge is quite narrow and sufficiently rough to make you thankful that you are ascending not descending!

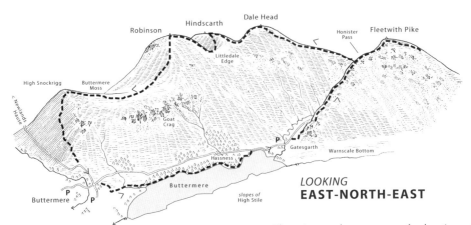

LOOKING
EAST-NORTH-EAST

The final few feet lead inexorably to the summit cairn of **Fleetwith Pike**. If ever a breather was appreciated it was here, and the view may leave you breathless too! At 648m/2126ft this may not be the highest fell top in the vicinity (for instance Dale Head is some 107m higher), but it certainly is an impressive culmination of the wonderfully rewarding north-west ridge ascent.

There is a welcome sense of relaxation when strolling on **Fleetwith's** fell top, weaving by knolls of heather and tiny tarns, though the steep fall of the northern cliffs may concentrate the mind. In fact, this edge will inevitably hold greatest attraction and tempt walkers to clamber as near as they can to the top of Honister Crag to gasp at the sheer fall. One may find the top quarryman's shelter and the associated slate hollows. Exploration in this area is tricky, the workings are far from safe, and the newly created fixed-wire Via Ferrata is only accessible from lower down.

Hindscarth and Dale Head from Fleetwith Pike

High Snockrigg and Hassness House from Birkness Comb

The ridge path keeps right to link up with the quarry road, crossing it almost as soon as it is joined and aiming for the top of the old Drum House incline, an obvious causeway feature on the saddle to the south of Honister Crag. Follow the incline path, which becomes a new pitched way eventually descending steeply to the environs of the **Honister Mine** workshop and visitor centre (with mine tours into the 11 miles of tunnels).

Cross over the road and, after stepping over a stile, ascend with the fence to the left. The fence is lost halfway up the seemingly endless grassy slope, but climb on north to gleefully reach the stout cairn marking the top of **Dale Head**. Here, at 753m/2470ft, is another memorable place to stand. This time the view is north through the deeply entrenched Newlands valley towards Skiddaw. Over to the right, the line of cliffs below High Spy forms a strong subject for the camera.

The ridge is followed due west alongside traces of an old metal boundary fence. At the depression one may keep to the western edge of the ridge or follow the lateral path curving right onto the top of **Hindscarth** 727m/2385ft. Backtrack only a few yards and veer half-right following an easily angled path curving down the western slopes to reach the ridge again at the very head of Little Dale. **Littledale Edge** is followed, now with a metal fence restored, and climbs onto **Robinson**. Leave the fence to reach the summit at 737m/2418ft. The cairn rests on a lower rib of rock beside a parallel outcrop.

About turn and aim for the guide cairn situated 100m to the south-west. This gives access to a comparatively comfortable descending path which comes onto the spongy morass of **Buttermere Moss**. After all the firm footfalls this is nice and soft – too soft in places! In wetter seasons it's a trial to keep the boots afloat! Traverse the damp hollow to the crest of **High Snockrigg**, overlooking the Newlands Hause road, with a handsome view of the Grasmoor group ahead across the Sail Beck valley. Bear right to find a cairn marking the grooved top of the **Buttermere** path. Follow this quite steeply down the scarp slope, with some zig-zags and but one small rock-step to ponder, and on to the road.

Green Gable and the Gable Girdle
from Seathwaite

*I*t is difficult not to extol the qualities of Great Gable, as the fell offers the fell walker, scrambler
and hardened rock climber well-rounded entertainment and many thrilling situations. So it is no
wonder that a tour can be undertaken that gives the walker tentative entry into the world of the
scrambler and rock climber without setting foot on tough rock nor even venturing to the summit,
though obviously one may do so.

In seeking the base of the cliffs the Gable girdle route traverses rough but accessible ground,
slinking under Gable Crag and angling down beneath the magnificent southern facade of the Great
Napes. The anti-clockwise orientation of the route will be understood when you climb the one
double-move bad-step (it is much easier to climb it than to tackle it in descent). Hence the walk
begins with the cascades of Sourmilk Gill and rises through Gillercomb onto Green Gable, bringing
the walker handsomely onto the climbers' path at Windy Gap. The route then departs from the girdle
at Sty Head and troops back into the beautifully wild depths of upper Borrowdale to end a quite
memorable mountain adventure.

↑ *Sour Milk Gill and Gillercomb Buttress*

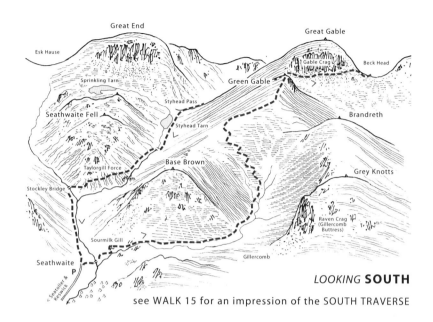

LOOKING **SOUTH**

see WALK 15 for an impression of the SOUTH TRAVERSE

ROUTE INFORMATION

Distance	13.75km/8½ miles
Height gain	713m/2340ft
Time	7½ hours
Grade	strenuous
Start point	GR235123
Maps	(Harvey Superwalker)
	Lakeland West
	(Ordnance Survey)
	OL4 North-western area

After-walk refreshment

There is a tearoom at Seathwaite Farm itself, but better in terms of timing is the Yewtree at Seatoller, the Langstrath at Stonethwaite or the Scafell and Royal Oak at Rosthwaite

The Start

The Borrowdale valley road comes to an abrupt end at Seathwaite Farm. The verges from the road bridge over the River Derwent through to the turning-circle at the farm entrance, dependent on the day, to varying degrees function as the car park facility, GR235123.

The Route

The key to access into Gillercomb is the mid-barn gate at **Seathwaite Farm**. Find the signposted gate almost opposite the farmhouse, and slip through the barn canopy and along the lane to cross the gated footbridge.

> **Seathwaite**, 'the clearing where sedge grows', is synonymous with water, loads and loads of it; the rain-gauge on the top of Seathwaite Fell records it as recipient of the highest rainfall in England.

Head on up the pitched path to the ladder stile crossing the wall. Embark on the flagged way, with the tilted Seathwaite Slabs close left, an excellent training ground for rookie rock climbers. The path runs alongside **Sourmilk Gill**, notably one handsome cascade that spills in petulant display into the rowan and birch ravine midway up the rough slope.

One tends to think of central Lakeland as the pre-serve of Herdwick sheep, but in the past dual-pur-pose shorthorn cattle played an important part in community subsistence. That Keswick, 'the cheese farm', is so named is an indication of the role of dairy farming in the region, as too is the name Sourmilk Gill, being derived from an everyday commodity.

There are a handful of robust encounters with bare rock en route to a hand-gate in the wall set just below the rim of Gillercomb, meaning 'the hanging valley with an abundance of gills'. The path strides confidently into the combe, swinging left beneath Base Brown. Notice the projecting rock known as the **Hanging Stone**. The footloose walker will find irresistible the notion of clambering up the steep ridge left of the block to include the summit of **Base Brown** in the day's affairs, and why not? Most will content themselves with adherence to the regular way, which has had major pitching repair along much of its course and notably on the steepening rise up the southern side-wall of the combe.

Reaching the grassy saddle, with the narrow path from the top of Base Brown linking in from the left, bear naturally up right, south-west, on a steady ascent towards Green Gable. There is a cairn where the route links with the Brandreth ridge path, more commonly frequented by walkers coming off Moses' Trod, at the fence stile on Brandreth's west ridge.

The enigmatic **Moses** was a quarryman who reputedly distilled elicit whisky in the top of a gully high on Gable Crag. He concealed his potent liquor amongst the slate hauled in pony panniers down to Wasdale Head on the regular seaward journey to Ravenglass via Miterdale.

The cairn on **Green Gable** at 801m/2628ft receives a steady flow of visitors through the walking day, who find the cairn the ideal situation to consider Gable Crag, which casts its long shadows into Stone Cove below. The majority will be continuing on to Great Gable. They pause, prudently taking mental and physical refreshment before tackling the all too apparent task ahead. For those about to engage in the Gable girdle the prospect is altogether different – their eyes will be trying to pin-point the line of the climbers' traverse beneath the north-facing cliff and probably finding it an uncertain science. The view down Ennerdale and around the compass is extraordinarily good, with

Green Gable from the climbers' traverse beneath Gable Crag

Great Gable obscuring little of note. The fell name Green Gable provides a stark contrast to the barren dome of stone that is Great Gable.

Descend promptly south upon the loose trail into the draughty flue of Windy Gap. From the cairn bear right upon the northern traverse, stepping only slightly down. A clear path of sheep-trod proportions clings to the under-cliff. The resident ravens are unlikely to leave you in any doubt that you are being observed, their rasping calls echoing round your head from on high. The traverse reaches looser ground only as a short-cut off the north-west ridge aiming onto Moses' Trod is crossed, the northern traverse ending at a cairn perched on an outcrop.

Descend the loose trail of the ridge, bearing half-left into the broad saddle of **Beck Head**, its grass floor a brief respite. Continue south, keeping a left-hand bias, and before the ground begins to fall away into the stony depths of the **Gable Beck** valley, find a cairned trail contouring along the boulder field along the western scree-draped slopes of the mighty fell. Under the fragmented outcropping of the White Napes a loose scree run is crossed, Little Hell Gate, which leads to the one obstacle in a heavenly tour – a quick bad-step ascent of little more than two moves. In descent this would be more problematic.

The way now angles down the broken base of **Great Napes** following a part-rake, part-shelf feature. Wainwright said of the route 'here one never has the feeling that the end is nigh'. True, but sadly the end of the fun does come, not before one gets a glimpse up at the towering Napes Needle and a silhouette view of the Sphinx Rock. The crossing of Great Hell Gate has no perils, though you'll probably wobble a bit on

South traverse approaching Kern Knotts backed by Great End

the unstable stones. The continuing path takes you over less distinctive surroundings, but always when you stop your attention will be set upon Lingmell, Piers Gill and the craggy wall of the Scafells. The route works down to the base of Kern Knotts, passing under massive fallen boulders, then contours and steps up onto the low ridge to end at the stretcher box, in harmony with the popular path descending south-east from the summit of Great Gable.

The walk bids farewell to the high fells, turning left and passing the western shores of **Styhead Tarn** to cross the subsequent footbridge following **Styhead Gill's** true right bank. Descend the pitched trail via hand-gates to cross the picturesque **Stockley Bridge**, and by following the gated track return through the farmyard at **Seathwaite**.

← *Great Napes from the south traverse – spot the climbers on Eagle Nest Ridge and the paraglider, human flight contrasting with the plane vapour trails in the blue sky above*

Rosthwaite Fell and Glaramara from Stonethwaite

A natural horseshoe, wandering over the rugged high fell pasture of Rosthwaite Fell from the head of Comb Gill, then slipping up through Comb Door onto Comb Head, and crossing a damp hollow onto the summit rock castle of Glaramara. Turning north, the route descends the popular ridge path down Thorneythwaite Fell, a memorably scenic finale as late afternoon light traces across distant Derwentwater and Skiddaw. Do not undertake this walk in misty conditions – Rosthwaite High Fell and the connection to Glaramara is no place for first-time visitors to these confusing fell tops.

The Start
A suitably discreet lay-by, GR261139, has been created about half-way along the minor road from Borrowdale primary school to the beautifully situated hamlet of Stonethwaite.

The Route
Walk through the tiny community of **Stonethwaite**, sharing the route of the Cumbria Way. The setting is sublimely Lakeland; the cottages authentically old and harmonious.

↑ *The Jaws of Borrowdale and Stonethwaite from Stanger Gill*

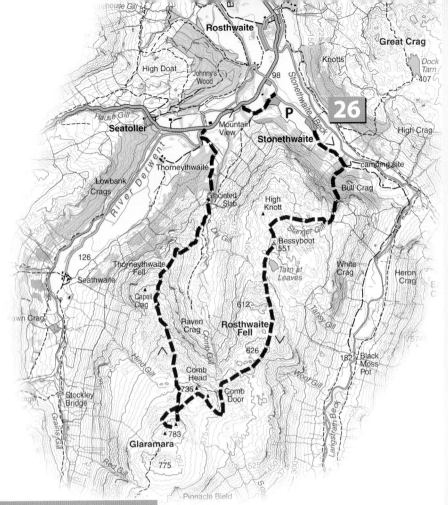

26

ROUTE INFORMATION

Distance	10km/6¼ miles
Height gain	762m/2500ft
Time	6½ hours
Grade	strenuous
Start point	GR261139
Maps	(Harvey Superwalker) Lakeland Central (Ordnance Survey) OL4 North-western area

After-walk refreshment

The Langstrath Hotel and Peathouse tearoom in Stonethwaite

The tarmac ends on a ramp rise above The Keld cottage, advancing a little above the meadow level. For all the roughness of the track the potential for car encounters persists, as this is also the access to the National Trust camp site. The site lives up to the hamlet-name, for it is indeed 'a woodland-sheltered stony clearing' on the strath next to **Stonethwaite Beck**.

The **camp site** entrance is the key for the start of the fell ascent. Go through the green metal gate on the right, directly facing the entrance. The path quickly enters the open wooded environs beside the excited waters of **Stanger Gill**, an impressive series of fuming cascades. The path was pitched some 15 years ago, but the ascent is not plain sailing. There are a few awkward moments, and in damp weather the roots and stones are slippery with the algae, so watch how you go. Climb to a stile in a short wall projecting from **Alisongrass Crag**, and the path hugs the under-cliff to zig-zag onto grass.

Take your breath here and look back. It is a majestic scene: the craggy walls of Hanging Haystack framing the deep green vale of Stonethwaite, looking beyond the Jaws of Borrowdale to Skiddaw. The gill is renowned as a place to spot ring ouzel, a declining bird species elsewhere, but flourishing here.

The path enters a tiny amphitheatre where the wind can swirl, confronting the walker emerging

Honister Pass from Bessyboot

from the comparative shelter of the steep pitched trail. Keep right beside the beck, hop over a ford then pass the end of a short wall that leads to a more awkward ford beneath the top waterfall in Stanger Gill. The narrow path climbs the opposite bank. Ignore the more obvious path leading straight on and bear left on the narrow trod, effectively keeping company with the headwaters of Stanger Gill.

Drift slightly right as peaty ground intervenes, and on meeting exposed peat hags the path swings left under a bank. The last of a succession of rocky ridges, known as **Racom Bands**, comes close left. This can be clambered up as a direct route (no path) to the cairn on **Bessyboot**, 551m/1808ft. Alternatively, keep with the natural southward progress of the narrow path, climbing to the summit of Bessyboot from the head of Dry Gill, though this does mean backtracking to continue.

> The charming name **Bessyboot** either derives from a lost sheepfold (booth/bothy), presumably named after a particular shepherd's wife, Bessy (the local pet form of Elizabeth), or it might just refer to the reasonably sheltered part of the fell. Consistent with several spots on this ridge the view west is best: across upper Borrowdale to Gillercomb, with Sourmilk Gill and Honister Pass prominent.

Descending from the cairn, **Tarn at Leaves** comes fully into view – a barren place, made all the more lifeless by the knowledge that it is devoid of fish. It was a long-held practice of miners to stock any decent body of high fell water – they didn't here! The name is intriguing, and what is meant by 'at Leaves' has not been satisfactorily explained.

The ridge path passes under a bank surmounted by a large erratic boulder, then takes a damp line holding an eastern bias onto the rising ridge. **Rosthwaite Cam** lies off the popular ridge way, a thin path taking a right-hand bias to gain the elevated subsidiary summit via a gully.

Rosthwaite Cam is a worthwhile detour – the top of the Cam is an easy rock scramble (from the west side) and a superb viewpoint, particularly across the deep re-entrant Comb Gill valley to Raven Crag. The crag is the sole preserve of serious rock climbers – the easiest route, known as 'Corvus' (named from the Latin for a raven), being in a league beyond fell walking. The cliff, almost permanently in shadow, is split by a gully out of which gushes a fuming white waterfall in wet weather.

COMB GILL VALLEY

The Comb Gill valley, infrequently visited by fell walkers, is a geologically designated SSSI: featuring

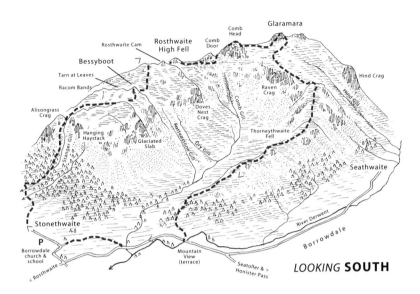

LOOKING **SOUTH**

the ravine of Comb Gill itself at the head, and Doves Nest Crag with its massive rock-slip caves and chimneys. Neither are places where fell walkers should venture – though one may climb out of the valley on the steep sides of these features.

The term Cam derives from the Norse for 'a haircomb', hence the stones surmounting a field wall became known as cams. This large rock was apparently likened to a solitary wall stone. From the Cam you can comprehend the final rise of Rosthwaite High Fell.

From Rosthwaite Cam traverse Great Hollow (no path) or, if you are keeping to the conventional ridge path, very poorly evidenced on the ground, make purposefully onto the summit of **Rosthwaite High Fell**. The cairnless top at GR11282565 is a suitable outcrop on which to sit for a few moments. The crest effectively forms the culmination of the Cam Crag ridge out of Langstrath, a popular scramblers' route rising from the Woof Stones howff. At 626m/2052ft this true summit is 75m/244ft higher than Bessyboot. It is a fine viewpoint for upper Langstrath and over Stake Pass to the Coniston Fells.

Step down from the peak, rejoining the ridge path as it strides over a short length of broken wall. Embark upon a traverse of a broad boggy hollow, aiming south-west. Coming immediately above **Comb Gill's** upper ravine, switch up the bank, off the narrow path, reaching **Comb Door's** obvious gap (a

variant on Mickledore, only a considerably narrower rock passage). Small sheets of water go some way to fill the flat ground beyond – good photographic subjects. Keeping under the cliffs an obvious path continues. Descend briefly before switching sharp right onto a prominent bare slab edge. Set at an easy angle this glacially smoothed feature makes for easy route identification. Complete the ascent onto **Comb Head's** cairned top, and anticipate a stunning view into the deep Comb Gill valley and over Rosthwaite High Fell.

If you are lucky you will see peregrine falcons soaring in this vicinity; they make Raven Crag a permanent base. Traverse the tarn-jewelled hollow

Rosthwaite Cam   157

south to join the popular path leading to the base at mid-point of the **Glaramara** rock castle. A 6m scramble ensues, though the well-rounded rock makes an easy ascent; it is harder in descent, and treacherous when iced up. The summit cairn, with shelter tucked into the rocks, well rewards efforts expended. The view south features Bowfell, Esk Pike, Great End and Great Gable. The summit is prone to lose its cairn from time to time, but the situation is reassuringly solid enough.

Leave the summit, initially heading south into a shallow depression, then follow the natural weakness west. This puts easy ground at hand. Swing round the summit outcrop, right, to join the main path. The path negotiates several headstreams and weaves over marshy ground mingled with boulders, keeping on a fundamentally northward declining line. You will notice numerous instances of path landscaping and restoration, particularly lower down on the steeper section, where heavy rain had washed away former stone pitching.

The descent provides a dream of a view, the perfect end to a day on the fells. Attention is drawn into the heart of upper Borrowdale, with the distant focus of Derwentwater and Skiddaw beyond the Jaws of Borrowdale. As the path approaches the kissing-gate in the wall, Comb Gill offers one last fine exhibition of cascades, compelling you to stop and admire the water's crazy antics. Complete the descent through open woodland on a track, eventually swinging left, and as the track veers left again keep the wall close right to reach a kissing-gate joining the **Thorneythwaite Farm** access lane. Go right to reach Strands Bridge, where the valley road spans the River Derwent.

Turn right following the roadside verge by the prominent white-washed **Mountain View** terrace. Keep to the verge. Directly after the road crosses Comb Gill go through the kissing-gate on the right. Follow a footpath leading across a pasture, with a tractor track your underfoot guide. En route a pair of grey fell ponies may seek your attention. Pass a stewardship access waymark as you advance to a gate entry into a confined lane leading to Chapel Farm. Go through the yard and, after St Andrew's, the parish church of Borrowdale, reach the **Stonethwaite** road. Turn right, and pass the primary school to complete the day's encounter.

Looking south-east over Stake Pass to the Coniston Fells from the summit of Glaramara

Eagle Crag, Sergeant's Crag, High Raise and Ullscarf from Stonethwaite

*T*his route follows the Greenup Gill skyline, taking in the striking twin craggy heights of Eagle and Sergeant's Crags en route to the scarp edge of High Raise. Thereafter the route follows the broad ridge north over Ullscarf, the most centrally situated fell in the Lakes, before descending to Dock Tarn and the steep steps close to Willygrass Gill. For most of the walk you'll be away from the crowds, but from time to time you'll be reminded of the heavy visitor concentrations on particular paths – the Coast to Coast Walk and Cumbria Way being major influences. High Raise is inevitably a focus for walkers from three directions – Grasmere, Great Langdale and, to a lesser extent, Borrowdale. The ridge path used on this walk will be appreciated by discerning fell walkers, who will also revel in the solitude of Ullscarf.

↑ *Eagle Crag from sheepfold on the Greenup Edge bridle path in the Stonethwaite valley*   159

27

The Start

Scope for car parking in Stonethwaite is modest, and it is far better to use the lay-by on the approach road, off the main Borrowdale road, beyond the primary school at GR260139.

The Route

Walk into the hamlet of **Stonethwaite**, turning left at the red kiosk signed 'Grasmere via Greenup Edge'. The bridle lane crosses **Stonethwaite Beck**, with the view upstream framed by trees and focused neatly upon Eagle Crag. Pass through a gate to reach a T-junction, and go right via a second gate. The bridle lane passes a sheep-fold. Continue to where the river bank has been washed away by the beck and cross a plank bridge spanning the foot of **Willygrass Gill**. At the next gate pass between a tall sheep-fold and a roofless barn. After the next gate cross a frequently dry, stony gill-bed, the product of converging gills, hence the adjacent hinged fence for damage limitation during a storm. Passing above Galleny Force reach a fenced pen where the path forks. Go right through the hand-gate to cross the Greenup Gill footbridge, in harmony with the Cumbria Way.

Bear right off the bridle path, crossing the stile in the light fence, to keep alongside Greenup Gill with a fence on the left, initially over marshy ground. Passing through a hand-gate continue to a confined corner, stepping up to begin the ascent proper accompanying the steeply rising wall. The path drifts left as the crags of Bleak How loom, and winds up to cross a wooden stile at the top of the ridge wall, where it abuts the crag, draped in birch and heather. The path ascends under the crag to ultimately reach a weakness, a short easy scramble up the gully overhung with a solitary birch. A short spur left can be

ROUTE INFORMATION

Distance	15km/9½ miles
Height gain	811m/2660ft
Time	6½ hours
Grade	strenuous
Start point	GR261139
Maps	(Harvey Superwalker) Lakeland Central (Ordnance Survey) OL4 North-western area

After-walk refreshment

The Langstrath Hotel and Peathouse tearoom in Stonethwaite

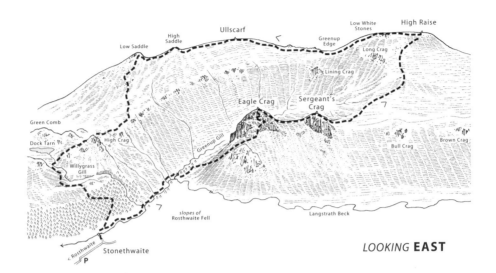

LOOKING **EAST**

considered, just to look at the actual Eagle Crag; otherwise follow the path right along the ledge streaked with ice-like quartz.

A brief zig-zag and the path keeps south, with impressive views towards Sergeant's Crag and the great gulf of Langstrath, backed by Rosthwaite Fell and Glaramara. Another zig-zag and the path continues

a little further south before working up through the rock bands and a garden of heather. The upper realms of **Eagle Crag** are a magical place to explore, and all too soon it seems the summit platform is rounded at 520m/1706ft. The view is no better than experienced during the ascent, for the best outlook is up Langstrath to Bowfell, Esk Pike and Great End.

Outcropping near the summit of Sergeant's Crag

High Raise summit looking south to the Coniston Fells

Follow the ridge path south, stepping down at the wall corner. Keep the wall close until the natural flow of the ridge draws the path slightly right to mount onto **Sergeant's Crag** at 574m/1883ft. The summit cairn is a place of quiet contemplation, for few walkers come this way. The best view from the fell is down the ramped rib to the north-west, which provides a dramatic outlook into Langstrath.

The path heads south from the summit, crossing the ladder stile onto the broad damp moor. A faint path can be detected, and dry ground arrives as the slope begins to rise and the path promptly disappears. Keep south-east, avoiding the rocks of Long Crag and Low White Stones to the right to reach the scarp-topping summit of **High Raise** at 762m/2500ft.

The plain plateau of **High Raise** ensures that eyes are most keenly trained in the arc from south-west to north-west. A wall shelter and stone-built OS pillar provide the focus and a brilliant foreground for photographs across Langstrath to Bowfell and the Glaramara ridge.

Leave the summit north-north-east to an outcrop topped with a metal post. Head north to **Low White Stones** and on down the easy, if eroded slope to **Greenup Edge**. Crossing the Coast to Coast Walk bridleway, the ridge path follows on with the remnant fence line, skirting a pool hollow, and with a prominent cairned knoll to the right. A final pool is skirted before the steady pull to the summit cairn on **Ullscarf** at 726m/2382ft. To all intents you are standing at the centre of the Lakeland fells, yet you'll probably cross the summit with little sense of event.

The old estate boundary fence, the metal stumps of which may have caused the occasional inadvertent stumble, comes back to life at the northern end of the plateau, where a stock-proof fence has been reinstated, running on from here along the spinal ridge to and beyond Bleaberry Fell. Follow on, passing the old metal strainer post to reach the peaked end of a fence. Bear left, crossing the fence as convenient. The stiles are in a poor state, but the plain netting is no hazard. Follow the ridge down via **High Saddle** and then traverse the saddle to the more prominent **Low Saddle** at 655m/2149ft. The cairn provides a good view down on Blea Tarn towards Watendlath.

Step back to avoid the initial drop, and begin the main descent north-westwards; grass is easily found among the sporadic boulders. You may aim direct for the heather-clad High Crag or drift slightly more left to join and accompany the wall a little earlier. Contour through the heather where two gills cause the wall to break left. Hug the wall then bear half-right through a small saddle, passing through a hollow to rejoin the wall alongside **High Crag** and descending to ford the outflow of **Dock Tarn** and join the popular footpath from the tarn.

A visit to **Dock Tarn** is much to be recommended. The lillies that form a 'S'-shaped swirl on the tarn's surface explain the tarn name (from the Old English word *docce* meaning 'water-lily'). The scene is one of great beauty, with heather-clad knolls to either hand, and the air of mystery can border on the spooky. The rough little summit of Great Crag is a worthy addition, situated a little to the north-west of the tarn.

Return with the popular path to cross a stile, from where the path swings right in a combe, with handsomely framed views down the Willygrass Gill ravine towards Eagle Crag. After descending Lingy End by a small ruin, join the thoroughly well-pitched steep steps leading down through the birchwood close to **Willygrass Gill**. The path crosses a wall-stile and completes its descent on the pasture, reconnecting with the bridle lane at the scenically sited sheepfold.

Eagle Crag, Sergeant's Crag and Langstrath from High Crag

High Spy, King's How and Brund Fell from Rosthwaite

*A*n unusual walk exploring the Jaws of Borrowdale on a grand scale. The walk provides the best of all perspectives on the Derwent gorge, regarded as the most beautiful square mile in Lakeland by that doyen of Lakeland commentators, Alfred Wainwright. Certainly the mix of trees, water and crags surrounded by beautiful fells is hard to fault. Walkers might not usually consider embracing both sides of the gorge, but it makes a jewel of a day, contrasting the high craggy rim of High Spy with the richly wooded dale and the complex of heathery knolls upon Grange Fell. A no less entertaining, and certainly less taxing, alternative route avoids High Spy and instead takes in Castle Crag en route between Rosthwaite and Grange-in-Borrowdale. This reduces the walk by a good two hours and slices a hefty 1200ft from the day's tally. Whatever your combination, time spent in this place will be well rewarded.

↑ *Castle Crag backed by Goat Crag*

ROUTE INFORMATION

Distance	13km/8¼ miles
Height gain	549m/1800ft
Time	6 hours
Grade	energetic
Start point	GR258148
Maps	(Harvey Superwalker) Lakeland Central (Ordnance Survey) OL4 North-western area

After-walk refreshment

The Scafell and Royal Oak Hotels and the Flock In tearoom in Rosthwaite

The Start

Head south from Keswick along the shores of Derwentwater, passing Grange to thread through the Derwent gorge and arrive at Rosthwaite. Directly after the bus stop (regular hourly 'Borrowdale Rambler' bus service) and opposite the village shop turn right to reach the National Trust car park. If full use the adjacent Community Hall (parking fee for hall funds), GR258148. Failing that, use the bus!

The Route

Follow the village lane leading between the Flock In tearoom and Yewtree Farm, a genuine working farm which boasts periodic royal patronage. The ensuing lane leads to and alongside the River Derwent to cross the neatly cobbled New Bridge. Turn immediately left and cross the first of a pair of footbridges and the mid-point stile. Follow the beck to a gate, crossing a small footbridge to a stile, where you bear away from the beck. Climbing the bank into bracken, pass through a gate at the top and continue uphill, heading straight across the Seatoller/Grange path.

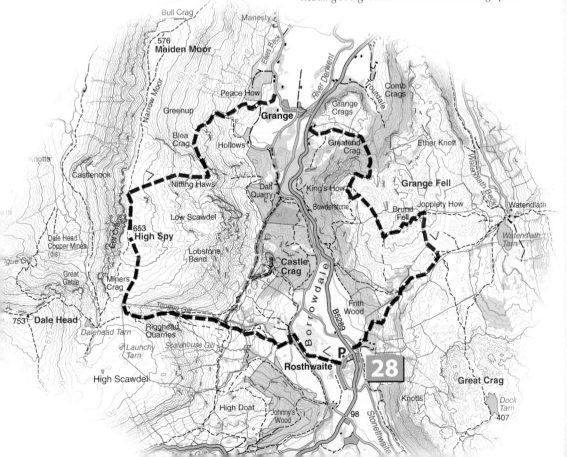

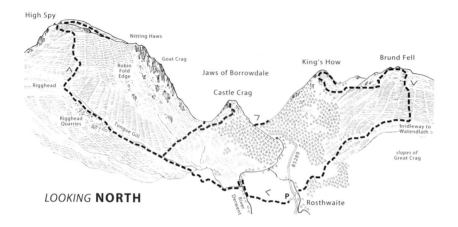

LOOKING **NORTH**

ALTERNATIVE ROUTE VIA CASTLE CRAG

At this point one may ignore the main route, which involves the mighty pull onto High Spy, and instead take the option of wandering north upon this contouring path. This delightful way, part of the Allerdale Ramble, threads through the valley 'behind' Castle Crag, with an inviting spur path climbing steeply right onto the diminutive pulpit peak itself – a moment of no less charming elation than High Spy. The route reaches the bonny banks of the Derwent amidst scenery reminiscent of a Scottish glen. The bridleway weaves through wood-flanked pastures onto a minor road leading directly into the community of Grange.

Those stubbornly resolved to stick to the main route should now turn their minds to the ascent to Rigghead. A stony path rises on the left bank of **Tongue Gill**. Higher up, and evidence of the old slate quarry incline, is a path leading to a fence stile, where the old quarry incline swept through the gill. Some pitching is evident as the path mounts through the slate spoil and remnant workings of **Rigghead Quarry**. The dark interior of two mine levels may invite furtive glances before the path duly arrives upon the moor at **Rigghead**, veering right to cross the stile in the right-hand corner of the fence.

Embark on a easy ascent upon grass to the summit of **High Spy**, passing an intermediate cairn brow. The large cairn is a place of congregation and conversation with fellow fell-folk, almost all engaged in the Newlands Horseshoe. Head north with the ridge. After 200m a breach in the Eel Crags scarp allows access to the top of an arête, adorned with

heather. Descend the short way to sit on the nab end above the western brink and absorb the grandeur of Hindscarth and the depths of the upper Newlands valley. It's the perfect place to sit for a while, away from the flow of ridge walkers.

Stepping back onto the ridge, continue a further hundred or so metres to find a small cairn indicating the start of a path to the right. This descends the shallow combe beneath the obvious prow of Minum Crag, towards **Nitting Haws**, following the left side of an emerging gill. Reaching a cairn short of the headland, the path is guided left on a shepherd's droveway known as High White Rake that slants beneath a low crag – a deft piece of route invention, unlocking the seemingly impenetrable cliffs when seen from below.

The path passes a large square rock topping Cockley How (a name identifying a former courtship area used by woodcock during the mating season), delivered to the spot by glacial action, and sweeps down the bracken slopes, with the mass of heather on the eastern slopes of Maiden Moor a striking sight up to the left. The path leads to a kissing-gate in a fence and passes tight by a pumping house compound to reach a gate beside a private wood. The path leads through **Peace How** to a gate onto the road almost opposite Borrowdale Gates country house hotel.

Go right through **Grange-in-Borrowdale** (two tearooms), crossing the Derwent via Grange Bridge. Turn right. Immediately after the house find a bridleway hand-gate up the bank left from the road. Follow the path naturally through the open birchwood and marshy flushes, crossing a low ridge to a hand-gate in a wall. As the path descends fork right, just before

Squat Knotts on Hindscarth from High Spy →

the next hand-gate, with the path dipping through a stony hollow in the woodland beneath **Greatend Crag**. The path sets off on a steady ascent, soon supported by firm steps – a magical staircase to the upper storey. As the path emerges from the trees it levels out. Keep to the stepping stone trail, rising again to curve right of the damp lateral valley and climbing to the north end of **King's How**. Ascend via the Edward VII memorial plaque set into a rock alcove directly below the summit.

Skiddaw and Derwentwater from King's How

The cairnless top of King's How, 392m/1286ft, is the most prominent of the three 'summits' that comprise **Grange Fell**. Ether Knott, 'the heather eminence', is the most northerly and just one metre lower than Brund Fell. Brund Fell, the highest at 416m/1365ft, lies to the south and is the final objective of the walk. The name Brund is thought to refer to a tradition of heather burning.

Continue naturally over the top, watching for a break left as a small stone marker is seen ahead. Traverse the end of the marshy lateral valley, crossing the fence stile, and continue past a ruined fold to cross a ladder stile. Rise beyond a second ruined fold, and when it seems that the path is missing the main summit the path turns acutely left. Advance up past the first rock turret to reach the narrower rock castle, the actual summit of **Brund Fell**. Note the volcanic swirls in the rock. Nearby stands the jaunty-sounding outcrop **Jopplety How**. The path continues down to a new ladder stile over the bounding wall, where you turn right, initially avoiding the marshy ground. Then keep by the wall, descending to the top of the Watendlath/Rosthwaite bridge-path at the gate. Go through and follow this down by a series of three further gates by Hazel Bank to cross the Stonethwaite Beck bridge into **Rosthwaite** opposite the bus stop.

Jopplety How and Brund Fell from King's How

Catbells, Maiden Moor, High Spy, Dale Head and Hindscarth from Hawse End

*O*ne of the all-time favourite horseshoe walks, on a par with the Fairfield Horseshoe – but this
round has a kick in its midst, the pull onto Dale Head from Dalehead Tarn. The views are consistently uplifting and more than compensate for the extra effort in holding to the complete round.
Catbells may seem a little fell, but it has a big heart and a peerless view both over Derwentwater and
into the Newlands arena, catching the best of all perspectives on a cluster of bold ridge-ends. The
continuing rising ridge forms a remarkable escarpment to the Newlands valley, starting upon Maiden
Moor and reaching its zenith on High Spy. Dale Head just could not be better named, enjoying a
peach of a view down dale to Skiddaw. Hindscarth reflects the High Spy ridge and then attempts to
go one better in Scope End, giving the walk an excitingly narrow heather-clad ridge-end.

↑ *Catbells from Maiden Moor*

Distance	19.25km/12 miles
Height gain	1052m/3450ft
Time	8 hours
Grade	strenuous
Start point	GR246212
Maps	(Harvey Superwalker)
	Lakeland Central
	(Ordnance Survey)
	OL4 North-western area

After-walk refreshment
The Swinside Inn, 1km north-west of Hawse End

The Start
In spite of the popularity of the Catbells ridge walk, parking is at something of a premium at the northern tip of the Skelgill Bank ridge, GR246212. However, there is some scope for parking along the open road above Brandelhow, the first land acquired by the National Trust in the Lake District.

The Route
Take your pick from one of two paths in making your first step onto the Skelgill Bank ridge-end. The ridge path mounts without complication, passing an old memorial slab over the first top, **Skelgill Bank** at 338m/1110ft. After two quick depressions the path climbs heroically to the summit of **Catbells** at 451m/1480ft. Walkers scrutinising their maps will notice that the south top bears the name Mart Bield. This latter meant 'pine marten's lair', while Catbells was 'the bell-shaped hill frequented by wild cats' – the two tops might explain the plural in the name.

Descend the grassy bank south into the sweeping depression of **Hause Gate**, where a cross-ridge bridleway from Little Town to Manesty intersects. Keep faith with the rising ridge path, and climb above Trap Knotts onto the brow of **Maiden Moor**. The popular path strides merrily on to Narrow Moor, missing the actual summit.

High Spy summit cairn

Do make a point of veering right to find the **Maiden Moor** cairn at 576m/1890ft. It rests close to the great fall into the Newlands valley and has the most sumptuous of views over the Bull Crag brink onto Scope End, with its ancient mine-spoil bank prominent. Follow the edge, peering down on the Carlisle Mountaineering Club hut and across to the chiselled profile of Hindscarth.

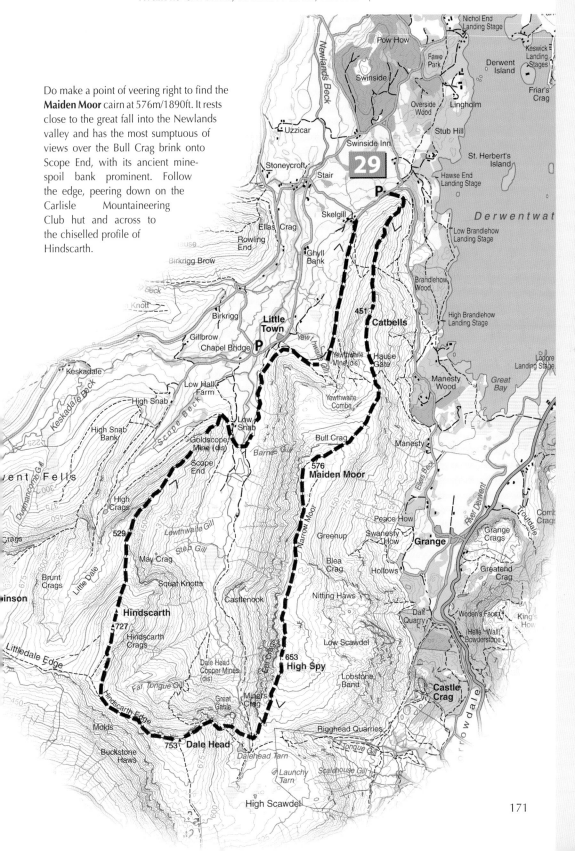

171

LOOKING **EAST**

The route reconnects with the popular path at **Narrow Moor** which, as its name implies, squeezes the ridge, and leads on to the next modest ascent onto the north top of High Spy at 630m/2067ft. The ridge path takes the line of easiest progress, as

may be expected, but the real thrills lie closer to the western edge. The ridge makes one final shallow dip before marching up to the main summit cairn of **High Spy** at 653m/2142ft.

HIGH SPY

Like High Spying How on Striding Edge, the name must suggest 'a good vantage' – and it is very good! The considerable cairn attracts walkers like moths round a bulb. Invariably the walk to this spot has put them in good humour, and conversations hit a cheery note.

If you were thinking of taking your lunch break at this point, might I suggest you backtrack a matter of 150m to where there is a breach in the scarp and a narrow heathery arête dropping into the bosom of Eel Crag. There you will find the perfect lone perch, hidden from the flow of walkers and offering a marvellous airy outlook into the upper Newlands valley.

Backtrack past the summit cairn, follow the ridge path and step down towards **Dalehead Tarn**, fording the beck short of the tarn to embark on the steep, partially pitched path climbing the eastern slope of Dale Head. Gain the shoulder of Great Gable, a second cousin to its more famous Wasdale namesake; strictly speaking, this is the top of Dalehead Crags. Meet a narrow path, emerging from the copper mine located in the high cove directly beneath the fell summit. Finish the ascent up the north ridge, reaching the **Dale Head** summit cairn at 753m/2470ft, a serious rival to that on High Spy. More than ever it is the view that will grab the emotions – the deeply entrenched Newlands Beck valley hemmed in by

Dale Head summit cairn

Catbells and Maiden Moor from Scope End

craggy walls leads the eye north to Skiddaw, while all around the grandest of fells liberate the senses and permeate the consciousness with a gratitude that you are at this moment in this high place.

Continue west to descend **Hindscarth Edge**, avoiding stumbling on the stump remains of an old metal boundary fence. Attention will be glued on the steep wall of Honister Crag and the heathery edge of Fleetwith Pike, with High Stile's triumphant trio of fell tops above Buttermere beyond. As the path forks, curve north on an easy angle rising onto **Hindscarth** at 727m/2385ft. The fell name is enigmatic – 'pass of the deer hind' – there being no obvious gap to which to attach the description. While it offers a fine viewpoint, a better place is perhaps the larger alcove cairn near the northern lip. The ridge path continues north, stepping with increasing steepness onto the narrow neck above Littledale Crags, and thereafter

leading onto **Scope End**. To experience this ridge-top path in late summer, when the heather is in full bloom, is pure magic.

The path skips down in neat stages to meet the intake fence. Turning right, descend to join the track above **Low Snab** and bear right beneath the spoil banks of the old Goldscope copper mine, then left by the wall over the footbridge to join the track from the upper dale. The track leads towards **Little Town**. Watch for the green path forking up right as the track starts to curve. As it does so, it loses the notably photogenic view back to Scope End. Follow this rising grass path which leads above the hamlet as a bridle path coming beside a wall, which is retained to a footbridge among the spoil banks of **Yewthwaite Gill**. The succeeding track leads north to a gate at **Skelgill**, where the tarmac road is joined and followed to complete the round trip.

Robinson,
Knott Rigg and Ard Crags
from Rigg Beck

*T*he North-Western Fells divide neatly upon Newlands Hause, from where the shapely mass of Robinson handsomely dominates, enhanced by the fuming presence of Moss Force. The road wending up the Newlands valley draws over the considerable slope of Rowling End, bound for Keskadale, and catches a glimpse to the right of an impressive razor edge looming over Rigg Beck. This ridge, which includes the summits Knott Rigg and Ard Crags, combines beautifully with Robinson to make an entertaining skyline horseshoe.

The walk is recommended in a clockwise direction because of one minor rock-step near the foot of Robinson's north ridge. As a route of descent in adverse weather it would unduly tax most fell walkers, whereas in ascent the scramble can be enjoyed in a far more relaxed frame of mind.

↑ *The Grasmoor group of fells from Robinson*

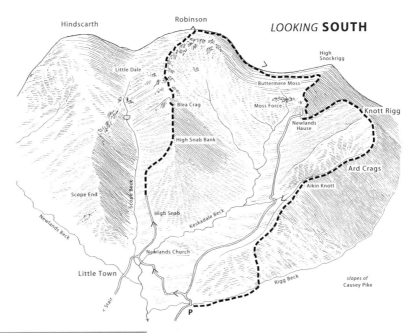

LOOKING **SOUTH**

Distance	13.5km/8½ miles
Height gain	924m/3030ft
Time	5½ hours
Grade	energetic
Start point	GR229202
Maps	(Harvey Superwalker)
	Lakeland West
	(Ordnance Survey)
	OL4 North-western area

After-walk refreshment

The Coledale, Royal Oak and Middle Ruddings at Braithwaite, The Swinside near Stair, and the Fish and Bridge at Buttermere

The Start

Situated along the Newlands Hause road less than a mile south of Stair, a small alcove quarry serves as a car park at the foot of Rigg Beck, GR229202.

The Route

Stride over the Rigg Beck bridge upon the Newlands Hause road. At the top of the initial rise, where until recently stood a purple-painted timber chalet-house (sold at auction so a new abode is sure to take its place), turn left on the road signed left to Newlands Church.

The narrow road twists and turns. Follow the next right-hand turn, again signed to the church. Pass on from the open common in front of the charming white-washed chapel in the dale, rising beyond and passing the access to **High Snab Farm**. Go through a gate where the tarmac ends and pass close by the delightful traditional Lakeland cottage Low High Snab. A short woodland track leads to a gate. Follow the green lane beyond and, as this opens, bear up right. Climb on the path evident through the bracken onto the skyline of **High Snab Bank**.

A largely grassy ridge, like the roof of a house, commands lovely views over the Keskadale valley to Ard Crags backed by the massive Eel Crag ridge, which guides the eye right to the distinctive undulating profile of Causey Pike. The ridge path leads over the knoll of **Blea Crags** ('blue rocks'), where you may spot evidence of speculative mining. Down to the left at the foot of secretive Little Dale, see an old header pond that formerly served the Goldscope Mine via a water channel, and now serves as a place for quiet reflection.

The ridge dips then embarks upon Robinson's outcropped north ridge. A scramble is unavoidable; in wet or icy conditions this demands the utmost care, and in descent requires a high degree of competence. The climb is otherwise simple, and provides opportunities to enjoy scarp-edge

175

Robinson from High Stile

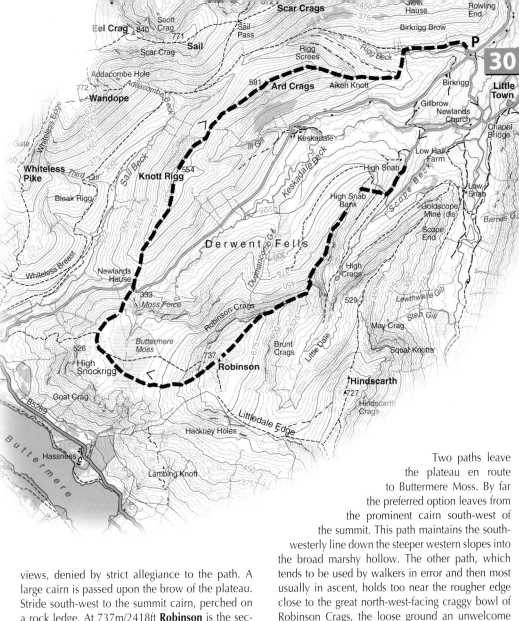

views, denied by strict allegiance to the path. A large cairn is passed upon the brow of the plateau. Stride south-west to the summit cairn, perched on a rock ledge. At 737m/2418ft **Robinson** is the second highest of the handsome group of fells east of Newlands Hause.

From **Robinson's** summit, being a shallow dome, valley views are obscured, but the senses are stirred by the surround of mighty fells. The Grasmoor group to the north-west is shown off to wonderful effect; indeed, the all-round view is fit for any king's table. The cairn rests on the westernmost of two low, parallel rock-ribs and thus provides Spartan shelter in a gale. It is common to find personal names attributed to fells, but only on this one fell is it the sole name. The family of Richard Robinson owned lands in the Buttermere area in the 16th century.

Two paths leave the plateau en route to Buttermere Moss. By far the preferred option leaves from the prominent cairn south-west of the summit. This path maintains the south-westerly line down the steeper western slopes into the broad marshy hollow. The other path, which tends to be used by walkers in error and then most usually in ascent, holds too near the rougher edge close to the great north-west-facing craggy bowl of Robinson Crags, the loose ground an unwelcome travail worth side-stepping as described.

As a spongy carpet the path traverses **Buttermere Moss** – not the most endearing terrain, especially after it has been raining! Its one virtue is as a gathering ground for the magnificent cascades of **Moss Force**, a spectacular waterfall feature above Newlands Hause. Avoiding wet feet is not an easy process, and neither is sticking to any form of common path. The upper edge of the Goat Crag ravines might prove an interesting lure, especially as they do provide a fine view down on Buttermere lake and across the valley to the great corries either side of High Stile, Birkness and Bleaberry Combs. Only sheep paths can be found, so be sure not to drift down too far.

Robinson and Keskadale Farm from Ard Crags

The headland of **High Snockrigg** rises like a merry wave, assuring dry feet once more, and from its southern tip there is a magnificent view over the Buttermere vale. Once firmly set upon the grassy ridge-top, head north down the ridge. Ignore the footpath breaking left destined for Buttermere village. As the ridge steepens, a grooved path works down the outcropped nose, with pitching in its latter stages serving the inevitable increased attention from visitors provided by the hause-top car park.

Cross straight over **Newlands Hause** due north, following the steep grass path onto the comparatively narrow ridge of Knott Rigg. The scenery is a pure delight, especially the great heathered slopes of Wandope and Eel Crag rising impressively across the Sail Beck valley to the left. The summit of **Knott Rigg** is a modest gathering of stones at 554m/1818ft, with a view down the narrow cleft of Keskadale. As the ridge path dips grass is replaced by heather in mounting onto **Ard Crags**, 581m/1906ft, where eyes are most surely drawn to the ridge-end summit of Causey Pike across the deep fold of Rigg Beck. The old coppiced woodland is quite a feature of the fell's steep southern slope, similarly evident on the steep Keskadale bank directly below the summit.

The ridge path, loose in places, plunges down from **Aikin Knott**. The headland's name meant 'the oak-clothed height', though there is nothing left on this side of the Rigg Beck valley to suggest the former presence of an oakwood. As the ridge eases, bear half-left on the clear path through the bracken to ford **Rigg Beck**, where the cross-ridge enclosure fence meets it. Follow the Rigg Beck track easily down to the quarry car park.

Eel Crag and Sail from Knott Rigg

Grisedale Pike, Hopegill Head, Eel Crag, Sail, Outerside and Barrow from Braithwaite

*A*pproaching Keswick along the A66 it is the North-western Fells, rising west of the town, principally Eel Crag and Grisedale Pike, that draw most avid attention. This impressive walking tour tightly embraces the skyline of Coledale and includes the summits of Grisedale Pike, Hopegill Head, Eel Crag, Sail, Outerside and Barrow. The omission of Causey Pike is the natural by-product of a focus on Braithwaite.

The village of Braithwaite was once a much larger, industrial community – home to miners, woollen-millers and pencil-makers. The Cumberland Pencil Company had a factory here from 1868 to 1898, when a fire resulted in its demolition and the transfer of manufacturing to Keswick.

Should you decide to take the alternative return route via Scar Crags ridge and claim the Pike, be aware that the initial descent east is fraught with rock-step obstacles that may cause you problems.

↑ Grisedale Pike, Coledale and Skiddaw from Eel Crag

ROUTE INFORMATION	
Distance	16km/10 miles
Height gain	1160m/3806ft
Time	6½ hours
Grade	strenuous
Start point	GR227237
Maps	(Harvey Superwalker)
	Lakeland West
	(Ordnance Survey)
	OL4 North-western area

After-walk refreshment

Braithwaite offers the Coledale Inn, Royal Oak and Middle Ruddings Hotel – cask ale and good food all round

The Start

From the village of Braithwaite follow the Whinlatter road up the initial rise, passing the Hope Memorial Camp, to find a track access left to Coledale and the Force Crag Mine at the valley head. Short of a gate there is room for six tidily parked cars (GR227237).

The Route

Climb the flight of steps rising immediately to the right. (Note: The track beyond the barrier leads easily into Coledale proper and could be a useful return route if, later in the day, the weather deteriorates and you have to retreat from Coledale Hause.) The path gives fine views over the Bassenthwaite Vale to the Skiddaw massif as it rises to a stile. After this the path climbs a little further before levelling along the **Kinn** ridge overlooking Coledale. Here eyes will be focused on the headwall drama of Force Crag. The valley is of simple form, long and straight, reserving all its visual drama for its upper reaches, where a rock band intervenes causing the valley beck to step down two great mare's tail falls. Pitch up again onto the heather bank of **Sleet How** above Hospital Plantation to climb ever more sternly up the conical east ridge to the summit of **Grisedale Pike**. Path erosion is inevitable on such a singular and popular path.

The summit of **Grisedale Pike**, at 791m/2595ft, has a block of tilted slate providing a naturally sheltered eastern shelf. The outlook is superb, and while the remainder of the walk includes a succession of handsome tops, none is better than this spot.

Sail, Eel Crag and Force Crag at the head of Coledale

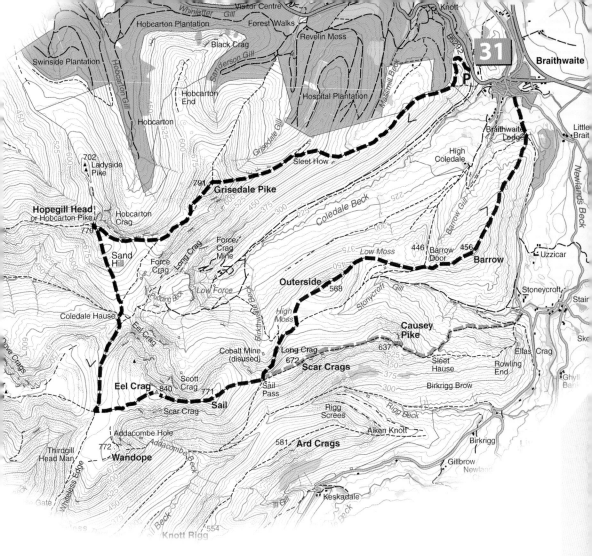

A broken wall accompanies the continuing ridge path over a intermediate top to end where the path forks; the left-hand path leads directly down to Coledale Hause. Keep to the ridge now above the remarkable craggy headwall of the Hobcarton valley, revelling in the views back along the edge to Grisedale Pike, and climb to the peaked summit of **Hopegill Head** at 770m/2526ft. **Hobcarton Crag** falls majestically beneath one's feet, its grassy ledges threaded by perilous sheep trods. To the west the continuing ridge jinks to end on Whiteside, with Crummock Water peeping into view down Gasgale Gill. To the west the ridge steps attractively down to Ladyside Pike.

Turn south and follow the path over **Sand Hill**, with shards of slate not sand underfoot. Descend into the broad hollow of **Coledale Hause**, a path intersection. (Note: To shorten the walk you may follow the clear path left down into the Pudding Beck

hollow to join the Force Crag Mine access track, which leads easily down the north side of the valley directly to the car park.) Due south the north ridge of Eel Crag rises in two abrupt craggy steps. It is far better to follow the re-structured path rising beside the upper course of Gasgale Gill south-south-west on an easy gradient.

This duly comes to a T-junction of paths (shown as a cross-path junction on the map) by a pool, with the Grasmoor ridge connection right. This is peak a worthy add-on for the extraordinary panorama from that summit; return to the main track to continue.

Turn left, still upon an engineered path climbing the plain slope; a brief traverse right provides a sumptuous parade of fells over Addacombe Hole. An Ordnance Survey column stands on the broad, featureless summit of **Eel Crag** at 838m/2753ft. Stride the few paces north-east to peer down on the Force Crag Mine and upper Coledale.

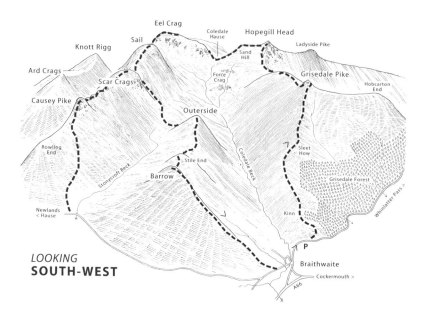

LOOKING
SOUTH-WEST

Force Crag Mine was the last working mine in the Lake District, closed in 1991. Lead, zinc and barytes had been extracted there since the 1830s. The National Trust have acquired the buildings and internal machinery and periodically provide guided tours – contact Keswick 017687 74649.

The east ridge descends with continuing grand views on either hand. There are two minor scrambly sections – one near the top and the other near the foot of the ridge. A small col leads to a steady climb onto **Sail**, 773m/2536ft. The actual summit, bypassed by the common flow of fell walkers, is

Hobcarton Crag, Hopegill Head and Ladyside Pike

Ridge to Scar Crags and Causey Pike from Sail, with the Rigg Beck valley near right

marked by a tiny cairn in a shallow pool. Descend east-north-east to a lower, more substantial hause.

One may continue up the facing ridge onto **Scar Crags** en route to **Causey Pike**, a major landmark fell, but the descent off the ridge east is less than pleasant. However, the preferred route takes its leave of the ridge at this point, and a clear path angles north-east to descend beneath the outcrops on the western side of Scar Crags. As this becomes a track on **High Moss**, veer smartly left across the marshy hollow to climb the grassy ridge of **Outerside** at 568m/1863ft.

Being a less frequented summit this is an excellent place for a longer pause, the view devoted to Coledale. The heathery path descending the east ridge contends with minor gullying caused by sudden rain wash-out. Reach the pool in **Low Moss** and stride over the shoulder of **Stile End**, advancing via the gap of Barrow Door up onto **Barrow** at 455m/1493ft. It is quite the place to linger after the rigours of the day and really soak up a fabulous prospect across the woods surrounding Swinside to Derwentwater and Keswick, backed by the mighty Skiddaw and Blencathra. Follow on naturally down with the ridge north to **Braithwaite Lodge**, joining the track at gates which lead most sweetly into Braithwaite, a lovely last lap.

Ullock Pike, Long Side, Carl Side, Skiddaw Little Man, Skiddaw and Bakestall from Bassenthwaite

*S*kiddaw is a much loved landmark fell. The cornerstone of the northern Lakes, it has been revered down the generations by native and tourist alike as a gracious backdrop, particularly to views from Derwentwater and Bassenthwaite. It is a massif in its own right, with a company of supporting fells leading to a remotely sited summit. Built of slate and therefore almost bereft of crags, its upper slopes are strewn with scree. Many who climb the fell do so as a one-off fell-walking event – they see the sleek slopes and judge it an 'easy' ascent to a magnificent viewpoint. They are correct. But judgement and a little local knowledge are needed to avert tedium and fashion a memorable mountain day.

To unlock Skiddaw's finest qualities begin your walk from the charming little village of Bassenthwaite, which lies in the vale immediately to the north-west. Eyes turn quickly to the razor-edge leading to Ullock Pike, Long Side and Carl Side. The route follows on from these grand-galleried viewpoints to traverse the southern slopes of Skiddaw and gather up Skiddaw Little Man, possessing the most comprehensive and expansive fell-top view in Lakeland. Backtracking over the main summit, the route descends via Bakestall to the beautiful waterfall of Whitewater Dash. It follows on down the enchanting Dash valley and subsequent green pastures to regain Bassenthwaite, where it all began.

↑ *Long Side and Ullock Pike from Bassenthwaite*

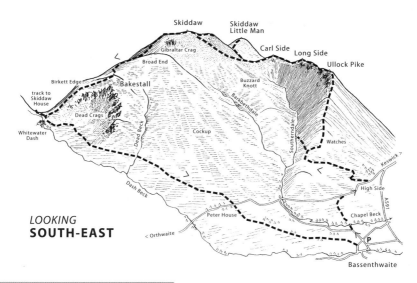

LOOKING
SOUTH-EAST

ROUTE INFORMATION

Distance	19km/12 miles
Height gain	1045m/3430ft
Time	9 hours
Grade	strenuous
Start point	GR230321
Maps	(Harvey Superwalker)
	Lakeland North
	(Ordnance Survey)
	OL4 North-western area

After-walk refreshment

The Sun Inn at Bassenthwaite, Pheasant Inn at
Dubwath and Snooty Fox at Uldale

The Start

Park wisely in Bassenthwaite – either in the trian-
gular village centre near The Avenue, GR230322,
or on the verge at the junction of School Lane and
Burthwaite, GR230321. Alternatively, one might
start from the lay-by at High Side on the Orthwaite
Road, GR236310. Quite the majority do, but they
miss the genuine pleasure of the green-pastured out-
walk and final setting-sun strides... to the door of the
Sun Inn!

The Route

Leave the tree-shaded Avenue at the centre of the
village, south, and follow the road to the junction
with School Lane. Keep left along Burthwaite, a
vergeless lane blinkering a view of Skiddaw, dead
ahead. At the tight left bend cross the stone-flag stile
and descend the pasture to the gated footbridge
spanning **Chapel Beck**, its waters draining Barkbeth
and Southerndales. Once across, bear left, rising up
the shaded bank to a new fence and stile – spot the
Victorian spired parish church down to the right.

Cross the stile and follow on with the hedge to
the left. As the pasture recesses left, cross the stile
ahead, now with a fence right, advance to a stile and
curve round left with the next field corner. Some 60
metres short of the gate, find a stile beneath a mature
oak tree, then cross and ascend the pasture diagonally to a stile onto the road. Turn right, following
the road passing **High Side House** to reach the start
of a bridleway, left, at a gate. Note the lay-by just
beyond, an alternative starting point for the walk.

Go through the gate, with a bridleway signboard
to 'Skiddaw – Barkbeth and Mellbecks' (farms), then
ford the gill and follow the line of gorse. As an old
hedgeline is met bear right with the thorn, continuing beyond, where they have been grubbed, to angle
up left to a ladder stile spanning a wall. A green way
leads across the pasture to another ladder stile, after
which the green track curves right with an open view
into Southerndale (which means 'the valley south of
Bassenthwaite village').

Arrive at a gate and perilously perched stile. Cross
and, leaving the track, go immediately right, ascending beside the intake wall. At the brow bear off left
onto the ridge path. This rises to an intriguing area

185

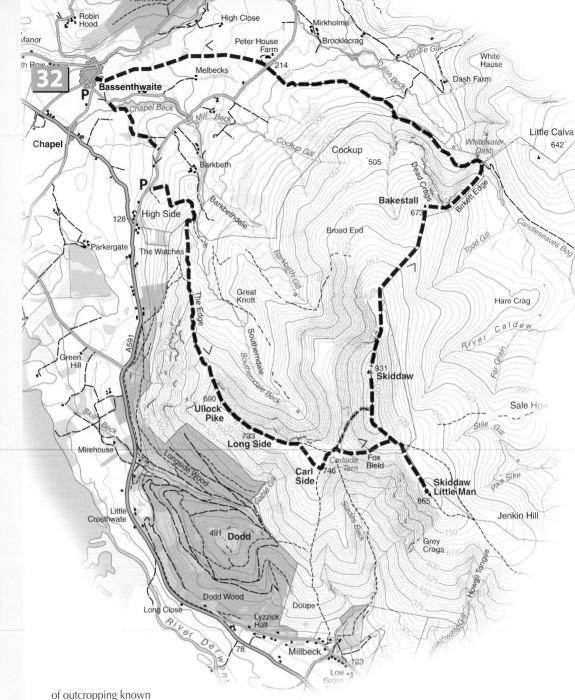

of outcropping known as **The Watches** – time for your first a stop. Rock features are rare on the massif and geologists have paid them attention, as can be judged by several pneumatically drilled bore holes.

The path pursues the ridge which soon starts up more steeply, after being joined by a side path from Ravenstone. Views over the pastures and woodland to Bassenthwaite lake give heightened pleasure to any moment's pause. Higher up, the path has been decommissioned from the precise edge, though the new line is taking a pasting too, so further work will inevitably be done on this section. A short stair of rock leads onto the first top, leading on to the cairned summit of **Ullock Pike** at 690m/2264ft.

Ullock Pike is a worthy place to deliberate on Skiddaw across the barren headwall of Southerndale and, on a broader front, ridge upon ridge of Lakeland's wonderful fells spread out to the south. The fell name derives from a combination of 'the pike espied from Ullock', where Ullock (GR245231) itself meant 'the place where wolves play', from *ulfa leikr*.

The ridge path dips and rises along a comparatively narrow crest, looking down upon the forestry-relieved upper dome of Dodd to the right and the greater sparkle of Bassenthwaite lake. Rise to the cairn at 733m/2405ft marking the summit of **Long Side**, and attention ever more focuses on Skiddaw, its scree-draped slope suggesting a torrid ascent. The ridge leads down to a depression, with the obvious path skirting the edge above Southerndale. Take the opportunity to follow the ridge path direct to the summit cairn on **Carl Side** at 746m/2448ft, 'the ridge of the old man'. Enjoy the view down the slope to the sub-ridge of Carlsleddam and across the vale to Keswick and Derwentwater.

But of more pressing importance is where next to travel. The obvious path up the impending Skiddaw looks less than inviting. Upon seeing universal scree, 999 out of every 1000 walkers will turn with the more obvious path, cursing and stumbling to the mid-point on Skiddaw's summit ridge. However, from Carl Side the wily orienteering fell walker will observe the potential for a different scenario. Using simple deduction they will judge the right-hand slope to be less steep and sense a more agreeable route to Fox Bield. Therefore, descend to pass **Carlside Tarn** and, rising briefly to an obvious quartz boulder, bear half-right on grass. Embarking on firm, stable slate scree, rise at a comfortable angle with no hint of a path. Pause upon reaching the large quartz outcropping of **Fox Bield**, the name suggesting the traditional hidey-hole of reynard. Then bear more acutely uphill for only a matter of 45m to step onto grass, and then follow on a shallow ascending line retaining pasture to the ridge path. How sweet is that?

At this point one may simply turn left to complete the easy-underfoot ascent of Skiddaw. However, the route described here takes this golden opportunity to visit **Skiddaw Little Man**. Descend, and at a fence corner continue with the fence close left to then rise to the conical top. At 865m/2838ft the cairn sits off the main course of Skiddaw's daily procession, yet right at the middle of the most comprehensive view you are ever likely to get of this fabulous mountain district. Given the weather, indulge yourself with time to soak up the prospect, outstripping Skiddaw's

Long Side from Ullock Pike

South along the summit ridge of Skiddaw

in terms of Lakeland detail. Backtrack and continue up the south slope of Broad End to the first of a line of cairns leading duly along the slate trail to the summit of **Skiddaw** at 931m/3054ft.

On **Skiddaw**, a topograph, with an inevitably rudimentary fix on detail, a wind-shelter and an old concrete triangulation pillar form the summit focus. Being so far back from the southern fells, the outlook is more directed to the Solway Plain, with the distant sweep of Dumfries and Galloway holding the promise of distant high lands. Back o'Skidda's apron of heathery hills fills the foreground, with a less than exciting back view of Blencathra. Skiddaw House, among its huddle of trees, seems a lonely place in the midst of it all.

Pass on by a second wind-shelter, winding down the north slope to come beside a fence. Looking ahead notice the curious patchwork of heather on Great Calva, cut in irregular strips to provide younger growth for grouse. The fence turns right as the slope breaks north-east. This leads down Broad End to reach a saddle containing a dishevelled bield-cum-fold, after which you veer half-left to reach the summit cairn of the shoulder-height **Bakestall** at 673m/2208ft. The fell name, like Stool End in Great Langdale, suggests a distant (from the north) likeness to a baking-stool. Even more enigmatic is the name of the cliffs directly below – why Dead Crags?

Keep right along the heather and bilberry rim to rejoin and continue down **Birkett Edge** with the fence, and subsequently wall, to meet the Skiddaw House track adjacent to a gate. Turn left, paying keen attention to the beck, and as the track begins to bear left find the opportunity to sneak closer to view the handsome waterfall **Whitewater Dash** – most of the time it well and truly lives up to its name. The lower portion is harder to reach, but merits the adventure.

Follow the track below the shadowed amphitheatre of Dead Crags to join the farm drive from Dash Farm, admiring the intriguing mass of quartz across the valley known as Brockle Crag, 'the place of badgers'. The backing fell is called Great Cockup, which meant 'the lekking place of black grouse'. The road passes through four gates to meet the road at **Peter House**. Cross straight over via the broad gate and pay little heed to the farm track, a waymark board guiding slightly left straight across the pasture to a gate to the right of a wood. The bridleway continues by three further hand-gates, then passing a line of trees veers half-right down to a gate midway along the fence line. It continues on by further gates into a lane and so into the village centre.

← Skiddaw from Long Side

Carrock Fell and High Pike
from Stone Ends

A simple round encircling the Carrock Beck valley in the far north-east corner of the national park. The tour claims two sentinel summits. The first, Carrock Fell, is an Iron Age hill-top refuge; the second, High Pike, is the northernmost outpost of the Lakeland fells, surveying the land towards the Solway and the backing hills of Dumfriesshire.

'The Caldbeck Fells are worth all England else'. The proud boast, coined in Victorian times, referred to the great mineral wealth extracted from the mines above Caldbeck – principally lead and copper, but also an amazing diversity of minerals. As a rocky ramble this walk holds further interest. Carrock Fell, the first high port of call, derives its name from the Celtic 'carreg', meaning 'the rock'. This relates to the hill-fort retreat, but could also have been a reference to the anti-magnetic volcanic rock gabbro, evident in the fell's crag and bouldered east slope.

Navigation is a problem because of the crazy effect that gabbro has on a compass pointer. Mountaineers will be familiar with this phenomena as this self-same rock, whilst absent elsewhere in the Lakes, predominates in the Black Cuillin of Skye.

↑ *Eastern aspect of Carrock Fell*

ROUTE INFORMATION	
Distance	10.5km/6½ miles
Height gain	533m/1750ft
Time	4½ hours
Grade	energetic
Start point	GR354337
Maps	(Harvey Superwalker)
	Lakeland North
	(Ordnance Survey)
	OL5 North-eastern area

After-walk refreshment

The Old Crown in Hesket Newmarket and the Mill Inn at Mungrisdale

The Start

An open common extends north from the hamlet of Mosedale (pronounced 'mowsdil'), flanking the road for a little over 2 miles in the direction of Hesket Newmarket. Find ample roadside parking some 200m north of the access track to Stone Ends Farm, GR354337.

The Route

Eyeing Carrock Fell from the roadside it is apparent that there is a break in its midst, drained by **Further Gill Sike**. Follow Rake Trod, an obvious shepherd's path, skirting the hollow remnant of the old Carrock End Mine and a sheepfold hugging a boulder, and make purposefully up the fellside to enter the gill. Pass above a rowan on a crag and below a solitary larch. The steep path is loose in places, narrow and trenched higher up where it reaches the heather moor. The impressive view back during the ascent extends

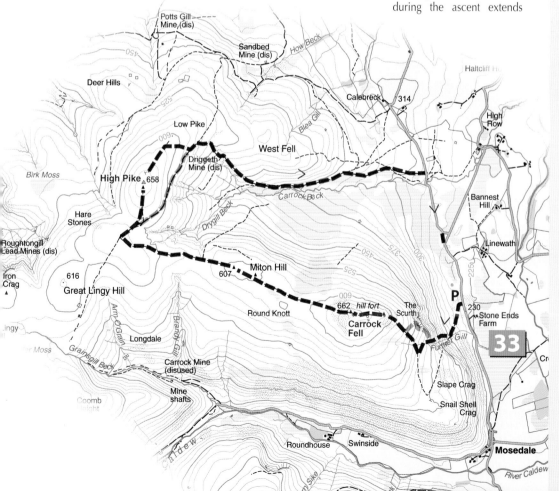

LOOKING **SOUTH**

over the lower limestone country beyond Stone Ends Farm. The intermediate woods and pastures of Greystoke Forest are succeeded by the distant Pennine chain, with Cross Fell centremost.

Nearing the initial brow there are two options. The first is to follow the eastern edge right, a narrow cairned path leading close to the craggy scarp edge, lending further dramatic opportunities to enjoy that eastward prospect, though from a final cairn the path is lost in the heather facing the gabbro crags of **The Scurth**. A direct pathless ascent to Carrock Fell is necessary – the going in rank heather is quite tough, though there are a few instances of boulder-fields to give contrast. Notice the prostrate juniper colonising these sites. Alternatively, the easier line from the top of Further Gill Sike is to keep with the more regular path, bearing half-left then switching right to mount to **Carrock Fell's** prominent east peak cairn, guided by a string of cairns.

CARROCK FELL HILL FORT

Visitors to this fell top have two thoughts uppermost in their minds: the promising view, and the desire to inspect the stone ramparts of the Iron Age hill fort. There are only a few instances of such forts in Lakeland, usually identified by the hill-name Castle Crag.

The scale of the stone ramparts, even today, suggests a highly organised community. It also leads one to think that the walls were used during and after the Roman period. It has been suggested that the Dark Age Celtic community welcomed and sheltered St Mungo on his southerly travels, hence the name Mungrisdale.

The rampart is an intriguing jumble, with hints of structure, and is great fun to explore. A complete tour, all around the tilting plateau, is heartily to be recommended. There are gaps, but the sense of history marches with your every stride.

Southern ramparts of Iron Age hill fort on Carrock Fell

Normally walkers plod straight up the middle to the west top cairn marking the summit at 662m/2172ft. The view is excellent, particularly south-west into the vast bowl at the source of the Caldew – once considered as a likely place for a reservoir.

The ridge path dips off the short western scarp and weaves along an often marshy moor – peaty patches and soggy moments unavoidable. Over to the left off the line of the ridge path a cairn sits invitingly upon **Round Knott**, and may be reached through a labyrinth of small pools. The continuing path strides west-north-west over the grassy, feature-less **Miton Hill** to be joined by Red Gate, an old miners' path arising out of the Carrock Beck valley. Keep on, and skirt the deep headstream gullies of Drygill Beck in swinging north towards High Pike. In so doing, cross a further miners' track coming across the eastern slopes of the fell.

North-east across the Caldew valley from Carrock Fell

High Pike 658m/2159ft is not the conventional 'pike', rather it is an unabashed domed pasture. The summit composes a novel three-piece suite of ragged, hollowed wind-shelter cairn, stone-built OS column and stout flag seat – the latter suggesting a much admired view. In fair weather the outlook is extensive.

High Pike summit, a high seat and saddle

On **High Pike** summit the sense of being detached from the normal Lakeland outlooks is understandable, so doubtless you'll be pleased to pick out the High Street range from Loadpot to Ill Bell. Through the Glenderaterra Gap, the major fells make a tantalisingly distant guest appearance from Bowfell and the Scafells to Great Gable. Elsewhere, attention is drawn in the northern arc across the Solway Plain to Criffel, and round by Roan Fell, Christianbury Crags and over the Roman wall to the Pennine range due east.

In leaving High Pike summit visit the northern cairn before turning north-east, pathless, down the grassy slope to meet the miners' track. Follow this left, encountering the upper rake of the **Driggeth Mine**. Pass a small enclosure defending an old open shaft. Where the track forks, go down right into the **Carrock Beck** valley, crossing spoil scree associated with the main area of the Driggeth Mine. The track has its damp moments but leads simply down the valley. Keep right (straight on) where it forks to reach the minor road on the common. Turn right and cross the footbridge by the road-ford. Where the road swings left to a junction, keep forward along a connecting track onto the continuing road, following the verge southwards back to the start.

Bowscale Fell,
Blencathra and Souther Fell
from Mungrisdale

*B*y contrast to the normal line of ascent up Blencathra, this walk tackles the peak on a more gradual course via Bowscale Fell, encircling the headwaters of the Glenderamackin to conclude over Souther Fell (pronounced 'sooter'). The walk is almost entirely on grass, but if the weather is dry and the wind relents an alternative return route – a scrambling descent of Sharp Edge – can provide a slice of real mountaineering for the confident hill-goer. It requires a steady head and competence on exposed rock, so most definitely should not be undertaken lightly.

↑ *Blencathra from the old A66*

ROUTE INFORMATION

Distance	14km/8¾ miles
Height gain	834m/2736ft
Time	6½ hours
Grade	energetic
Start point	GR364301
Maps	(Harvey Superwalker)
	Lakeland North
	(Ordnance Survey)
	OL5 North-eastern area

After-walk refreshment

The Mill Inn at Mungrisdale... try a pie and pint

The Start

There is parking on the sheep-cropped verge south of Mungrisdale village's contemporary Recreation Rooms, GR364301.

The Route

Follow the road past the Recreation Rooms, noting the old limekiln tucked into the bank behind, a sure indication of the near proximity of mountain limestone. Also spot the old mill-race falls tumbling from the north side of the **Mill Inn**, a great place for a drink at the end of the walk. The road swings right through the village, passing the diminutive church of

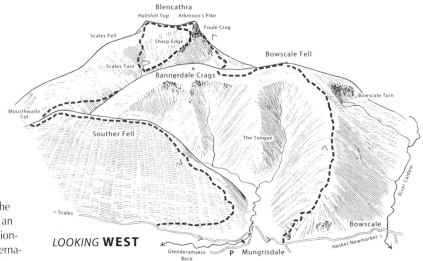

Blencathra
Hallsfell Top   Atkinson's Pike
Foule Crag
Scales Fell
Sharp Edge
Bowscale Fell
Scales Tarn
Bannerdale Crags
Bowscale Tarn
Mousthwaite Col
Souther Fell
The Tongue
River Caldew
< Scales
Bowscale
LOOKING WEST
Glenderamakin Beck   P   Mungrisdale
Hesket Newmarket >

St Kentigern. The dedication is to an early British missionary with the alternative name St Mungo, hence the village name.

Turn left where a lane begins, immediately after the Hutton Roof junction. Go through the gate and step onto the fell to the left of the old quarry. A clear path climbs quickly through the gorse onto the steadily rising ridge. Soon bracken is replaced by heather, and there are spacious views north over the Caldew valley to Carrock Fell. The contrast between the fells and the lower country to the east is very apparent, though geologically the lower-lying land is composed of more ancient rocks. When you cross the subsidiary summit, make a point of stepping down right momentarily to view **Bowscale Tarn** in its wild

Souther Fell from Scales Fell

Looking down on Sharp Edge from the saddle path

hollow, before heading on to the summit of **Bowscale Fell**, with its cairn and wind shelter at 702m/2303ft.

The path continues south, along the broad, damp ridge, and it is worth making a point of bearing briefly left to the edge overlooking the deep trench of Bannerdale. One can continue with the edge-path to visit the summit of Bannerdale Crags, though the main route veers right, south-south-east, declining to the small saddle at the head of the **Glenderamackin**.

> **Glenderamackin Beck** is a main feeder of the Greta and thus the River Derwent. The romantic name just might intrigue. As is so often the case this watercourse bears a really old name, in fact pre-Viking. It means the 'valley where swine forage' – from the British 'glyn' and 'moch'.

Cross directly over and climb the prominent ridge by the intermediate peak, where the ridge path from Mungrisdale Common meets the ridge at a wind shelter. The final steep climb of Blue Screes onto Atkinson Pike above Foule Crag is a marvellous moment. Stride south across the broad saddle, from which the fell's modern name, Saddleback, derives

(though the ancient name, Blencathra, similarly meant 'valley-head seat', which is to all intents the same thing). A pool frequently occupies the saddle. Pass the quartz cross set into the slope and rise to **Blencathra's** summit, finding no cairn but a circular plate marking the Ordnance Survey spot height at 868m/2848ft – and what a spot!

From **Blencathra's** summit the stupendous view south to the Helvellyn range and the fell surrounds of Thirlmere and Derwentwater encourages one to linger long in the breeze. The view down Hall's Fell is equally as impressive, while to the west and north lies the great rolling mass of fell Back o'Skidda, at the source of the River Caldew, with considerable tracts of heather lending rich mosaic tones of purple in late summer.

Leaving the summit one has two descent options to the outflow of Scales Tarn. The natural walkers' route descends east – watch for a half-left fork off the newly well-graded path. A path materialises and goes down into the hollow beneath Sharp Edge to reach the outflow of Scales Tarn. Alternatively, you could take the descent by Sharp Edge.

197

← *Walkers carefully negotiate the crux of Sharp Edge*

↓ *Solitary cairn on the west shoulder of Souther Fell*

ALTERNATIVE DESCENT
BY SHARP EDGE

For sure-footed brave-hearts Sharp Edge carries kudos but also a strong element of peril; first-timers should avoid the route in adverse weather. To follow this genuine scramblers' route, backtrack across the saddle, holding to the eastern edge path that rapidly plummets from Atkinson's Pike down the steep slick slabs of Foule Crag.

In themselves these slabs are challenging enough, but it is the cockerel's comb arete of Sharp Edge that really puts one on one's metal. The first unavoidable obstacle is the undoubted crux, oft times called The Postbox (see picture below), a slanting block stands proud beside a smooth tilted slab – pass with the utmost care.

Thereafter, suffice to say that by a mixture of steady steps and always having one's hands in play, one may make comparative light of the process. There are few weak-kneed cop-out options, so stay well clear if you are in any doubt. As the rock rib ends the path sweeps benignly down to the tarn's outflow to savour the glistening waters backed by the high bristling skyline of Sharp Edge.

Meeting the walkers' route off Scales Fell follow the beckside path to a ford, contouring above the Glenderamackin onto the broad saddle of Mousthwaite Col. Follow the ridge path straight on, rising onto Souther Fell, swinging north along the plain, damp summit ridge. The only cairn lies off the spine of the ridge, on the west. This is a fine spot from which to consider the dark wall of Bannerdale Crags, and particularly the short east ridge in its midst. There are no other cairns on the gently undulating ridge, and **Souther Fell** summit at 522m/1713ft is identified by the merest scrape of bedrock. The ridge path steps easily down to the north-east, but is denied a direct route to its natural destination, the Mill Inn, by landowner resistance. At a wooden waymark post veer right, descending to the enclosure wall which is followed amid dense bracken due south until at last the open road can be accessed. Go through the road gate, left, to finish the walk via the footbridge below the **Mill Inn**.

Blencathra
from Threlkeld

*T*he shortest walk in the book and perhaps the most immediately satisfying. The ascent of Hall's *Fell is a heady experience, with the last third of the ridge a cockerel's-comb rocky edge. It is the perfect crescendo to the route, which lands plumb on top of Blencathra. The line of descent, the adjacent Doddick Fell ridge, provides less daunting grassy footing. It offers lovely aspects of the near heather slopes, as well as back up to the summit's high throne; and always ahead is the wide southern horizon of mountain Lakeland, centred on the Helvellyn range.*

The Start

Modest parking in Threlkeld village street, or in the large park behind the sports pavilion on the south side of the A66 opposite the eastern entry into the village, GR325254.

The Route

From the bus shelter at the eastern end of the village street, follow the road forking left which leads up past the entrance to Four Seasons Foods. Take the farm access lane, left, a signed bridleway (a later

↑ *Blencathra from Doddick Fell*

ROUTE INFORMATION

Distance	7.5km/4¾ miles
Height gain	732m/2400ft
Time	5 hours
Grade	strenuous
Start point	GR325254
Maps	(Harvey Superwalker) Lakeland North (Ordnance Survey) OL5 North-eastern area

After-walk refreshment
Horse & Farrier Inn and Salutation in Threlkeld

sign indicating the horses and bikes are unwelcome). Pass up by a bungalow – the gnome, fox and huntsman weathervane a clear indication of your entry into John Peel Country.

Gategill Fell on Blencathra has a prominent rock outcrop called **Knott Hallo**. 'Cry hallo' was a hunting call associated with the local Blencathra Foxhounds, and the phrase features in the lyrics of the old musical hall song 'Da ya ken John Peel'.

Go through the gate/stile to the left of **Gategill** farmhouse. Hear and see the impressive falls of **Gate Gill** in the wooded gorge to the right.

On reaching a hand-gate by a tall-walled fold advance to the old mine dam, now a level ford. Floods have backfilled the retaining wall with slate debris, and evidence of the old lead and zinc mine is paltry. A moment's glance into the interior of the ravine reveals further cascades and little obvious scope for comfortable walking, with the soaring summit of Hall's Fell an inspirational peak at the head of the gill.

Cross the ford and step onto the ridge of Hall's Fell, mounting steadily on a firm, secure path. Quickly beating back the bracken, the path climbs into heather. Bilberries and sheep-cropped grass provide a pleasing near surround and ever-more handsome views back down on the green Threlkeld vale, backed by the plantation-embraced golf course and the 'granite' quarry at the base of Clough Head. The path veers diagonally right, gaining better prospects to the adjacent Doddick Fell – the return route.

Blencathra from St John's-in-the-Vale →

The thrilling flaky slate ridge eases and ends not on a jagged peak but, as if running out of ideas, on the most barren summit you'll ever encounter. There may be a scrap of stones, but – more likely – there'll be nothing except a small concrete ring marking the Ordnance Survey Triangulation Station at 868m/ 2848ft. Who needs cairns anyway? The view from **Blencathra** is everything, unfettered and all embracing. Most eyes will be drawn across the near scarp peak of Gategill Fell westwards towards the circle of fells backing Derwentwater. Back from the tip a gather of stones exists as if deferring from the high throne itself.

BLENCATHRA

The fell name means 'valley-head seat', combining the Celtic terms 'blaen', evidenced in the Welsh town Blaenau Ffestiniog, and 'cadeir', contained in the Welsh mountain Cadair Idris – the nearby hamlet of Catterlen carries the term too. It is stuff and nonsense that it means the 'devil's peak'. Interestingly, 16th-century references to the hill focus on the still prevalent legacy of Arthur, giving Blenkarthure.

The strength of north Cumbrian hold on the origins of Arthur are solidly founded. Arthuret, near Longtown (north of the Roman frontier), was the site of a famous Dark Age battle in AD573. The name Arthuret means 'Arthur's head', and it is said that a King Arthur was slain in this battle. This is the earliest genuine reference to a fighting leader so styled and the first recorded date in Scottish history.

Arthur was prefigured by the Roman legionary officer Lucius Artorius Castus, who commanded a thousand-strong cavalry of Salmatians both at Camboglanna (Castlesteads) on Hadrian's Wall near Brampton and at Bremetanacum (Ribchester) in the Ribble valley. His illustrious victories over Caledonian onslaught in AD183 made him and his cavalry the stuff of legend in their own time. Thus, in vulgar speech 'Arturius' became the Dark Age term for a leader, King Arthur.

By medieval times the descriptive nickname Saddleback had cropped up in written texts, from the mountain's likeness to a horse saddle.

Narrow Edge

Irresistibly the path mounts onto a narrowing ridge with increasing evidence of benign outcropping snaking up the ridge. The fell is inhabited by wistful sheep wondering why you are striding so happily onto their Spartan grazing. Little do they know your heightening anticipation. The path slips through a small rock cutting and engages with the top third of the ridge. A thoroughly entertaining sequence of scrambly slabs and coarse ribs ensues. When dry you'll want to climb up and down to repeat the delight; when windy, wet and worse you'll be greatly tested. In such conditions my advice is to choose another ridge altogether. This is no place for frivolous play, and accidents are, sadly, all too common.

Unlike many other summits, this is not one to picnic on comfortably, being exposed on all sides and a place of constant congregation. Either make

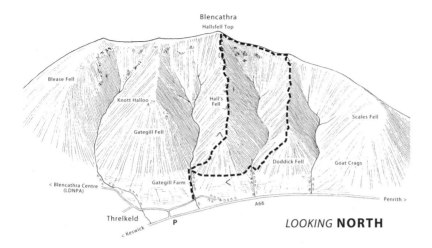

LOOKING **NORTH**

an earlier halt on the ridge just below, or save your sandwiches till at the top of Doddick Fell. Turn east, following the newly fashioned serpentine causewayed trail that snakes easily down towards Scales Fell. Observe walkers teetering along the serrated skyline of Sharp Edge above Scales Tarn to the left. Keep your eye on the edge, for when the first hint of outcropping appears seek to move down onto the rocky head of **Doddick Fell**. While the fell name could mean 'rounded ditch', it is more likely to mean 'the compact dodd or fell top'; this latter certainly fits the description.

The ridge descends on grass, with a bed of heather clothing the adjacent and intimate fell sides seamed with sheep tracks. The ridge draws down to a definite knoll with a remarkable view back upon the peak of Hallsfell Top, crowning Doddick Gill. The path scuttles down the south-west edge of the ridge-end to meet a wall. Keep right, curving right to ford Doddick Gill and effectively contour through bracken all along the base of **Hall's Fell**. The fell name derives from Threlkeld Hall, which lies along the access lane to Keswick Gold Club, and is now severed from the fell by the A66. Regain the base of Gate Gill and your return is assured.

Narrow Edge nearing the top of Hall's Fell →

Clough Head, Great Dodd, Watson's Dodd, Stybarrow Dodd and Hart Side from Dockray

*F*ancy doing the Dodds? This classic expedition links a cluster of predominantly grassy fells gathered in loose association at the northern extremity of the Helvellyn range. Five summits, three being Dodds ('dodd' being 'a rounded top'), give a real clue to the physical attributes of these free-flowing fells.

The walk uses the Old Coach Road as a convenient link to attain the northernmost summit, Clough Head. From Clough Head the walk strikes south down the broad ridge before climbing onto Great Dodd, from the curious rock tor of Calfhow Pike. The route zig-zags along the ridge to claim Watson's Dodd and Stybarrow Dodd, from where the route takes leave of the spine of the range, heading east via White Stones, then north above Glencoyne Head to reach Hart Side. After visiting the viewpoint cairn on Birkett Fell, the walk begins a steady, if sometimes wet, descent to the remote farming community of Dowthwaitehead.

↑ *Blencathra from White Pike*

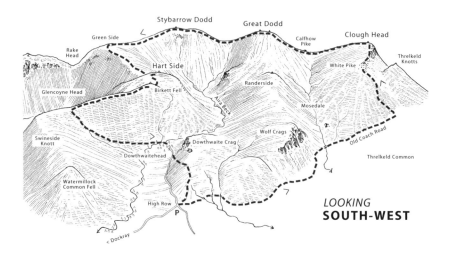

LOOKING
SOUTH-WEST

Begin a pathless, perhaps breathless ascent of **White Pike**, a spill of boulders shielding the topmost cairn. Follow on up the north ridge to reach the old Ordnance Survey column at 726m/2382ft on **Clough Head**. A small wall grasps the pillar to give visitors some relief from a gale. You'll be hard pressed to leave: the view south extends to the Conistons and Scafells and almost all else that is grand and noble in Lakeland, with the majestic facade of Blencathra to the north reigning supreme.

ROUTE INFORMATION

Distance	18km/11½ miles
Height gain	1143m/3750ft
Time	8 hours
Grade	strenuous
Start point	GR380219
Maps	(Harvey Superwalker) Lakeland Central (Ordnance Survey) OL5 North-eastern area

After-walk refreshment
Royal Hotel at Dockray

The Start
Park above the village of Dockray on the road verge at High Row, GR380219.

The Route
Embark on the Old Coach Road from the gate. Further on, Groove Beck ford can be a considerable flow, but fortunately it is supplemented by a foot-bridge. Remain with the track, passing along Barbary Rigg, set forward from the broken scarp of **Wolf Crags**. In a little over 2 miles go through the gate and cross **Mariel Bridge** spanning Mosedale Beck. Curving north above the great expanse of Threlkeld Common the track rises further, and at Hausewell Brow shapes to descend. Precisely here seek a stile in the fence to the left.

Thirlmere from below Calfhow Pike   205

A clear path heads almost due south, declining to the broad saddle beneath **Calfhow Pike**. The broken marsh is the result of peat cutting. Calfhow Pike, a welcome halt on the 2 mile trek to Great Dodd, means 'the tor of red deer fawn'. From here the ridge path climbs steadily south-eastward over **Little Dodd** onto the bare dome of **Great Dodd**; a small cairn marks the north top. To reach the shelter cairn on the south-east top cross the true summit at 857m/2812ft, devoid of cairned recognition. Looking south the serried summits of the range culminate on Helvellyn.

Follow on down the open ridge south-south-west. The majority of walkers, as can be judged by the state of the path, follow the trod curving round the head of Browndale Beck, but the easily reached cairn on the top of **Watson's Dodd** well merits inclusion. At 789m/2589ft the cairn is perched right on the brink of a sublime sweeping slope. Follow the edge-path east-south-east to a pool depression then rise south-east, making a conscious move off the worn edge-path onto the north top and true summit of **Stybarrow Dodd**. Though it has to be conceded that the best view is found from the south top, should you wander round to that point it is also best to backtrack to continue. The small summit cairn at 843m/2766ft, sporting a flake of slate, lies a few yards from an eastwardly orientated bield

wall, partially fashioned in to a wind break.

Descend south-east from the western tip of this wall, picking up a path from a cairn heading east. Cross the pool depression onto Green Side, marked by four cairns. From the highest point bear north-north-east, marching ¾ mile upon firm turf via a peat grough and pool step, rising gently via the miners' trench to the summit of **Hart Side** with its cluster of cairns at 758m/2487ft. On this final summit of the round take a moment to sit and reflect on the day, gazing back north over Randerside to Clough Head. Walk east across marshy ground to stand beside a proud little cairn with a plaque inscribed '**Birkett Fell**', which is by some measure a better viewpoint.

South top wind-shelter, Great Dodd

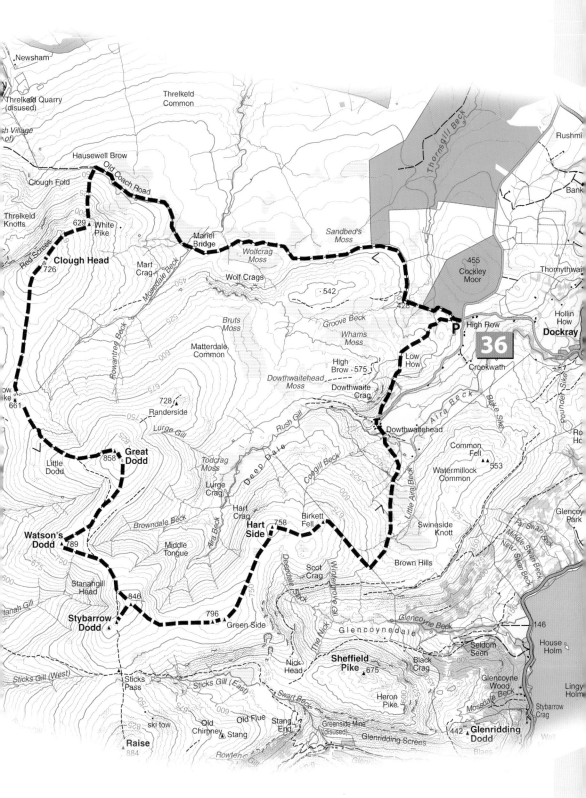

The **plaque** was erected in 1963 in memory of Lord Norman Birkett in appreciation for his successful defence of Ullswater against proposed damming for water extraction. A similar plaque is set on Kailpot Crag on the shores of the lake below Hallin Fell. This states 'He loved Ullswater. He strove to maintain its beauty for all to enjoy.'

Advance to the partially restored wall and follow it downhill, to the right. The wall may have been rebuilt within the last five years, but it would appear the craftsmanship has been found wanting by the elements. Whole sections have prematurely given way, which is disappointing, and this might explain why the wall has not been completed over Birkett Fell to where an old miners' path cuts through the wall. Go left with this down damp slopes to a kissing-gate in the intake fence. Further damp ground is traversed down to a footbridge spanning Aira Beck which leads on via a gate into the little farming community of **Dowthwaitehead**. Having passed the farmhouse onto the tarmac road, one might be content to follow this back up to **High Row**. Alternatively, follow the footpath rising as a green way from a hand-gate up under Dowthwaite Crag to a small gate at the brow. Join a tractor track on **Low How** which is followed easily down to the Old Coach Road at the gathering folds and gate.

North-western Fells from Stybarrow Dodd

Raise,
White Side and Helvellyn
from Legburthwaite

A combination of perspectives on a famous mountain. The route approaches Helvellyn from the west via Sticks Pass, the highest regular cross-range bridle route in Lakeland, and then traverses the northern spine of the range by Raise and White Side. Western approaches to Helvellyn suggest that the walker will reach a graceful peak, whereas the ground near the summit falls away into deep combes, providing a view over the most amazing amphitheatre. The route then pitches off the west ridge to conclude the walk along the scenic shores of Thirlmere. Alternatively, one may return by traversing the lower slopes of the range immediately above the intake wall, starting either off the old White Stones Route or from the foot of Helvellyn Gill on the approach to The Swirls car park.

↑ *Browncove Crags from Helvellyn Lower Man*

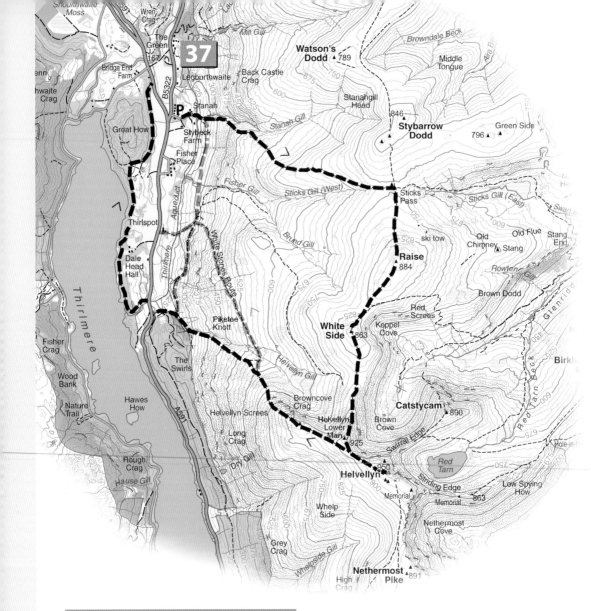

ROUTE INFORMATION

Distance	14.5km/9 miles
Height gain	960m/3150ft
Time	7 hours
Grade	strenuous
Start point	GR318189
Maps	(Harvey Superwalker)
	Lakeland Central
	(Ordnance Survey)
	OL5 North-eastern area

After-walk refreshment
The King's Head at Thirlspot, near the end of the walk (follow the A591 back to the start)

The Start
Suitable car parking exists close to the Thirlmere Community Hall at Legburthwaite, GR318189, situated where the St John's-in-the-Vale road meets the A591.

The Route
Follow the lane up from the road, either climbing the ladder stile at the top or taking the bridle path that sweeps right around the cottages at Stanah Farm by gates. Climb the ensuing paddock to a gate and stile beside the open Thirlmere supplementary water channel, which appears to slip beneath a giant roche moutonnée – a French term describing

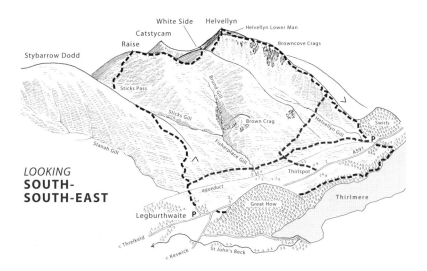

White Side Helvellyn
Helvellyn Lower Man
Catstycam
Browncove Crags
Raise
Stybarrow Dodd
Sticks Pass
Brund Gill
Sticks Gill
Sticks Gill
Brown Crag
Helvellyn Gill
Swirls
Stanah Gill
Fisherplace Gill
P
A591
Thirlspot
LOOKING
**SOUTH-
SOUTH-EAST**
aqueduct
Thirlmere
Great How
Legburthwaite P
< Threlkeld
< Keswick
St John's Beck

ice-sculpted rock. The aqueduct gathers side streams from Ladknott Gill through to Helvellyn Gill that would otherwise slip the net of Thirlmere. By clever engineering the water in the channel seems to flow uphill, just like the reservoir itself, which flows by gravity south under Dunmail Raise to Watchgate and on down by Bolton to Manchester – undeniably amazing engineering.

The path comes to a bridle gate and little bridge crossing the excited waters of **Stanah Gill**. Above, the main path rises through bracken. Ignore the wooden footpath fingerpost (directing right on a predominately contouring route to The Swirls car park, though this may come into its own as an alternative return to the Thirlmere shoreline path). Climb a groove to reach an old sheepfold above the bracken level, then cross a marshy patch and trace the turf trail over the swelling slope of Stybarrow Dodd's west ridge with a sequence of three marker cairns as guide. Continue towards the Sticks Pass.

Like Stake Pass between Langstrath and Great Langdale, the name **Sticks Pass** suggests an old trade route once marked not by cairns but by seasonally installed stakes, to give confidence to travellers in mist and snow.

The top of **Sticks Pass** is marked by a cairn, amid a marshy hollow, the transverse ridge path very

apparent. Turn right, circling the peaty patch, to climb onto the firm stony slope mounting to the summit of **Raise**. At 884m/2900ft this is a rare moment of coarse rock outcropping, the summits of the range otherwise being uniformly grass pasture. The distinctive rocks are suggestive of gruyere cheese, fashioned by gas bubbles during vulcanisation. The view is extensive and only bettered by Helvellyn, inevitably. The fell's only visual flaw, caused by cairn-builders' exuberance, is a plethora of cairns lining the continuing ridge path.

Follow this south-west to the saddle, where the old pony route from Glenridding is joined. From here a pinky-brown gravely trail curves up to the solitary cairn at 863m/2851ft marking the summit of **White Side**, named after a rash of quartz stones on the west slope, out of sight from the top. Continue down to the next depression, tripping over the superfluity of cairns, with Browncove Crags to the right and Brown Cove itself over the brink to the left. Head on up the gravely path due south, huffing and puffing, to a marvellous culmination at the loose shaly cairn of **Helvellyn Lower Man**. At 3035ft you have made it to the magical Munro point of the walk. Trend south-east and join the popular path from The Swirls to reach the stone-built Ordnance Survey pillar on the top of **Helvellyn**.

Helvellyn from Helvellyn Lower Man

HELVELLYN

At 950m/3116ft there is no doubt one is at a heady height. The sudden fall of the eastern edge to the vast bowl of Red Tarn is quite profound and uplifting. Catstycam and Striding Edge form the strong visual arms to the eastward outlook, and westwards all of Lakeland is on display – savour and enjoy.

The moment of arrival is euphoric. Even the most taciturn can slip into hearty conversation with complete strangers – the summit of Helvellyn is that kind of place. The cross-wall wind-shelter a few yards down to the south of the top is a common retreat in hostile or fair weather. If you want seclusion then you've chosen the wrong mountain.

The fell name means 'mountain lake of the hunting ground' – in modern Welsh this would be spelt Helfa-llyn. It is therefore a transposed name from nearby Red Tarn, much as Lochnagar in the Cairngorms is named after the corrie lake in that mountain's great embrace.

Backtrack north-west towards Lower Man, keeping company with the popular trail over the top of **Browncove Crags**. As the slope steepens new pitching has been installed all the way down to cope with an unending tide of walkers.

ALTERNATIVE ROUTE

The old pony route leading to the King's Head at Thirlspot, known as the White Stones Route, can be followed, though the modern pitched trail tends to obliterate its natural first moves right to a ford of Helvellyn Gill. Old cairns can be found, though the white-washing that gave the route its name has been all but extinguished. As this path switches left down to the intake wall, bear right, keeping above the wall. Ford Fisherplace Gill en route to reconnecting with the Sticks Pass bridle route that leads back down to Legburthwaite.

The main path down to The Swirls strides on to a hand-gate and subsequent footbridge. Enter the car park at a hand-gate. Alternatively, before the car park you could bear right with the path that follows the intake wall, crossing footbridges over the succession of gills back to Stanah.

← *Helicopter delivering rock for pitching above Helvellyn Gill*

Those following the edge of Thirlmere should pass through the car park and over the main road diagonally right. Pass by the Station Coppice car park through the hand-gate and follow the path that descends close to Helvellyn Gill where it enters Thirlmere. A shoreline path, predominantly a woodland trail, leads right and briefly opens at the break in front of Dale Head Hotel. Passing through a gate it becomes a forestry track and comes beside the bounding fence on the right. Bear right at the field corner short of **Great How** and descend east then north below the hill to a gate onto the road, turning right to complete the walk.

Great How from path alongside the intake wall above Thirlspot

Helm Crag, Gibson Knott, Calf Crag and Sergeant Man from Grasmere

*S*tudious tourists and serious trekkers have long paid homage to Grasmere. The village means a variety of things to a variety of folk, but whether you're a devoted fan of Wordsworth, Heaton-Cooper or Wainwright the green vale with its sparking lake owes its ultimate charm to its glorious encirclement of fells. Wordsworth and the Heaton-Coopers were inveterate fell walkers, and their respective study centre and art gallery are creative acknowledgement of the village's beautiful setting.

    The inspiration for this walk is not only the obvious enticement of Helm Crag and its consequent curving ridge over Gibson Knott and Calf Crag to the head of Far Easedale, but the attainment of the remote brass knob summit of Sergeant Man, backtracking into the wild bowl cradling Easedale Tarn. The outward route is complemented by a return via the greater Easedale circuit – it's an all-round treat.

↑ *The Howitzer, the summit of Helm Crag, and Dunmail Raise*

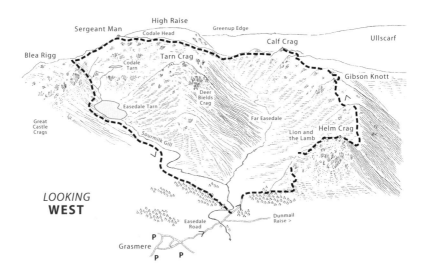

LOOKING
WEST

Distance	16km/10 miles
Height gain	808m/2650ft
Time	7 hours
Grade	strenuous
Start point	GR335073
Maps	(Harvey Superwalker)
	Lakeland Central
	(Ordnance Survey)
	OL7 South-eastern area

After-walk refreshment
Grasmere has an abundance of pubs and cafés

The Start
There are three pay and display car parks within the village, with only modest free parking opposite White Bridge Forge and the long lay-by beside the A591 north of the old Swan Hotel junction.

The Route
The start point of this walk is Sam Read's Bookshop, right at the heart of the village, which was opened one hundred years ago. Opposite the shop is a bus stop for Stagecoach buses, so this is definitely a walk you can entertain minus your car.

Head off up **Easedale Road**, crossing Goody Bridge. Keep to the tarmac roadway through the open meadow to Little Parrock, then fork right upon the bridleway which promptly becomes a narrow,

slate-cobbled path close by Kitty Cottage. Reaching a gate, note the wicket gate right for later reference. The signed path leads through woodland to Lancrigg Hotel where 'walkers' teas' in gracious surrounds may be enjoyed – at walk's end.

Pass through the wide gate, now in a broad walled lane that quickly constricts. Bear right at a yellow waymark to 'Helm Crag'. A damp embowered passage leads smartly to the steep bracken and rock slopes at the foot of Helm Crag proper. Veer right and quickly left on a rising path, and cross the small patch of quarry spoil to rise by wooden handrails. Momentarily the ground levels, beside an old quarry, thoroughly restored in nature's raiment. Rise again on a pitched path close by a wall, veering left under the yew-clothed White Crag and clambering by ice-smoothed rock shelves. Enjoy fine views down into the verdant pastures of lower Easedale and across to Silver How and Great Castle How, with Swinescar Hause between and the juniper forest of Blindtarn Moss.

The path dips, then presents a lovely view up Far Easedale. Switching right, climb on grass to a saddle of the ridge. Peer over the brink to Town Head and the Great Tongue leading up to Seat Sandal, Grisedale Hause and Fairfield. The lion's share of the Helm Crag climb is all but complete. Walk up the ridge to the first eye-catching outcrop, a lion if ever there was, with a jumble of boulders cluttering the rift hollow beneath. The ridge path is a joy to tread and leads majestically to **Helm Crag's** main summit outcrop at 405m/1329ft, a tilted jagged mass of rock that will draw a camera from any

The roller-coaster ridge to Gibson Knott from Helm Crag

Deer Bield Crag from the head of Far Easedale

pack. The scramble and subsequent descent may require hands to rock, but are not really difficult as long as you have the basics of scrambling. Be consoled, the view from the top is little different from the grass below. This is a fine spot from which to view Steel Fell and Dunmail Raise with its backdrop of the Helvellyn range.

The speedy A591 **main road** through the vale below follows an age-old path, a trade and travel highway from time immemorial. Its course is defined by the natural break in the high fells from the north to south made by the pass of Dunmail Raise. Travellers of old doffed their caps to the mighty cairn at its crest saying 'Good day your majesty' in a bid to ingratiate fine weather from the sleeping monarch.

Travellers knew well the striking rock-topped fell to the west. **Helm Crag** is one of Lakeland's most distinctive heights, the term 'helm' meaning 'cloud-capped hill'. Two rock tors stand at either end of its summit ridge lending scope for tourist guides of former years to offer a plethora of descriptive names to entertain their passengers: The Lion and The Lamb, The Howitzer, The Old Woman Playing the Organ. These tops are hard for the average hill-goer to climb – notably the tilted summit tor, the Lion Couchant, which probably receives the attention of barely one in every hundred visitors.

The main attraction is the enticing ridge continuing to the north-west over Gibson Knott. The path pitches down easily from directly behind the main outcrop to reach Bracken Hause. As the route continues it contrives to hold a leftward bias off the true ridge-top leading to the summit knoll of **Gibson Knott** above Horn Crag 421m/1880ft. With its small cairn, this is a good spot to pause. The ridge continues pleasantly undulating; note the throne among a mass of boulders on the right. The path dips briefly through a trough then slants steadily over Pike of

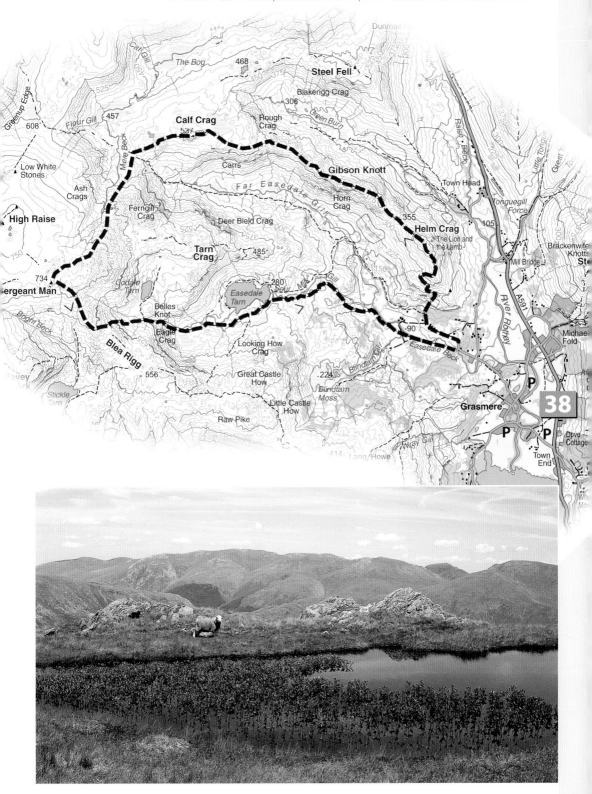

Bog bean in a pool on Codale Head backed by the Helvellyn range

Carrs and patches of eroded peat – hence the stepping stones, inserted to reduce pedestrian impact.

The wet ridge to Steel Fell drifts right, but the main path strides on to the cairn on **Calf Crag**, 537m/1762ft. The outlook features Deer Bields Crag, invariably hard to see, being in heavy shadow. The whole mass of high ground backing the crag, Tarn Crag, leading to Codale Head, fills the southern gaze, while westward the flat horizon of Greenup Edge leads the eye round right to Ullscarf, often considered the centre-point of Lakeland (Walk 27).

The ridge path, never in doubt, arrives at the saddle at the very head of Far Easedale marked by a white cairn and the remnants of a metal fence. Head on up the facing slope south-south-west, following the remnant fence by pools onto Codale Head and round a marsh to clamber onto **Sergeant Man** at 736m/2414ft. Being the lynch-pin of walks off the High Raise plateau towards Grasmere means the path trending off the top south-east is as plain as plain.

Follow this, fording the marshy outflow down the ridge to a large slab where the path veers left, descending the outcropped ridge to a path intersection where you go left. The well-pitched path leads down by **Belles Knott**, which from lower down takes on the appearance of a majestic peak. The path leads past **Easedale Tarn**, its austere setting enhanced by sunlight dancing on its waters and round the abundant moraine. From the outflow follow **Sour Milk Gill** down the continuing pitched trail, making the all-important side move to inspect the lower section of the gill's cascades. The path leads by gates on through the meadow to a footbridge onto **Easedale Road** opposite Oakhow.

Sergeant Man from Codale Head

Low Pike, High Pike, Dove Crag, Hart Crag, Fairfield, Great Rigg, Heron Pike and Nab Scar from Ambleside

A *n all-time favourite horseshoe ridge walk. A chain of eight edifying summit viewpoints give the Fairfield round pre-eminence. Ridges always provide the very best of fell walking, especially when they are graceful and the outlooks generous. In this instance, weather dependent, satisfaction is almost certainly guaranteed.*

The Start

The Rydal Road car park, GR375046, is capacious as it serves the bustling tourist haven of Ambleside, yet it is insufficient at times. Hence parking can be an issue. At such times Miller Ground car park at White Platt Fields GR373041 can come to the rescue. Some walkers opt to place the cars in the shaded back lane near Miller Bridge, GR371044, from where a footpath strides efficiently north-east to Rydal Road via the cul-de-sac Stoney Lane.

↑ *Great Rigg, Fairfield and Hart Crag from Heron Pike*   219

ROUTE INFORMATION

Distance	19.5km/12¼ miles
Height gain	1050m/3443ft
Time	9 hours
Grade	strenuous
Start point	GR375046
Maps	(Harvey Superwalker) Lakeland Central (Ordnance Survey) both OL5 North-eastern area and OL7 South-eastern area are needed to cover this walk

After-walk refreshment

The Golden Rule in Smithy Brow above the main car park; in the Market Place The Queens and Salutation Hotels and the White Lion, plus a generous choice of tearooms

The Route

Cross Rydal Road at the mini-roundabout and ascend Smithy Brow by the Golden Rule, bearing left into Nook Lane. Tarmac is sustained to Nook Farm, after which go through the gate descending to cross **Low Sweden Bridge**. For all the Norse names in the Lakes, the term Sweden has nothing to do with the Scandinavian country, being the dialect word 'swidden' for 'the land cleared by burning'. The nearby Birk Hag in Rydal Park has similar connotations, being 'the birch plantation with trees marked for felling'.

The ensuing track switches up right above the bank then goes left, keeping the wall to the left. Beyond the next gateway the path forks, with a way bearing up left accompanying the ridge-top wall. It goes via a ladder stile and negotiates the **High Brock Crags** 'bad step', which is the most minor of physical obstacles. Some walkers chicken out, opting instead for the alternative scarp path to the right. The main way leads on through two further gateways before bearing up through **Low Brock Crags** ('badger rocks') onto the ridge, skipping over some peaty ground before climbing by the wall to the exciting little summit of **Low Pike**.

At 507m/1663ft this is a great moment, with a very real sense of standing high, for all one might say the peak is measured in inches when compared to

Inviting ridge to High Pike – the path to the east of the wall is the normal choice, gaining shelter from a westerly breeze

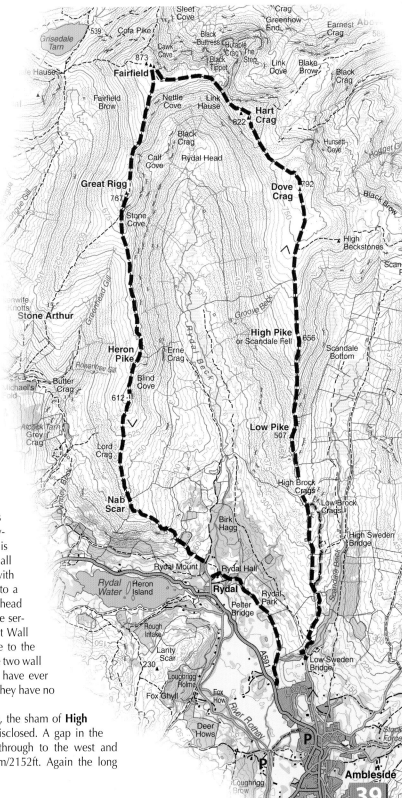

Fairfield. The ridge wall muscles in, snaking over the top to claim the proudest ground, and (to be honest) hampering appreciation of the westward view. Indeed, the best of the panorama lies in this south-western arc from the Coniston Fells, round via Crinkle Crags, Bowfell and the Langdale Pikes, with the briefest of glimpses of Scafell Pike to the right of Harrison Stickle. Walkers have erected a small cairn as a mark of respect and passing affection for what is the only genuine peak on the Fairfield Horseshoe. High Pike is more of a sham, for all it appears to lord it from this spot, merging into the broad-ening ridge behind.

Although Low Pike is but the first rise on a grow-ing ridge, nonetheless it is a fell that falls sharply on all sides. Hence step down with care, cross a ladder stile to a small depression, then head uphill in harmony with the ser-pentine wall, a mini Great Wall of China. On the last rise to the top of High Pike notice the two wall stiles. Neither appears to have ever been used, and certainly they have no contemporary purpose.

On arrival at the cairn, the sham of **High Pike's** peakless peak is disclosed. A gap in the ridge wall gives access through to the west and the highest point at 612m/2152ft. Again the long

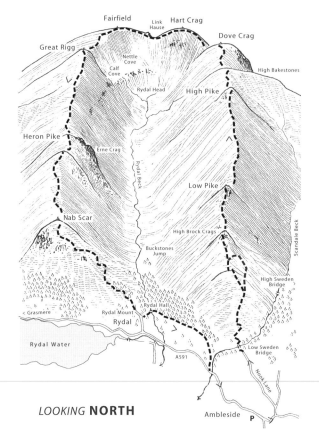

LOOKING **NORTH**

down the ridge to Little Hart Crag. Keep heading north with the depleted wall to reach the lack-lustre summit cairn of **Dove Crag** at 792m/2599ft. Walkers will race over this top oblivious of the fell's greatest glory. If the weather is settled and clear one may consider visiting the top of Dove Crag to view the depths of Dovedale. To achieve this, traverse the splintered plateau in a north-north-east direction guided by cairns, a length of sheep-baulking wall defining the limit of safe exploration. Backtrack to the ridge wall to continue your horseshoe walk.

Keep faith with the broken wall through the broad depression to rise onto the rough south-east top of **Hart Crag**. The cairn at 822m/2697ft rests among a confusion of great flaky boulders, the fell top being infested with loose stone and the traversing ridge path weaving a slalom-course lurching to the north side to find the firmest footing. The most all-consuming component of the view is the empty Rydal Beck valley.

view west offers a crowd of familiar fells. To the east the sudden fall of the slope into Thack Bottom gives exaltation to the view from the cairn. Beyond Scandale Pass see a tight skyline of Far Eastern Fells from Loadpot Hill to Kidsty Pike, and a brief swell of High Street between Caudale Moor and Red Screes. The view down Scandale draws attention towards Windermere beyond Ambleside, and to Esthwaite and Coniston Waters.

Continue alongside the wall as the ridge broadens. Ignore the path right at a cairn. This is bound for the prominent cairn on High Bakestones and down the ridge east to Scandale Tarn and Pass – though this makes an excellent alternative return via Scandale should the prevailing weather show signs of serious deterioration. It is a useful face-saver to keep up one's sleeve if leading a party, as there is nothing worse nor more embarrassing than a backtracking retreat.

The consistent wall ends where a ridge fence bears right, with an accompanying path leading

Caiston Glen from Scandale Pass

Walkers congress on Fairfield's broad summit, 'a fair stony field'

Head to the northern of the two summit cairns and angle half-right for a few paces to join the main ridge path. To enjoy the full grandeur of Scrubby Crag buttressing the east wall of Fairfield, one may cautiously wander across to the solitary cairn set off to the north of the path. Otherwise, keep rigidly to the well-trod way into the narrow saddle of **Link Hause**. Climb the easy rock step onto the broadening plateau guided by an abundance of cairns. With the benefit of good weather, one may indulge in a spot of edge walking to glimpse the best of this fine mountain, as sheep trods cling to the rim above Scrubby Crag and the northern precipices. A trio of cairns mark **Fairfield's** 873m/2864ft summit, two fashioned into windbreaks.

The summit of **Fairfield** is without question the scenic crescendo of the walk. Stroll to the north edge to gasp at the fabulous outlook north upon the Helvellyn massif, with St Sunday Crag a monster presence to the north-east. Elsewhere the most liberal array of Lakeland fells are on show … enjoy!

The ridge path now turns slightly west of south with cairns too many to count guiding down to the depression for the brief hop onto **Great Rigg**. The summit cairn at 767m/2516ft, a sorry heap, is dignified with the name Greatrigg Man, a good spot to rest and look down into the lonesome hanging valley of Nettle Cove.

Head on down and along the south-trending ridge, with pools punctuating the undulating ridge. The wall-topped Erne Crag is correctly the summit of **Heron Pike** at 767m/2516ft. Wainwright preferred the featureless south top, which has no cairn and only an exposure of quartz to catch the eye.

The all too palpable ridge path steps down by **Lord Crag** with a broken wall for company to the large cairn marking the top of **Nab Scar** at 455m/ 1490ft. While this is not a fell by the normal measure, being the ridge-end shoulder, it is an excellent viewpoint, giving every good reason to stop to gaze over Loughrigg Fell, picking out the gaping mouth of Loughrigg Cavern and the bird's-eye view of Rydal Water. Modern pitching down zig-zags into a walled lane ensures the descent to **Rydal Mount** is comfortably achieved. Pass down by Wordsworth's old home taking the left turn by **Rydal Hall** (walkers' café) to follow the drive through the park onto Rydal Road, completing the round to the clamour of cars.

Red Screes, Little Hart Crag, High Pike and Low Pike from Ambleside

*A*mbleside is all about shops, cafés and cars. Well not quite all, but nearly! The fells form a discreet backdrop – one knows they are there, but unlike Keswick or Patterdale one is not subjected to their impending shadow. So this walk from the town centre allows time to sense the scenic swell and enjoy remarkable backward glances towards Windermere and the seeming far-off Coniston Fells.

Travellers of yore knew of the taxing drive over Kirkstone, and this walk puts you through your paces in climbing Red Screes to view the pass from on high. The walk then sweeps across the head of Scandale to the beacon cairn on High Bakestones and helter-skelters down the exciting High Pike/Low Pike ridge. The route offers the natural option of cutting back down Scandale after the ascent of Red Screes, if that is a long enough day – as well it might be in winter.

↑ *The red screes of Red Screes looking over Kirkstone Pass to the Ill Bell range*

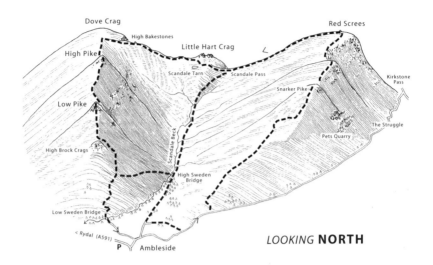

LOOKING **NORTH**

ROUTE INFORMATION

Distance	18km/11¼ miles
Height gain	1000m/3280ft
Time	8½ hours
Grade	strenuous
Start point	GR375046
Maps	(Harvey Superwalker)
	Lakeland Central
	(Ordnance Survey)
	OL5 South-eastern area

After-walk refreshment
The Golden Rule in Smithy Brow above the main car park; in the Market Place – The Queens and Salutation Hotels and the White Lion, plus a generous choice of tearooms

The Start
The Rydal Road car park, GR375046, is capacious as it is serves the bustling tourist haven of Ambleside (insufficiently at times). Hence parking can be an issue. At such times Miller Ground car park at White Platt Fields GR373041 can come to the rescue. Some walkers opt to place the cars in the shaded back lane near Miller Bridge, GR371044, from where a footpath strides efficiently north-east to Rydal Road via the cul-de-sac Stoney Lane.

The Route
The first move replicates that of Walk 39, crossing the mini-roundabout to ascend **Smithy Brow** by The

Golden Rule. However, on this occasion continue with the Kirkstone Road to go left into Sweden Bridge Lane, and then right with Ellerigg Road. Bear right on a footpath by Eller Beck Cottages. This leads via wall gates to a stile and on into a gated lane, with a pleasing view down over the town. At a gate the lane re-emerges into the Kirkstone Road above the town. Ascend the road and, some 300m beyond Sunny Bank Cottages, find a wooden hand-gate to the left.

Pass through the cattle-holding pen, ascending the broad, irregular walled lane winding up to a stile, where a holding pen intervenes in the lane. Keep within the lane and enjoy extensive views over Rydal Water to a backdrop of Coniston and Langdale Fells. Pass through a hand-gate in a wall, and follow the broad green lane, frequently challenged by marshy ground, rising to a ladder stile.

Kirkstone Pass Inn from Red Screes   225

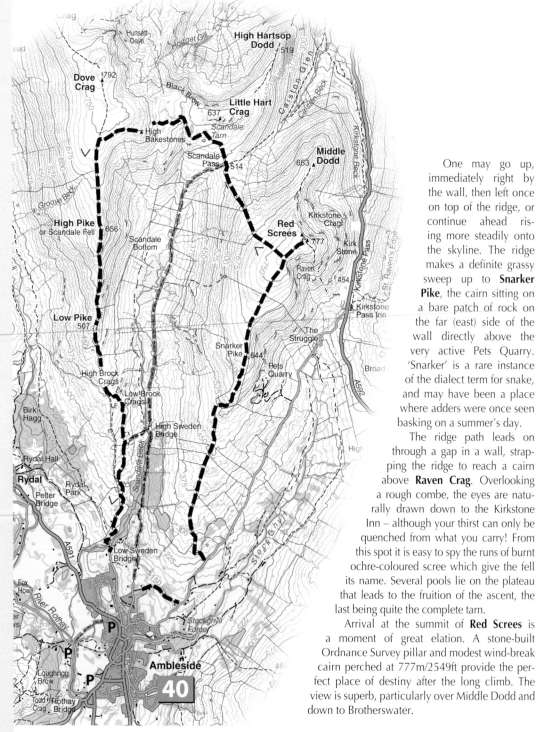

One may go up, immediately right by the wall, then left once on top of the ridge, or continue ahead rising more steadily onto the skyline. The ridge makes a definite grassy sweep up to **Snarker Pike**, the cairn sitting on a bare patch of rock on the far (east) side of the wall directly above the very active Pets Quarry. 'Snarker' is a rare instance of the dialect term for snake, and may have been a place where adders were once seen basking on a summer's day.

The ridge path leads on through a gap in a wall, strapping the ridge to reach a cairn above **Raven Crag**. Overlooking a rough combe, the eyes are naturally drawn down to the Kirkstone Inn – although your thirst can only be quenched from what you carry! From this spot it is easy to spy the runs of burnt ochre-coloured scree which give the fell its name. Several pools lie on the plateau that leads to the fruition of the ascent, the last being quite the complete tarn.

Arrival at the summit of **Red Screes** is a moment of great elation. A stone-built Ordnance Survey pillar and modest wind-break cairn perched at 777m/2549ft provide the perfect place of destiny after the long climb. The view is superb, particularly over Middle Dodd and down to Brotherswater.

Scandale Tarn backed by Little Hart Crag →

The link with the Fairfield range begins by crossing the plateau due west to a wall junction, from where you descend north-west with the wall to the left, passing the Rose Kershaw cairn, poignantly perched with an eternal view down Caiston Glen. Reaching **Scandale Pass** one may cross the ladder stile and turn left, following the ancient bridle path down into Scandale. After a gate enter a walled drove lane leading naturally back into Ambleside, passing close by the picturesque High Sweden Bridge. The prime route runs straight across the Scandale Pass saddle – keep beside the wall then, as the broken fence takes over, follow the path half-left which curves above **Scandale Tarn**.

One may wish to include the enticing outcropped summit of **Little Hart Crag** by following the fenceline up and bearing right. This is not obligatory, and there is every good reason to patronise the lower path, which gains height most pleasantly with a last pull to reach the 7ft cairn of **High Bakestones**. This provides a fine viewpoint down the flanks of High Pike and through Scandale, which meant 'short valley' as compared with the adjacent Rydal Beck. The path winds on to meet the ridge wall where it turns left, descending to the cairn on **High Pike** at 612m/2152ft. From this approach one has little sense of it being a peak.

Follow on down beside the ridge wall. Heavy use by walkers too hastily chasing off the Fairfield Horseshoe has made footing inevitably unstable in places, and some walkers may opt to wander down on the west side for greater comfort. The ridge dips to a ladder stile and climbs onto **Low Pike**, a shapely little peak at 507m/1663ft. Continue via a wall gateway and follow the prominent path which veers left, thereby avoiding the 'bad step' by the wall on Sweden Crag. This route forks – with the path trending left leading down to cross the picturesque **High Sweden Bridge** and so join the dale-bottom track leading back into Sweden Bridge Lane. Otherwise, more naturally, continue down via gates to cross **Low Sweden Bridge** and re-enter the town by Nook Lane.

High Bakestones, a cairn of distinction

Caudale Moor
from Cowbridge

*A*fter starting with one of Lakeland's most delightful strolls, along the shores of Brotherswater, this walk then sets course across the foot of Dovedale and Caiston Glen to join the ancient path up Kirkstone before launching onto St Raven's Edge for the easy wall-side ridge ascent of Caudale Moor. A thrilling ridge descent plummets straight back down to Brotherswater to complete a comparatively short but stirring round that includes two inns – doubly refreshing!

The Start

Park at Cowbridge National Trust car park, GR403134. Do not be lured into parking at the top of Kirkstone Pass – the holistic feel of beginning deep in the vale beside Brotherswater is a fundamental part of the experience.

The Route

From the car park follow the tree-shaded track, soon taking pleasure in the views across the glistening lake to the shapely Hartsop Dodd and up the Pasture Beck valley to Gray Crag backed by The Knott. Further right the sharply defined Rough Edge ridge

↑ A long view of Caudale Moor from the upper reach of Ullswater

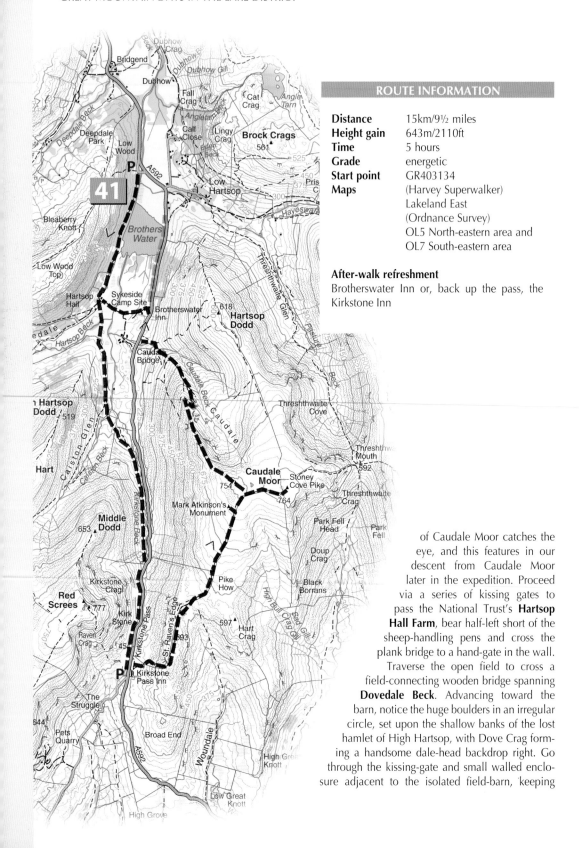

ROUTE INFORMATION

Distance	15km/9½ miles
Height gain	643m/2110ft
Time	5 hours
Grade	energetic
Start point	GR403134
Maps	(Harvey Superwalker)
	Lakeland East
	(Ordnance Survey)
	OL5 North-eastern area and
	OL7 South-eastern area

After-walk refreshment

Brotherswater Inn or, back up the pass, the Kirkstone Inn

of Caudale Moor catches the eye, and this features in our descent from Caudale Moor later in the expedition. Proceed via a series of kissing gates to pass the National Trust's **Hartsop Hall Farm**, bear half-left short of the sheep-handling pens and cross the plank bridge to a hand-gate in the wall. Traverse the open field to cross a field-connecting wooden bridge spanning **Dovedale Beck**. Advancing toward the barn, notice the huge boulders in an irregular circle, set upon the shallow banks of the lost hamlet of High Hartsop, with Dove Crag forming a handsome dale-head backdrop right. Go through the kissing-gate and small walled enclosure adjacent to the isolated field-barn, keeping

The grand surround of fells about Brotherswater from Angletarn Pikes

the wall close left, via a further kissing-gate. The wall drifts left, and the path gently rises in a stony field with some light woodland. Notice high to the right juniper amassed on the eastern flanks of High Hartsop Dodd. Watch for the faint fork in the path half-left. This leads down the short bank to a footbridge spanning **Caiston Beck** at a wall junction.

The path is less than obvious from here across the rough, damp slopes of **Middle Dodd**, but becomes more concerted as it draws closer above **Kirkstone Beck**, with the old packhorse path in a groove. Pass through a wall squeeze-stile, and rise up the valley beneath the steep slopes of Middle Dodd, right, and the dauntingly barren scree slopes of Caudale Moor to the left. For all the benefits of car travel you'll be grateful that your experience of Kirkstone Pass is based on being on the ancient path; though it, too, is drawn onto the road at steps.

There is no need to tread the tarmac. Slip through the wall gap immediately right and stay shielded from traffic through the bouldery pasture up to a stile into the Red Pit viewpoint car park. Exit in like manner, rising on to pass close by the distinctive **Kirk Stone**, showing flecks of former white-washing, and passing on over quite damp pasture reach the car park at the top of the pass.

Kirk Stone, with hints of white-wash still evident   231

Mark Atkinson's cairn on John Bell's Banner

Go through the car park to cross the road, keeping left of the **Kirkstone Pass Inn** by the bus stop and ascending the steps to a fence stile. Aim half-left to reach a stile in the enclosure corner. The path ascends, with some pitching, and quickly reaches a large cairn on the crest of **St Raven's Edge**. The long curving line of the ridge wall now guides progress through a damp depression onto the high ground of **Caudale Moor**, with the little-visited Woundale down to the right. Inevitably you will wish to visit the fell summit, though an aside left is recommended before you do. Cross the wall just short of where it curves most noticeably right on that area of fell known as John Bell's Banner to locate **Mark Atkinson's cairn** with its wooden cross – the last resting place of a father and son who clearly knew and loved these fells.

Return to the far side of the wall and continue in its company all the way to a wall junction, stepping over to bear half-left after some 100m to the obvious cairn, short of the steady fall towards Threshwaite Mouth. Also known as **Stony Cove Pike** the summit, at 763m/2503ft, embraces a wide panorama, with the beacon cairn on Thornthwaite Crag and the distinctive peaks of Froswick and Ill Bell the main attention seekers east and south-east.

While you may choose to follow the wall leading north from the wall junction along the spine towards Hartsop Dodd, it is far better to backtrack. This time you may wish to stay on the north side of the wall, and en route to inspect the saddle tarn before reaching the large cairn marking the ultimate point of Rough Edge. After the initial downward step encounter a striking cairn superbly situated at the top of the north-west ridge.

Brotherswater and Ullswater come strikingly into view, as too the whole mass of the Near Eastern Fells from Red Screes through Dove and St Sunday Crags to Helvellyn and beyond. The Atkinson's certainly knew a good place to rest for eternity.

Follow the ridge down. Don't be in any hurry – it should be savoured. The Caudale slate quarry comes into view down to the right, and this may be visited on a path to the right – a fascinating place to investigate, and a vivid reminder of the labour of man in the service of domestic shelter. Whether you visit the quarry or stick with the ridge, eventually the grooved quarry sled-gate is joined, and lower down this becomes braided – the result of many changes in belaboured pony-drawn sledge journeys. Whichever

Cairn at the brink of Caudale Head →

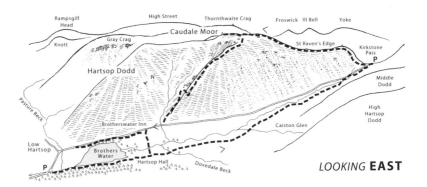

LOOKING **EAST**

your line of descent the path duly passes a wall corner to reach a ford at the base of a pleasing fall in **Caudale Beck**. The combe above, being north facing, was known as the 'cold valley', hence Caudale. The footpath fords the beck, aiming down to a ladder stile on the road, though the depth of the ford may reasonably cause you to stop and follow the wall down to a wall-stile.

Follow the road right to reach the **Brotherswater Inn**, where you have a choice of routes. You can pass on by to join the permissive path at the second road entrance to **Sykeside** camp site, which leads along the bank next to the road to reach the eastern shore of **Brotherswater**. This path regains the road and follows the footway passing the bus shelter at Low Hartsop to regain **Cowbridge**. More efficiently, go straight down through the car park of the Brotherswater Inn following the track down through Sykeside camping ground and traversing the dale bottom to reconnect with the outward route at Hartsop Hall.

Dove Crag, Hart Crag
and Hartsop above How
from Brotherswater

*T*he best of fell-walking territory from start to finish. The walk runs up through Dovedale to attain the skyline via Houndshope Cove, visiting Dove Crag and Hart Crag before backtracking down the lovely sickle-shaped ridge of Hartsop above How. There are various named connections with deer in the greater Patterdale valley, but Hartsop is the only reference to the red deer stag in a valley context, all the remainder are in high-fell situations.

The Start

The Cowbridge car park access point for Brotherswater is perfectly sited to engage in this very special expedition, GR403134.

The Route

Pass through the kissing-gate and follow the woodland track beside Brotherswater's out-flowing beck. The shining lake is quickly encountered, with all eyes focused across the mirroring waters to the shapely fells encircling Low Hartsop – a scene frequently

↑ *Dovedale from the Brotherswater Inn*

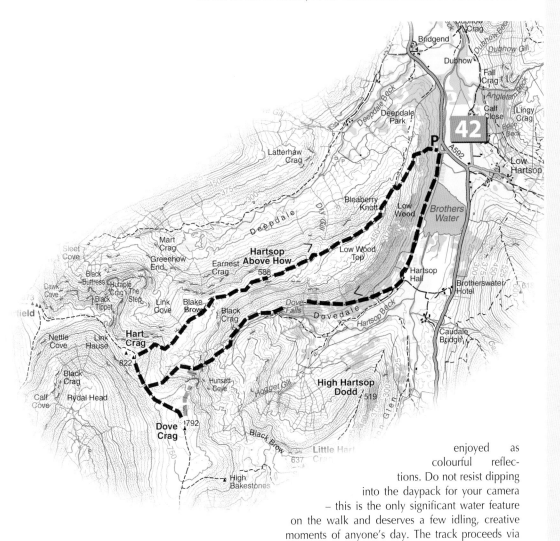

Distance	11.25km/7 miles
Height gain	823m/2700ft
Time	6½ hours
Grade	energetic
Start point	GR403134
Maps	(Harvey Superwalker)
	Lakeland Central
	(Ordnance Survey)
	OL5 North-eastern area

After-walk refreshment
The Brotherswater Inn

enjoyed as colourful reflections. Do not resist dipping into the daypack for your camera – this is the only significant water feature on the walk and deserves a few idling, creative moments of anyone's day. The track proceeds via a series of kissing gates to pass the National Trust's **Hartsop Hall Farm**. Remain with the track, passing the out-barn and stock pens and heading south-westwards into Dovedale proper.

As the larch spinney is passed, bear off the track part-right onto the green way. This leads via gates under the spoil banks of the old Hartsop Hall Lead Mine, abandoned in 1942 after at least 400 years' exploitation. Running on with a wall on the left, the path rises gently through woodland to emerge at a hand-gate above Dove Falls and almost directly beneath **Dovedale Slabs**, seen high above like a shield on the slopes of Hartsop above How. The path wanders on up the fell valley with **Hunsett Cove** ahead, the scene dominated by the impressive cliff of Dove Crag. Welcome pitching has restored secure footing to this popular path,

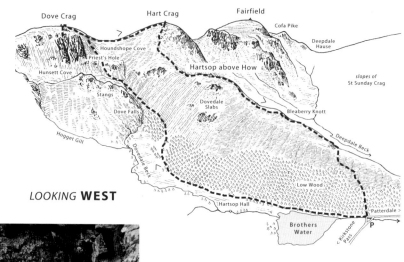

LOOKING **WEST**

Priest's Hole cave beneath Dove Crag

which is specially valuable as the path climbs up a steep section, passing a ruin. This old building is thought to have been a religious retreat, a secretive place of a pilloried Catholic sect escaping persecution. The path climbs, not without the odd loose stumble, up a gully and emerges onto the peaty shoulder, close below the precipitous cliff.

In fair weather walkers with a head for heights may diverge to inspect **Priest's Hole**. The approach path is not too difficult to locate. Bear half-left from a solitary erratic boulder, and go up the grass bank and boulder scree to find a path leading onto the cliff. Once begun there are no hazards until the cave is reached: the fore-shelf offers no security from a precipitous 600ft drop! Please respect the climbers' metal casket which holds a visitors' book and bare provisions for benighted 'tigers' (the

Nepalese Sherpa term for a British rock climber). The cave is entirely natural and may have been used deep back in pre-history. Long may the sanctuary be adored and respected.

Those who have visited Priest's Hole should retrace their steps, precisely, to resume the steady ascent of **Houndshope Cove** and duly meet the broken ridge-top wall. Turn left, south-east, to reach the 792m/2599ft summit of **Dove Crag**. There is every inducement to venture back due north over bristling outcropping to where a transverse wall forms the limit of safety, built by shepherds to prevent sheep from falling over the edge. From here the view is superb back down into Dovedale. Backtrack and follow the ridge wall right, retracing your ascent, and go on through the depression up the less than grassy rise onto the stony top of **Hart Crag**. The likelihood is that you'll encounter walkers on the Fairfield Horseshoe hereabouts. Wish them well, and know that you're on a pretty good walk yourself.

Having enjoyed the views into Rydal Beck valley and the stunning view into Link Cove and Scrubby Crag from the northern edge, thoughts turn homeward, or rather towards Hartsop above How. The early stages do not have a cairned path, and in mist this can be treacherous. Head north-east and a grass strip leads to an area of scree glitter. Either

Dovedale from the top of Dove Crag

hold to the rocky edge or slip down the unruly scree gully on the right. Once the steep ground is cleared, with no little pleasure, a largely grassy rolling ridge is pursued. The path takes two lines to **Blake Brow**, and to the north avoids a final rocky step down. Peat hags are encountered in the depression before the easy pull to the cairnless top of **Hartsop above How**. It is likely that most walkers pass the summit oblivious of the event. At 586m/1923ft Hartsop above How is a pleasing viewpoint overlooking the wilds of Hunsett Cove.

The apparently simple ridge is lined with crags on either flank, making it imperative that the ridge path is adhered to henceforward. However, as a special treat after some 300m you might venture down right to stand beside The Perch above Dovedale Slabs for an exclusive view of Dove Crag, though good conditions are definitely needed for this somewhat erratic pathless diversion.

The continuing grassy ridge descends north, a lovely parade that comes into harmony with the ridge wall. Watch for a ladder stile over the wall directly after a rock step. The path veers left crossing a broken wall and passing cairns to plummet down through **Low Wood**, eventually leading through a deer-exclusion pen, via weighted gates, to reach **Cowbridge**.

Low Hartsop from above Low Wood   237

Fairfield
and St Sunday Crag
from Patterdale

*M*ountain magic distilled – a round for the connoisseur. The route wanders into the depths of Deepdale to witness the drama of the dale-head unfold, then energetically and cannily over-comes the impressive blunt craggy ridge of Greenhow End to gain the panoramic top of Fairfield. It descends the narrow ridge by Cofa Pike through the saddle of Deepdale Hause. Mindful that Greenhow End will not be to every walker's taste, the natural continuation up through Sleet Cove onto Deepdale Hause is shown on the map. While this cuts Fairfield from the day's equation, it does major on the no less impressive harmony of Deepdale and St Sunday Crag. Sweeping over St Sunday Crag you gain arguably the finest prospects of the Helvellyn range and Ullswater – stretching away into the haze of distance and leading the eyes towards the Eden vale and the Pennines.

↑ *Dollywaggon Pike, Nethermost Pike and Helvellyn peering over Deepdale Hause from Greenhow End*

ROUTE INFORMATION

Distance	17km/10¾ miles
Height gain	911m/2990ft
Time	8½ hours
Grade	strenuous
Start point	GR397159
Maps	(Harvey Superwalker) Lakeland Central (Ordnance Survey) OL5 North-eastern area

After-walk refreshment
The Patterdale Hotel and Side Farm Tearoom

The Start
Across the road from Patterdale Hotel find a modestly proportioned pay and display car park at GR397159. The regular Stagecoach shuttle buses from either Ambleside, Keswick or Penrith turning at the entrance are a possible hazard for motorists, but a valuable contribution to sustainable travel for walkers.

The Route
Follow the footway south along the main road passing **Patterdale Youth Hostel** and **Bleaze End**, the name a reference to a no longer discernible pale patch on the fellside above, after the stamp of a horse's blaze. Branch onto the bridle track at the cattle grid, right, and this leads via gates past Greenbank to Lane Head. Follow on with the gated track bound for Wall End, passing to the right of

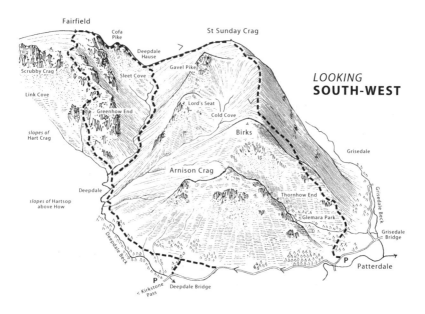

Deepdale Hall Farm to enter the open dale. Once the flagstone bridge spanning **Coldcove Beck** is crossed the dale's countenance, bereft of trees and cattle, turns wilder and, in certain light, austere. The valley path diminishes as it advances along the floor to weave over the drumlin field, with Greenhow End in all its glory looming ahead, a praetorial guard to fortress Fairfield.

VARIANT ROUTE

If Greenhow End looks a bridge too far then you can continue up the valley path into Sleet Cove to scramble up the eroded head-wall bank onto Deepdale Hause, thereby making St Sunday Crag your sole goal – and this makes a more than worthy prize.

Fairfield from Cofa Pike

Those with conviction for the full route (and to avoid wetting the boots while traversing the Mossydale dale-bottom basin) should pass beyond the moraine and, as two becks run parallel to the left of the path, ford the becks. Thereafter slant up in front of **Mart Crag**, a sought-after remote testing ground for the climber, the name hinting at the former presence of pine marten. Hold to the steep pathless grassy slope, to the right of an eroded gill, close under **Greenhow End**. Resist the temptation to step onto a grassy shelf, unless you are a suitably competent scrambler. The broad slabby buttress is a very happy hunting ground for the free-climber, often preceded by scrambling within the challenging recesses of Linkcove Gill.

An obvious line of weakness between rock bands permits a steep line up a narrow grass and boulder tongue to a point where the rock band relents to suitably easier ground, where you climb to a notch on the skyline. From the notch a thin, sketchy ridge path climbs left up **The Step** directly above **Hutaple Crag**, with a constant heaped plate of impressive rock architecture to absorb as rich reward. On reaching the plateau weave along the wild escarpment edge, with sheep tracks as guide, to get the best of views down into Cawk and Sleet Coves as you continue to the summit of **Fairfield**.

Three cairns, of which the northernmost is perhaps the highest by a whisker, stand at 873m/2864ft, providing a wonderful outlook panning wide across Lakeland's mountain world. The plethora of cairns on the plateau is indicative of visitors' caution. Safe ground lies due west and south, while to the north-east lies sure peril in mist. After an appropriate rest and the inevitable summit conversation with walkers, who will in the main be engaged in the old-time favourite the Fairfield Horseshoe from Ambleside, thoughts turn to the continuing journey and the excitements of St Sunday Crag, whose strong profile fills the gaze to the north-east.

Turn north, then either head west over stony ground to where a path angles right, or, in good visibility, head directly north upon a well-etched way working down the emerging ridge. This clambers over **Cofa Pike**, a weird devil's-tooth-like feature. Take your time in scrambling down the loose outcropped ridge to where it is constricted at **Deepdale Hause**. At two points paths bear off to the left, bound for Grisedale Tarn, and the only way into Deepdale itself, right, starts down a steep eroded gully. However,

241

these are of no consequence, for our mission is to stay resolutely on the main ridge rising purposefully and sweetly north-east to the summit of **St Sunday Crag** at 841m/2759ft. En route walkers can revel in the view back over the coves and ridges of Dollywaggon and Nethermost Pikes and the Striding Edge skyline of Helvellyn.

St Sunday Crag derives its name from St Dominic, who from the 15th century was known as St Sunday. One can only presume that as the fell dominates the head of Ullswater, and thus the community of Patterdale, the observance of the Christian day of rest was uplifted by gazing at this heavenly height. This dates the fell name some seven centuries later than such as neighbouring Dollywaggon Pike, which is from the Old Norse 'Dolr vegin', meaning 'the elevated giant' – quite a contrast to St Dominic.

Two ragged cairns in a loose litter of stones mark the summit, though such distractions are quickly transcended by the beauty of the all-round mountain view. Off the domed summit to the east, across the nape of The Cape, **Gavel Pike** provides a wonderful second scenic station from which to marvel at the amazingly rugged Deepdale face of Fairfield.

Regain the summit before heading north to a prominent cairn with the best of all views of the upper two reaches of Ullswater, backed by Place Fell and the distant Cross Fell range. Descend the north-east ridge, dipping from a saddle between Cold and Blind Coves. The popular trail trends down the western slopes of **Birks**, becoming a grooved way towards a stile crossing the park-wall at **Thornhow End**. Continue down through the open wooded **Glemara Park**, which in late spring is gloriously carpeted with bluebells. On meeting a track bear right, following this via a park-wall gate to slip through **Mill Moss** by a hand-gate to the rear of the **Patterdale Hotel**.

Dollywaggon Pike from St Sunday Crag

Dollywaggon Pike, Nethermost Pike, Helvellyn and Catstycam from Patterdale

*T*he phrase 'great mountain day' matches the spirit of this walk to a tee. The route ventures up the deep U-shaped glacial valley of Grisedale, with the option of climbing either Nethermost or Dollywaggon Pikes via their exciting east ridges, or sticking with the trade route via Grisedale Tarn, en route to Helvellyn and Catstycam. Lose yourself for a day in a Lakeland mountain environment of unsurpassed beauty and rugged grandeur, and see a less familiar side of Helvellyn.

The Helvellyn range is notable for its high east-facing hanging valley 'coves' – each is distinct, and all are worthwhile, frequently exciting places for the fell-wanderer to visit. Contrast the great basin in which Red Tarn lies, due east of the main summit, with petite Cock Cove on Dollywaggon Pike, or the wild hollows of Nethermost and Ruthwaite Coves. The latter harbours its own treasured pool, Hard Tarn.

↑ *Nethermost Pike and Cove*

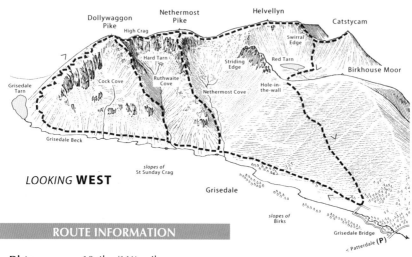

LOOKING **WEST**

ROUTE INFORMATION

Distance	18.4km/11½ miles
Height gain	1007m/3230ft
Time	8 hours
Grade	strenuous
Start point	GR397159
Maps	(Harvey Superwalker)
	Lakeland Central
	(Ordnance Survey)
	OL5 North-eastern area

After-walk refreshment
The Patterdale Hotel, Side Farm Tearoom

The Start
Car parking for Grisedale is limited to the small park opposite the Patterdale Hotel, GR397159.

The Route
From Patterdale follow the roadside footway, passing the charming little parish church dedicated to St Patrick. It appears the saint's name was originally attributed to the valley, hence Patterdale. The Patrick in question was probably not the Irish patron saint from the fifth century, for all the claims for his Cumbrian origins, but a later namesake. At **Grisedale Bridge** follow the side road leading into Grisedale – the name meaning 'the valley where swine forage'. As the road swings right follow this, crossing **Grisedale Beck**, and at the next right-hand corner, where the by-road trends east towards the hunt kennels, go through the kissing-gate and ascend the pasture bank to the

hand-gate. Take the lower path, left, and ignore the ascending path – this is the highway to the Hole-in-the-wall, which we shall use at the end of the day. Pass on above **Braesteads Farm** (the farmstead on the eyebrow-shaped slope). Continue through the third hand-gate.

VARIANT ASCENT
VIA NETHERMOST PIKE
Shortly after the third hand-gate, with Eagle Crag looming ahead, the first optional ascent presents itself, the fabulous east ridge of Nethermost Pike. An old path branches half-right to a wall-stile. The path enters Nethermost Cove, climbing within a bracken- and boulder-infested groove to top the cascades. As this old miners' path dwindles and is lost, ford the gill and climb through the outcrops, admiring the fabulous views of the surrounding headwalls, on course for the ridge above Eagle Crag and all evidence of the copper mine. The ridge ascends in easy stages, with a better-defined path materialising as the dramatic upper ridge commences. There is no serious hazard beyond steepness, the sharp rocks giving plenty of hand-hold security all the way up to the summit of Nethermost Pike – brilliant stuff!

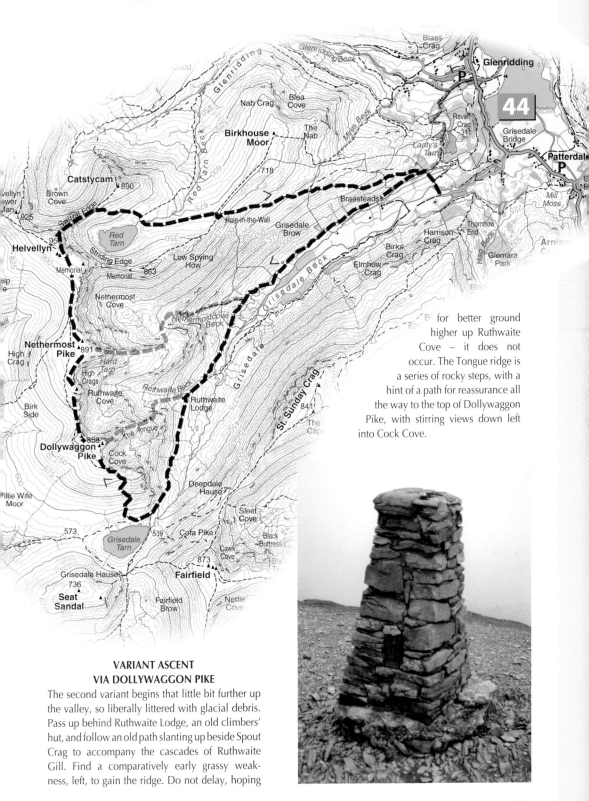

B' for better ground higher up Ruthwaite Cove – it does not occur. The Tongue ridge is a series of rocky steps, with a hint of a path for reassurance all the way to the top of Dollywaggon Pike, with stirring views down left into Cock Cove.

VARIANT ASCENT
VIA DOLLYWAGGON PIKE

The second variant begins that little bit further up the valley, so liberally littered with glacial debris. Pass up behind Ruthwaite Lodge, an old climbers' hut, and follow an old path slanting up beside Spout Crag to accompany the cascades of Ruthwaite Gill. Find a comparatively early grassy weakness, left, to gain the ridge. Do not delay, hoping

The most visited 3000ft summit in Lakeland, Helvellyn

245

Helvellyn from Swallow Scarth

Follow the edge to a cairn on the north-eastern brink marking the point of departure from the plateau. Descend **Swirral Edge** which, while steep, seldom taxes hands or posterior in normal conditions. Levelling at 793m/ 2600ft the ridge loses its craggy demeanour and begins a gritty, grassy climb to the conical top of **Catstycam** (pronounced 'cat stee cam') at 890m/ 2920ft. This airy perch has just about enough room for a cairn and seating for half a dozen walkers each facing in different directions, each getting a buzz from their particular portion of the brilliant view. Were all Lakeland fell tops this petite, we'd be calling it the Cumbrian Alps.

Backtrack to the col below Swirral Edge and follow the popular path down left to ford the outflow of **Red Tarn** and contour to cross the **Hole-in-the-wall** stile. Here there is a superb view of Grisedale as you look over at St Sunday Crag and right to the famous headwall fells traversed on this walk. Then begin the steady descent back down into the valley and back to the start.

The main path continues along the valley beneath the massive cliffs of Falcon and Tarn Crags, passing the Brothers' Parting Rock and to the right of the outflow of Grisedale Tarn. It embarks on the now re-engineered zig-zagging path up the steep south slope of Dollywaggon Pike. A huge amount of thought, effort, time and money has gone into the repair of this fellside, so please respect the solid pitched trail and pour scorn on anyone you see racing down the fellside off the trail – but do it nicely we don't want a fell fracas! The path gains height diligently, though once up high the popular way swings behind the summits, and you might find it more attractive to peel off right to reach the top of **Dollywaggon Pike** and link to **Nethermost Pike** via the intermediate top of **High Crag**. Follow on, dipping through the shallow depression of Swallow Scarth to join the trade route to the top of **Helvellyn**.

Pass on from the cross-wall windbreak, a place of general congregation, to reach and lean upon the triangulation column at the summit to appreciate the stupendous view.

↑ *Grisedale Hause and Tarn*   *Catstycam from the top of Swirral Edge* →

Birkhouse Moor, Helvellyn, White Side, Raise, Stybarrow Dodd and Sheffield Pike from Glenridding

*I*n amazing contrast to the abrupt western aspect of the range, the long ridge and valley system stretching east from the high summits of the Helvellyn range ensures that walks from Patterdale and Glenridding are full-day undertakings. Here is the lion's share of the good walking, the longer days. Here you'll find elegant peaks and chiselled ridges, wild corries and verdant straths all held in comparatively small compass – the romance of mountain Lakeland wonderfully disclosed.

Fundamentally this route is the Glenridding skyline walk. The first objective is Birkhouse Moor – its grassy pasture in stark contrast to the narrow serrated crest of Striding Edge, a ridge that attracts admiration, awe and respect from all who tread its devil's spine. Completing the ascent onto the headwall escarpment of Helvellyn, the walk sets to work gathering up a string of summits – Helvellyn Lower Man, White Side, Raise and Stybarrow Dodd – before striking east by Green Side and Sheffield Pike.

In its mid-section the walk has three well-engineered tracks back down to Glenridding, providing honourable bail-out points to suit prevailing conditions and/or your inclination. Discretion is always the better part of valour when venturing on these challenging ridges, especially as the weather can turn nasty very quickly.

↑ Helvellyn from Birkhouse Moor

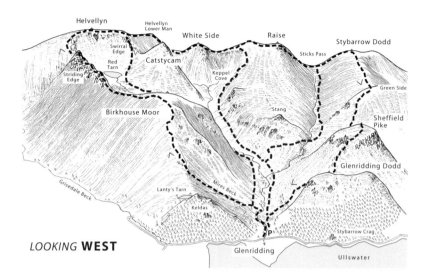

LOOKING **WEST**

ROUTE INFORMATION

Distance	17km/10½ miles
Height gain	1340m/4400ft
Time	10 hours
Grade	arduous
Start point	GR386169
Maps	(Harvey Superwalker)
	Lakeland Central
	(Ordnance Survey)
	OL5 North-eastern area

After-walk refreshment

The Inn on the Lake (Hikers' Bar), Glenridding Hotel (Ratchers Bar) and the Travellers Rest in the upper part of Glenridding

The Start

The large National Park Authority car park at the centre of Glenridding, GR385169, is the natural springboard for this expedition.

The Route

Either follow the path out of the top end of the car park by the health centre to follow the village road up past the Travellers Rest pub, then at the road-fork bear left to cross **Rattlebeck Bridge** (what a lovely name, redolent of clattering beck stones). Or, more in tune with the walking day, follow the lane from **Glenridding Bridge**, passing through Eagle Farm and along the beck-side bridle path by Gillside camping site.

Both routes come together beyond the farm signed 'Helvellyn via Mires Beck', passing via a stile up to a fork below 'Miresbeck' cottage, and rising right to the ladder stile crossing the intake wall. Paths splay to left and right. Join the well-engineered pitched path built to cope with rampant boots bent on Striding Edge. This fords **Mires Beck** and winds up Little Cove to the ridge wall keeping right. It then pulls away from the wall to gain the broad top of **Birkhouse Moor**, handy for the summit cairn over to the right at 718m/2356ft. Ahead is a superb view of the Red Tarn amphitheatre, with Striding Edge forming the left-hand side-wall and the peak of Catstycam, projecting proudly from Helvellyn's breast, to the right. Bear left to regain the wall, passing the Hole-in-the-Wall wall corner and now setting sights on the rocky headland connecting to Helvellyn.

If conditions look bad you may turn right at Hole-in-the-Wall, contour to the outflow of Red Tarn and follow the good valley path to early safety.

Approach the next stage of the journey with a steady head and bated anticipation for exciting situations. The walkers' highway runs on the north side

Bare rock on Striding Edge looking to Helvellyn

of **Low Spying How**, passing striated rocks to reach the top of the High Spying How, a good first vantage to survey the depths of Nethermost Cove and the changing fortunes of the westward-trending razor-topped ridge. Many walkers attempt to avoid the bare crest to varying degrees of success, and the net effect is unsightly erosion that could be healed only by giving the edge a 10-year sabbatical from boots. How likely, if desirable, is that? The ridge-name implies scope for confident strides, whereas it actually means 'the sharp ridge one can stand astride'. The edge ends with a rock tower, and equally difficult options to descend chimney clefts to right or left.

Step through the little col and scramble up the broken fellside, via a scree gully. Equilibrium and composure are restored at the plateau rim, and there is elation too, as the cross-wall is passed and the summit of **Helvellyn** reached at 950m/3116ft.

Final tower on Striding Edge linking to Helvellyn

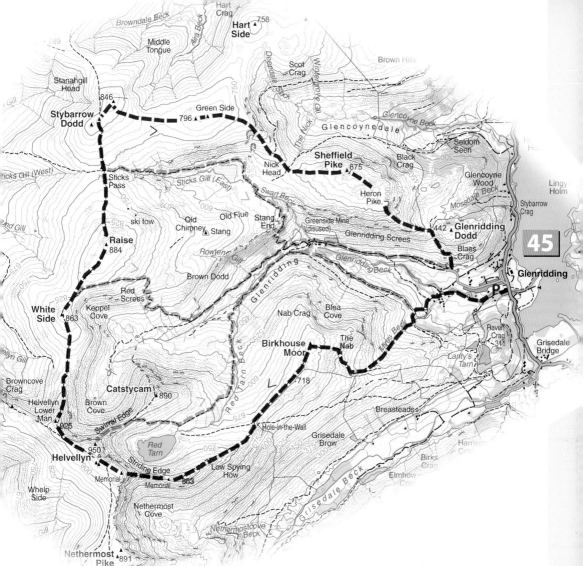

The contrasting views from **Helvellyn summit** to the cardinal compass points never fail to mesmerize the visitor. A daily procession of euphoric walkers stroll up, press against the summit pillar, and in time turn tail, well satisfied with the bounty of their day's endeavours. The proof of the panorama is the year-round, unending flow of walkers.

Follow the scarp edge north. One may break right at the first cairn and go down the crumpled spine of Swirral Edge, though this can be a slow descent. To take this route, from the col with Catstycam bear down to outflow of Red Tarn and join the Glenridding-bound made trail.

To continue on the main route, curve with the ridge the half a mile to the subsidiary top of **Helvellyn Lower Man**, with its dishevelled shaly cairn. Head on down the north ridge into the broad saddle rising to the summit of **White Side** at 863m/2851ft, the entire route super-served with cairns. The ridge path continues in similar vein. At the apparent fork, be aware that the right turn draws one down the renewed engineered pony route around the head of Keppel Cove and down into the Glenridding Beck valley – another useful return route. Keep to the skyline ridge by a string of cairns and continue to the coarse-rock top of **Raise** at 884m/2900ft. Continue north again down through a marsh to the cairn at the top of **Sticks Pass**. A right turn can curtail the walk and take you back to Glenridding via Stang End. But having come this far, why miss the final summits? They need only a little extra effort.

Sticks Pass in conditions fit for skiing, from Sheffield Pike

Strike due north up the grassy bank to the south top of **Stybarrow Dodd**, and curve with the edge to find the modest summit cairn at 846m/2776ft. Turn south-east and quickly east down the slope in harmony with walkers engaged on the round of the Dodds (Walk 36) to the cairns on **Green Side**, and here bear off south-east. In mist this apparently simple action has dangers, for the unprotected broken rim of the top mineral quarry catches the edge of the descending path. Striding through the cotton grass and peat of **Nick Head**, keep east to claim the splendid peak of **Sheffield Pike**. The name has nothing to do with the old Yorkshire home of steel and cutlers, being a mischievous corruption of 'sheep fold'.

The important path angles south-east over rough heather ridge to the brink of **Heron Pike** and continues down the ridge to trend down The Rake path from the saddle with **Glenridding Dodd**. With the last saps of energy one might visit this little vantage summit, giving the perfect view of the village below and, from the eastern edge, a brilliant view of Ullswater too. The Rake path comes down behind Rake Cottages, a terrace of converted miners' dwellings, to join the Greenside Road track.

Place Fell
from Patterdale

*T*o many Ullswater is the most scenic of all the lakes. It has the air of a mighty fjord snaking in a
succession of reaches – from no one point is there a complete view. At each of its turns comes
a wholly new perspective to adore. Place Fell rises solidly to the east of the water-head community
of Patterdale. Its high rugged sides and its eastward-curving shore are the basis of the upper two
reaches of the lake. Passengers on the lake-long steamer cruises may gaze most intently at the high
fells to the west, notably St Sunday Crag on their upstream journey. But travelling in either direction
from Glenridding Pier to Sandwick Bay all eyes will inevitably alight upon Place Fell's colourful mural
slopes. Place Fell is far more than a pleasing facade, it is a wonderful 'place' to walk. The prospects
from its summit are majestic, and the outlooks from its roller-coaster shoreline path absolute heaven
– making a very special day's walking.

↑ *Patterdale, with Sheffield Pike backing the White Lion*

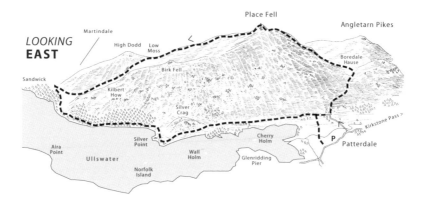

ROUTE INFORMATION

Distance	11km/7 miles
Height gain	550m/1800ft
Time	4½ hours
Grade	energetic
Start point	GR397159
Maps	(Harvey Superwalker) Lakeland Central (Ordnance Survey) OL5 North-eastern area

After-walk refreshment

Tearoom at Side Farm and the White Lion Inn, and several hostelries in nearby Glenridding

The Start

Across the road from the Patterdale Hotel find a modestly proportioned pay and display car park, GR397159. The regular Stagecoach shuttle buses from either Ambleside, Keswick or Penrith turning at the entrance are a possible hazard for motorists, but a valuable contribution to sustainable travel for walkers.

The Route

Regain the main road and walk left (south) from the **Patterdale Hotel**. The road bottlenecks in passing the curiously tapered White Lion Inn, obviously built on a jealously limited plot. The footway leads to a tight meander of the enchantingly named **Goldrill Beck**.

The stream name refers to marsh marigold, and to this day the valley pastures can glow with their rich yellow raiment. Turn left into the no-through road, crossing **Goldrill Bridge** to the rather exclusive community of houses known as Rooking.

Keep left, then go right at the gate signed 'Boredale Hause and Angle Tarn'. Bear up right, rising now with a bridleway and following up by the wall. Climb on, with truly lovely views growing with every step, initially framed by larch. As the path steps up through the bracken banks Arnison Crag draws the eye across the valley and, higher, to the backing St Sunday Crag. To the left are the majestic fells at the head of the valley surrounding Dovedale and the Kirkstone Pass, with Red Screes and Brotherswater on view. Pitching has helped secure the path, which is here part of the perennially popular Coast to Coast Walk. Keep to the higher path where it forks. Reach the open bowl of **Boredale Hause**, a proverbial Piccadilly Circus of paths of all complexions, purposes and destinations.

Boredale lies in the almost permanent shadow of Place Fell, tucked into a secretive fold of the Far Eastern Fells, between Place Fell and Beda Head. Both William Wordsworth and Alfred Wainwright fell into the trap of assuming that the name Boredale referred to pigs. Hence they preferred the erroneous spelling 'Boardale'. They were completely wrong. The Norse for swine was 'grise', as in Grisedale, and the British was 'moch', as in Glenderamackin. The name Boredale prosaically meant 'the valley with a storehouse'.

255

Pass the ruins of the so-called **Chapel in the Hause** to take your leave of the main trail by veering uphill left, north. Climb on a clear grass path onto the south ridge of Place Fell. Higher up, rainwater has gullied the path leaving a sorry sight and some wobbly moments for the ankles. Elsewhere, when pre-emptive repair has been possible, such unsightly difficulties have been avoided. Let's hope this can also be patched up in the not too distant future. During this ascent find any excuse you can to spot and look back towards the fells encircling Kirkstone – it is a stunningly uplifting scene. Passing pools, the path makes one final leap onto the high headland of **Place Fell** (meaning 'the fell top with open level space'), surmounted by a stone-built Ordnance Survey column.

Boredale Hause looking to Kirkstone Pass

Place Fell summit pillar

At 657m/2156ft **Place Fell** offers a superb all-round panorama, with the Helvellyn range pre-eminent. Also disclosed is the full length of Grisedale, and eyes will be trained on the massive slope of St Sunday Crag and the wild upper corrie galleries of Nethermost and Dollywaggon Pikes. Eastwards the skyline ridges embrace the land-locked Martindale valley system – a contrast as much as anything because the dales and ridges run north to south.

Leave the summit, with some regret – it's not a place to hasten from. The obvious path trends down by a large pool in a north-easterly direction. Ahead see the lower reaches of Ullswater and, beyond, across the Eden valley, the distant Cross Fell, monarch of the whole Pennine chain. The path inclines down the lovely grassy slopes to a cairn, then descends more purposefully to the depression at **Low Moss**. After passing a ruined fold take the left-hand path down the shallow valley to squeeze between a ruined roofless workshop and slate spoil. The ensuing turf path leads on invitingly. Keep left at the next fork, drawing closer into the fold of the Scalehow Beck valley.

Believe it or not **Scalehow Force** is a Victorian folly. The original owner of the scenically sited house that is now the Ullswater Outward Bound Mountain School sought to enhance his view, and successfully gun-powdered the beck to create a picturesque waterfall!

The path comes upon its own picturesque prospect – that of Sandwick Bay. It is a tautological name as, taken literally, it means 'the sandy bay bay'. It is curious that the Norse term 'wick' does not mean 'bay' in the town name Keswick, where it means 'cheese farm'. It all goes to show what a minefield place names can be in an area like this.

The path leads unerringly down to a junction with a lower track beside the open-wooded enclosure wall. Cut back left with this bridleway, crossing a footbridge spanning **Scalehow Beck**. This is one of the most popular paths in the district for all its

257

remoteness from a motor-road. Walkers use the lake cruise from Glenridding Pier to drop them at the jetty at Howtown Wyke and walk back beneath Hallin Fell and Sandwick on this section of pathway. The path descends and then makes a roller-coaster trip, coping with tree roots and small outcropping, never quite sure whether it should be up or down, but seldom making it to lake-level. The path has a sylvan canopy framing many a photographic opportunity across Ullswater to Sheffield Pike and Glencoyne.

The path curves round **Silver Bay** above the point to follow along by the enclosure wall adjacent to the wood-fringed Blowick meadows (Blowick meant 'dark bay'). The path becomes a track, leading by the camping ground into the yard at Side Farm. Bear right via gates following the access lane over grids and once more crossing **Goldrill Beck**. Regain the valley road at the George Starkley Hut, with the parish church of St Patrick (hence the valley name Patterdale) to the right.

Ridge path leading north from Place Fell

Steel Knotts, High Raise, Rampsgill Head, The Knott, Rest Dodd, Angletarn Pikes and Beda Head from Martindale

A world apart, Martindale provides the perfect 'far from the madding crowd' fell-walking experi-ence in truly beautiful surroundings. The route follows a natural horseshoe, climbing from St Martin's Church across the flanks of Steel Knotts to the head of Fusedale, then up onto the eastern skyline to join the Roman road (High Street) heading south to High Raise and Rampsgill Head. Breaking right at the Straits of Riggindale the route picks off The Knott and Rest Dodd and, passing Angle Tarn, claims Angletarn Pikes, before continuing north onto Beda Head. There are no obvious hazards; some paths are heavily used, some lightly trod.

↑ *Martindale Deer Forest from Beda Head*

Distance	19km/12 miles
Height gain	1012m/3320ft
Time	8 hours
Grade	strenuous
Start point	GR434184
Maps	(Harvey Superwalker)
	Lakeland East
	(Ordnance Survey)
	OL5 North-eastern area

After-walk refreshment
The Howtown Hotel, the Pooley Bridge Hotel or the Sun Inn

The Start

By car, approach Martindale from Pooley Bridge on the lakeside road. The 4 mile journey is narrow and tortuous, and should be driven carefully. Passing the lane to Howtown Hotel the road crosses a cattle-grid and embarks on a series of hairpin turns on the steep rise to The Hause, entry into the cul-de-sac world of Martindale. Park tidily on the open common beside Martindale Old Church at GR434184. Alternatively, take the steamer from Glenridding to Howtown and walk 2km/1¼ miles to the start of the route.

The Route

Leave the road on the north side of the churchyard. A path winds up through the bracken beside an enclosure wall to angle diagonally right across the fellside beneath Steel Knotts. Pass through a bridle gateway, almost reaching the ridge-top wall, and take a backward glance at the inviting summit of **Steel Knotts**. This fell top may (should) be included in the tour by following the ridge path, left, clambering over the wall and climbing simply to the prominent crest. The actual summit at 432m/1417ft is a curious rock feature, with an equally curious name, Pikeawassa. As a viewpoint its greatest charm is the prospect of the Martindale Deer Forest, centred upon The Nab, with its two flanking valleys, Rampsgill and Bannerdale. From the meeting of the waters of these two valleys flows **Howe Grain Beck**. Retrace your climb and rejoin the continuing path beyond the wall, initially keeping either beside the wall or along the edge overlooking the valley and facing the handsome bulk of Beda Fell.

Steel Knotts

The Roman road (running alongside the wall) north of High Raise

The ridge path drifts from the wall to traverse open fell towards **Gowk Hill**, but then prefers to slant left avoiding this pudding-topped ridge. The name 'gowk' means cuckoo, confirmation of the former richly wooded nature of the Martindale valley. Remnant alder and birch persist up the valley sides.

Crossing a damp rushy patch at the very head of **Fusedale** provides a tight view down dale to Howtown, Sharrow Bay and the lower reach of Ullswater. 'Fusedale' is agricultural Norse, distinguishing it as 'the valley of the cattle-shed' as distinct from Boredale, 'the valley of the storehouse'. Slipping through a wall skip over the beck and pass the ruins of a shepherd's bothy, a significant landmark in mist and a significant reminder of the lost farming life.

The path bears right, initially climbing beside a broken wall, then slants up a groove along the breast of the spinal ridge of the Far Eastern Fells. Looking down into the Rampsgill valley see the red-roofed holiday lodge The Bungalow. It was built in 1910 by the Earl of Lonsdale of Lowther Castle as a special retreat for Kaiser Wilhelm II on the occasion of a deer shooting visit, the exuberant rich orange tiles a startling addition to the green dale. Climb into a dry gully of **Mere Beck** – 'mere' meant boundary stream.

Ignore the gate ahead and keep left, completing the climb to quickly meet up with the Roman road coming south from **Wether Hill** – 'wether' means

'fattening pasture of castrated tups'. The ridge wall is joined beside a massive peat hag bank, a landscape reminiscent of the blanket bogs of the North Pennines across the Eden vale.

The open track heads south, slipping through the gap in the wall, eventually coming closer to a fence and crossing the rockless crest of **Red Crag**. It declines to an area of marshy pools skirting the largest, **Redcrag Tarn**. Avoiding the mire is quite a challenge, but a low order of hazard. The track passes through the fence at a bridle gate. Keeping the ridge wall left, the ground rises over **Raven Howe** to cross a stile where the wall ends. Pass up by the bridle gate to traverse the open top, enjoying fine views down into the Rampsgill valley – 'valley of wild garlic [ramsoms]'. The Roman way naturally glances over the brow avoiding the summit of **High Raise** at 802m/2631ft, so make a conscious break left through the boulder field to visit the cairn and maybe shelter in the adjacent windbreak before returning south.

The ridge path dips into the pool-filled depression and forks – the left-hand way leading to Kidsty Pike, while the Roman trail (and your route) heads up the facing slope over the brow of **Rampsgill Head** at 792m/2598ft. It misses the best view from the cairn, right, which offers views of the length of the Ramps Gill itself. Of note is the buttress arête falling from near the summit, framing the valley view.

Rejoin the Roman track which skirts the edge over **Twopenny Crag** to reach the wall above the **Straits of Riggindale**. Here, revel in the superb views down Riggindale to Haweswater and Rough Crags and the mighty form of the fell High Street, with the continuing Roman road tripping high across its western slope on course for Thornthwaite Crag and the Troutbeck valley.

Turn right, following the wall on the much-beaten path and taking the opportunity to visit the neat pimple of **The Knott** at 739m/2425ft by following the wall left. The cairn, quickly reached, occupies a fine vantage above water. Follow on, with the wall descending as straight as a die, crossing the regular path. The wall points directly to Rest Dodd, though some walkers will forego the pleasure, opting to keep to the popular path, the passage of Coast to Coast hikers.

Stouter types will gird their loins and keep faith with the wall's destiny down through the marshy depression and up the slope of **Rest Dodd**. Open for the final feet, the summit cairn at 696m/2283ft is hardly a treasured viewpoint, with a broad peaty hollow separating it from a second smaller cairn. The fell name suggests transferred association with an unspecified traditional place of transient rest during the age-old wearisome journey from Patterdale to Mardale.

Historic herd of red deer in Martindale

To the north the ridge takes a great sweep down through peat hags to rise onto the rounded tongue of The Nab. This lonely height lies at the heart of the Martindale Deer Forest. Peak-baggers who venture down to The Nab must religiously retrace their steps back up onto Rest Dodd to continue the route. But I must stress that a visit to The Nab is not to be condoned, as it is not sympathetic to the care and preservation of the unique herd of red deer that find sanctuary about the fell. The Dalemain Estate owns and sensitively manages all of Martindale, and is right to discourage fell walkers from casually wandering within these deer breeding grounds. The herd is the only pure red deer blood-stock in England, with no Sika cross-breeding, and on those grounds alone deserve us to keep a respectful distance at all times.

The path continues, initially heading north-west, then, before confronting the cross-ridge wall, it swings west to reunite with the popular path. The path enjoys views of Gray Crag and then, through a gap beside **Satura Crag**, goes into Bannerdale and across to Brock Crags, before it works down to the shores of **Angle Tarn**. The name is a clear reference to former stocking of the tarn for fishing sport. The peninsula often attracts backpackers as an appealing pitch location.

Note: Back from this point a path begins that slips over the ridge and down across the western flanks of Heck Crag into Bannerdale. Its upper course is exceedingly narrow and traverses a steep scree slope. Having sampled it I am well placed to provide a cautionary note on its use, though the peregrine falcon nesting on Satura Crag added audible excitement to my painfully slow, deliberate strides.

The main ridge path to Beda Fell branches off to the right of the Patterdale path in the proximity of the tarn.

EXTENSION TO ANGLETARN PIKES

Anyone considering adding the double-summited Angletarn Pikes to their day may either begin with the Beda Fell ridge path, breaking left through the undulating rocky hillocks, or continue with the Patterdale path to climb directly onto the western top at 561m/1840ft. For both routes, good visibility is essential. The two summits are separated by an area of eroded peat, the passage of walkers definitely not to blame in this instance. The outlook is superb – towards Red Screes beyond Brotherswater, to Fairfield through Deepdale, to the bold profile of St Sunday Crag, Grisedale, the very head of Ullswater, and to Place Fell.

The grassy ridge path bypasses the Pikes and strides north-east most pleasantly above **Heck Cove** to pass a stout cairn. It then descends to step over the bridleway emerging from Bannerdale and linking Martindale with Boredale Hause and Patterdale.

Should conditions dictate, you may choose to go right down this easy grass path, passing the remains of a bothy as it heads down to Dale Head Farm and the valley road. This path has the distinct advantage of coming close above the high-fenced valley enclosures harbouring the red deer herd. In the evening you'll hear what sounds uncannily like the calls of a distant shepherd – 'yoy', 'yoy'. During the day deer drift onto The Nab seeking grazing and use this method to reunite with their calves.

The ridge path crosses **Bedafell Knott**, descends again then steadily rises along the simple ridge to **Beda Head** at 509m/1670ft. This is a lovely viewpoint, intimate with the whole Martindale scene. The continuing path trends leftwards via a prominent cairn then slants right down a grooved path, pitching more steeply above Thrang Crag, another nesting site of peregrine. It is splendid way to end the day, traversing the rocky knot of **Winter Crag** to reach a seat, where paths splay three ways. Go sharp right down to meet the road beside **Wintercrag Farm**, crossing Christy Bridge to complete the round.

High Street, Rampsgill Head and Kidsty Pike from Mardale Head

A sensational skyline circuit embracing the great amphitheatre of Riggindale. The route climbs the wonderfully revealing Rough Crags and Long Stile ridge onto High Street before following the ridge wall down via the Straits of Riggindale to visit the summits of Rampsgill Head and Kidsty Pike. The tour concludes in the company of Wainwright's Coast to Coast Walk down the eastern slopes of Kidsty Pike via Kidsty Howes, thereby linking back to the valley path and regaining the dale-head car park.

The Rough Crags ridge can be side-stepped on a path leading up by the outflow from Blea Tarn to gain the Caspel Gate saddle. From here the walk can be extended to gather up High Raise in the company of the Roman road. The walk's embrace can also easily be widened to include Mardale Ill Bell via Small Water and the Nan Bield Pass, yet the simplicity of the core tour will always win the greater favour and linger as a richly rewarding memory.

↑ *Kidsty Pike from the Rough Crags ridge*

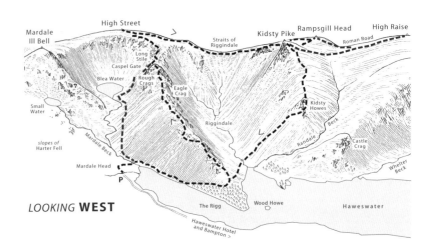

LOOKING **WEST**

ROUTE INFORMATION

Distance	10.25km/6½ miles
Height gain	760m/2490ft
Time	5½ hours
Grade	energetic
Start point	GR469107
Maps	(Harvey Superwalker) Lakeland East (Ordnance Survey) OL5 North-eastern area

After-walk refreshment
Haweswater Hotel 'Walkers' Bar', 2 miles back along the reservoir road, or go 4 miles to the Mardale Inn in Bampton, or patronise the village Post Office/shop tearoom

The Start
Park in the Mardale Head road-end car park at the head of Haweswater, GR469107, located 6 miles from Bampton, 4 miles from the dam, and 2 miles from Haweswater Hotel. Typically this free parking can reach capacity by 9:30am on a good summer's day, so an early start is always to be recommended.

Pre-amble
Haweswater is synonymous with Lakeland's most enigmatic bird of prey, the golden eagle. The return of this magnificent bird to its ancient breeding ground in the late 1950s was headline news. Since first nesting in 1969 three males have held tenure of this wild corner of the Cumbrian mountains, producing 16 young, though the female has changed several times over the period. The latest female, some 28 years old, successfully reared nine young, but sadly went missing in spring 2007; the RSPB are quietly confident that a new female will arrive soon to fill the breach.

At the last count 420 pairs of golden eagles inhabited the collective British eyrie, Riggindale being their only claw-hold in England. The water catchment land, owned by United Utilities, is managed in partnership with the RSPB on specific habitat issues in order to support the golden eagle. Every year the RSPB carries out a round-the-clock guard on the eagles and organises public viewing of the birds from a viewpoint sited at a safe distance in Riggindale valley, open during the breeding season, April to August, from 11am to 4pm.

The population has dwindled to one aging male, so ornithologists are encouraged to show due deference when observing the bird in the hope that nature will reward his vigil. Intriguingly there are two crags on the shadowed north face of Rough Crags named on OS maps as Eagle Crag and Heron Crag. The latter derives from the Norse term 'erne', identifying the sea eagle, as distinct from the golden eagle implied by the former!

Solitary male golden eagle soars forlornly in search of a mate

Anyone who has wandered in the verdant pastures of Kentmere or Longsleddale will know just how beautiful the valleys of the Far Eastern Fells can be. They are the product of generations of farming; the stewardship of nature and man. But step north over Nan Bield or Gatescarth Passes and witness an austerity that only municipal water extraction can bestow. Mardale, prior to the building of the dam in 1937, must have been equally as enchanting. Thus 'the valley of the mere', the derivation of the name Mardale, became Manchester's second Lake District dale-drowning, supplementing Thirlmere.

Prior to the dam building, the tiny farming community of Mardale Green had existed at the foot of Riggindale, centred on its church and pub. The Dun Bull Hotel evidently took its name from the droving of dun-coloured Shorthorn cattle through the valley. It might be noted that the reservoir was the second challenge to the valley's integrity. Prior to this, railway engineers had eyed the narrow valleys of Longsleddale and Mardale as a prime route for the west coast main line, tunnelling under the Gatesgarth Pass. In hindsight this would have saved the valley from drowning... but which fate would have been better?

The Route

Leave the Mardale Head car park via the kissing-gate and, as the path makes a three-way fork, bear right with the wall. Descend via a further kissing-gate and two footbridges, the larger spanning **Mardale Beck**, augmented by the outflowing becks from Blea Water and Small Water. One may bear left following the fell path up Bleawater Beck into the hanging valley – from the outflow of the tarn bearing up to Caspel Gate, a clear path persists throughout. But this is trumped for scenic delight by the majestic Rough Crags ridge, which is the principal route. Draw round the head of the reservoir and along the popular roughly made path leading above **The Rigg** conifer plantation to reach and cross a broken wall descending off the Rough Crags ridge.

Haweswater receives the catchment from Wet Sleddale, Swindale and even Ullswater. The water flows from the draw-off tower under Gatescarth Pass and down Longsleddale to the Watchgate Water Treatment Works, from where it runs by gravity, at some 3 miles an hour, down a pipe 8ft 3in square, the 80 miles to Greater Manchester.

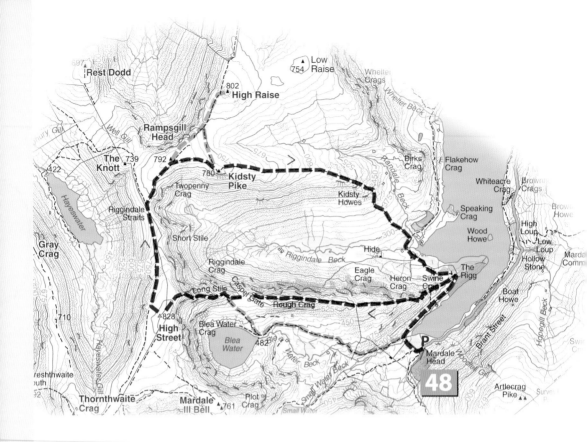

Bear immediately left, following this wall as it mounts the ridge, initially pleasingly adorned with birch. Soon the path threads through the wall as the ridge makes a sudden rise. With handsome views to the head wall of Harter Fell and down upon the lake-head car park, pass casual cairns as you climb back up to the ridge-top, now keeping the wall to the right. At the point where an old wall arrives from the left, **Eagle Crag** lurks under the eastern edge, unseen

and unseeable from the ridge. Nonetheless, from here on keep an keen eye out to spot the solitary male soaring from his eyrie and wheeling in the sky. The resident ravens frequently pester him to make evasive sweeps across Riggindale, a stirring sight as I witnessed on my own visits.

It is an utter joy to stride the ridge, which is consistently scenic and should not been hurried. The path eases until the wall breaks right, whereupon it steps up again towards the crest of Rough Crags. **Blea Water** is prominent, surrounded by the rim of broken cliffs forming Mardale Ill Bell and High Street. After crossing the top of **Rough Crags** 628m/2060ft, marked by a small stone man (cairn), the ridge descends to the damp depression of **Caspel Gate**, passing above a long tarn. At a small cairn, the path meets up with the dale path rising from Bleawater Beck, as the ridge steepens onto **Long Stile**, buttressing High Street. Climb up the middle of the ridge, with progressively better views down onto the blue sky-reflecting waters of the tarn. As might be guessed, 'blue' is the meaning of the tarn name.

Blea Tarn from Caspel Gate

Rough Crags from the top of Long Stile

The plateau is reached at **High Street's** inevitably bedraggled cairn. An obvious path leads southwest, eventually accompanying the ridge wall to the Ordnance Survey pillar at 828m/2717ft. This is one of several old triangulation columns that now form part of the Survey's National GPS Network; this replaced the former triangulation system, thereby making most of these landmark pillars redundant. New horizons to the west into the heart of Lakeland draw most attention, and Scafell and Great Gable will catch the eye, though the Helvellyn range is the more impressive mountainscape.

HIGH STREET

To get the best views from the summit, stride on due west down to the Roman road, from which the fell derives its name. The Roman 'street' connected forts at Brougham (Brocavvm) and Ambleside (Galava), and was probably a far more ancient ridgeway thoroughfare. Medieval charters refer to it as 'Brettestrete', 'the way of the Britons', adding further credence to the notion.

Until 1935 the fell top was a gathering place for inter-dale rivalry with the annual Mardale Shepherds' Meet each November. After shepherding matters had been resolved the men-folk would indulge in traditional sports such as Cumberland & Westmorland Wrestling and football, spiced with horse-racing, hence the fell's alternative name, Racecourse Hill. Huge quantities of ale were notoriously consumed, with inevitably much merry-making down in the Dun Bull.

Go right, descending with the Roman road – you might also go north directly from the Ordnance Survey pillar beside the ridge wall to the same effect, thereby gaining the eastern edge via the top of Short Stile with its superb views into Riggindale.

The name **Riggindale** derives from the Norse *rigga* 'to bind'. With this name, the roof-like shape of Rough Crags ridge was thereby likened to the taut rope-work on a sailing ship.

Ridge wall and High Street Roman road cross diagonally at the Straits of Riggindale

The popular ridge road slips through the wall where the spine of the ridge constricts, a place known as the **Straits of Riggindale**. Ascend by the wall until a clear path breaks right. This is where the Coast to Coast Walk is joined – arriving here from Patterdale. You can follow this edge-path directly over Twopenny Crag to **Kidsty Pike**. Alternatively, branch half-left to the summit of **Rampsgill Head** at 792m/2598ft. On the lovely day I wandered this way skylarks were hovering overhead singing an unending rhapsody, making life a sweet, sweet thing.

The northward-trending **Ramps Gill valley**, which drains into beautiful land-locked Martindale, is every bit as grand as Riggindale, and is renown for its considerable population of red deer. Of special note is the bold arête to be seen just below the summit, well worth a cautious closer view. Some walkers, keen on adding summits to their personal tally, will also visit High Raise at 802m/2631ft. Again it is easily knocked off along the open ridge, just a 12min walk to the north-east.

Backtrack and head east to reach **Kidsty Pike**. The fell name translates as 'the steep path where young goats were reared'. Once upon a time wild goats commonly inhabited the district's craggy ledges, hence the names Goat's Crag and Gatescarth Pass – both associated with Longsleddale. In fact, the goats would have been encouraged as a means of grazing the cliffs and dissuading sheep from neck-breaking situations. Kidsty Pike may seem a secondary shoulder, the term 'pike' shows this, but it contrives to hold greater than merited attention. It is a real landmark when viewed from the M6, for instance, and its visibility during the approach around the scarp rim, via Twopenny Crag, gives it further credibility as a summit.

A platform beside the cairn on **Kidsty Pike** at 780m/2560ft is a regular gathering point for Coast-to-Coasters, it being the effective end of their mountain Lakeland experience. Ahead they have a 38-mile trek via the Orton Fells and Kirkby Stephen for their next big pull over the Pennine ridge in traversing Nine Standards Rigg into Swaledale.

A simple path leads easily eastwards down comparatively gentle slopes to the next small knot in the ridge, **Kidsty Howes**. Traditionally walkers tended to veer half-left to follow the southern bank of Randale Beck to a footbridge at the foot. Oddly OS maps and the more recent habits of trail-walkers have created a path dipping off the edge directly south-eastwards. A recent cloudburst has further adversely damaged this path at the top, making progress quite dismal. So be advised, ignore the modern 'trail sheep' and trace **Randale Beck** downstream. It's far more comfortable and much better for the ecology.

The prominent craggy top opposite is known as **Castle Crag**, the site of an Iron Age hill fort. The crag was the scene of a fabled Border reiving skirmish, when Captain Whelter led the Kendal Archers in a bloody ambush on a troop of Scottish raiders, their bodies subsequently being buried in the hollow below.

Join the valley path and cross **Riggindale Beck** at Bowderthwaite Bridge. Note the curious paired stones defining and confining the path – they predate the reservoir and would appear to have been set by the farmer at the lost Riggindale Farm. Pass over a wall and spot traces of rigg-and-furrow cultivation under the path as it crosses a pasture. Probably oats were regularly grown here, a further reminder of the active agriculture practised before the waters consumed the valley. The path rises to regain the outward leg of the walk at **The Rigg** wall-crossing. The eye-catching peninsula plantation is destined to be felled along with most other softwoods around the reservoir to be replaced by native hardwoods. One might note that in their own native countries conifers are hardwoods, as they grow much slower and are thus more dense.

Kidsty Pike summit cairn

Yoke, Ill Bell, Froswick,
Thornthwaite Crag, High Street
and Mardale Ill Bell
from Kentmere

A glorious round concentrating upon the western skyline of the Kentmere valley. Climbing initially via the Garburn Pass, the route becomes special once the summit of Yoke is underfoot. Thereafter a succession of handsome fells – Ill Bell, Froswick and Thornthwaite Crag – lead with the Roman road to the top of High Street. The route then switches south and east onto Mardale Ill Bell to pitch off the high ground down the zig-zags from Nan Bield Pass. While strong walkers may choose to undertake the full skyline horseshoe via Harter Fell, Kentmere Pike and Shipman Knotts, our route does more justice to the scenic delights of the upper Kentmere valley, tracking down-dale and gaining new perspectives on the Ill Bell range and the green strath leading back to the village.

↑ *Froswick and Thornthwaite Crag from Ill Bell*

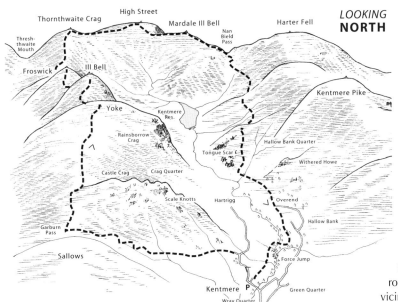

LOOKING
NORTH

ROUTE INFORMATION

Distance	19km/12 miles
Height gain	995m/3265ft
Time	8 hours
Grade	strenuous
Start point	GR455042
Maps	(Harvey Superwalker) Lakeland East (Ordnance Survey) OL5 North-eastern area

After-walk refreshment

Mags Howe in Green Quarter, Kentmere, for walkers' teas (open at weekends in winter and every afternoon in the summer); in Staveley, Wilf's Cafe at the Mill Yard or the Eagle & Child pub

The Start

There is parking at GR455042 beyond St Cuthbert's Church beside Kentmere Institute (£1 in courtesy box). Space is extremely limited, and demands an earlier than normal start. In high summer and for 28 days only a paddock beside the road bridge below the church is brought into commission by the landowner (parking fee). Otherwise roadside parking in the vicinity of the village is non-existent, though there is some scope in a lay-by after the road gate north of Green Quarter, close to the start of the Stile End bridle track GR464051. In summer the best option is to hop aboard the Kentmere Rambler bus in Staveley, which supports sustainable transport and uncluttered lanes. With these benefits, the valley deserves a year-round post bus shuttle.

The Route

Follow the road as it continues from the Institute, keeping left when confronted by a gate passing The Grove. On coming to a fork in the way, turn right, signed 'Troutbeck via Garburn Pass'. The rough track leads by a newly installed gate (thankfully denying access to 4x4 traffic) and along a walled section above the massive Brock Stone (**Badger Rock**) with its sprig o' heather. Look beyond to the pele tower at Kentmere Hall Farm and the narrow Kentmere Tarn – a tautological name, as 'tarn' and 'mere' both mean small lake. Pass through a further gate and continue on an open track winding up the trail – the gravel underfoot becomes a pitched track to the **Garburn Pass** gate.

Pass through and step onto the marshy ridge, right, accompanying the wall. The drier and more orthodox path branches right further west, where the adjacent wall turns left. By either means, the less than exciting ascent progresses up to a ladder

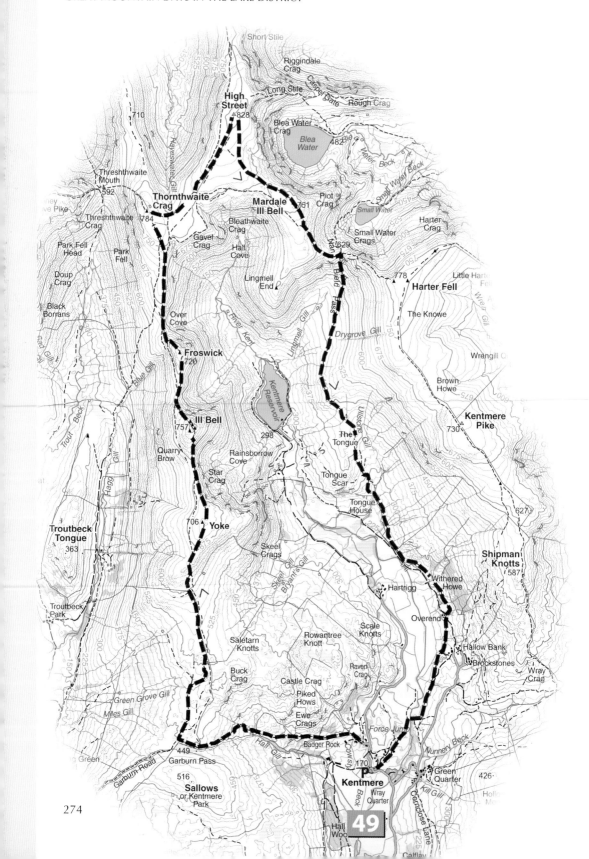

49

↑ Bleawater Crag from Mardale Ill Bell
← Thornthwaite Beacon, broken but not bowed – the handsome wall-end cairn

stile bound for the bare, gently domed summit of Yoke at 706m/2316ft. Each of the three summits – Yoke, Ill Bell and Froswick – has a lower by-pass path on the west side, created by the hasty passage of fellracers. Pass a solitary cairn at the brow leading on to **Yoke's** summit cairn, resting upon a small outcrop. The clear ridge path has recently been given a thorough make-over, inverting the substrate to create a firm, durable causewayed path through the eroded peat hags. The path descends, peering right over the brink into the barren Rainsborrow Cove, with old slate quarries at its foot. Climb from the depression steadily to the characterful peaked summit of **Ill Bell** at 757m/2484ft, the cluster of cairns and ribbed-slate outcropping hugely distinctive. Take time out to revel in the memorable situation.

The stony path heads north-west down to the next depression to climb again to **Froswick's** far less impressive cairn. After a moment's pause, descend to the next depression above **Over Cove**, climbing

now upon the Roman road, where hoof-prints and bike tread marks mingle with vibram treads. The 14ft beacon built into a wall corner on **Thornthwaite Fell** at 784m/2572ft is the inevitable lure. Leave the beacon right, following the ridge path which curves left around the head of the Hayeswater Gill valley, striding through an old wall. Choose harmony with the ridge-top wall rather than the Roman road, and pass a ruined fold to reach the OS pillar marking the top of **High Street** at 828m/2717ft. Though it is not the most immediately satisfying of summits, the wider panoramic horizon is amazingly extensive – westwards into Lakeland, and eastwards to the Pennines.

Leave the fading white-washed pillar south beside the wall, though after 250m veer half-left, being mindful that the broken edge of Bleawater Crag looms along the eastern edge of the grassy plateau. A path leads onto the tapering ridge of **Mardale Ill Bell**, gaining handsome views down upon the elliptical Blea Water and Bleawater crag. The fell summit is marked by a small cairn of no visual merit set at 761m/2497ft. The view is largely limited to the close surround of fells embracing Haweswater and Kentmere. The ridge path draws tighter, winding down south-eastwards into **Nan Bield Pass**. A three-sided wind-break, shielded to a southerly breeze, is located in the narrow hause; this is the remnant of a bothy. Nan Bield was an important north–south valley connection that would have figured in itineraries of all manner of travellers down the centuries. This is a wild spot, especially in winter, with little natural shelter, and the four tiny stone-bower shelters beside Small Water are evidence of the need for 'in-transit' storm refuge. 'Nan' is the dialect feminine pet form of Anne.

Turn right, embarking on the intense sequence of zig-zags dropping south from the pass. Drainage work has recently been done to minimise slippage. Down to the right attention is held by **Kentmere Reservoir**, created in 1848 to supply a head of water for the bobbin mills in Staveley. Above and below it Romano-British settlement sites have been identified. The Reservoir Cottage belongs to Blackburn Education Authority and is used for outdoor pursuits. The River Kent in the valley below is renowned as a haven for freshwater pearl mussels and native crayfish, for which is has been designated a Site of Special Scientific Interest.

Traversing the slopes of **Kentmere Pike** the path crosses by Smallthwaite Knott. Watch out for the bedrock inscribed 'WK 1879' and 'T Kitching 1877' – one wonders who these people were idling long enough to immortalise their visit. Wind down and pass an old slate waymarker 'To Mardale' off the modern line of the path, being at an old fork in the

way north to a long-defunct slate quarry in one of the headstreams of Ullstone Gill. There is further, more extensive slate quarrying on the west slope of **Tongue Scar**, with two big metal-barred levels.

The path from Mardale descends to a footbridge and continues above the valley-bottom wall as a green way via several gates to **Overend**. The met-alled road may appeal, but given even moderately dry conditions the best route is unquestionably the bridleway, which goes through the gates adjacent to the renovated Little Overend. This runs on to cross a bridge into Low Lane. Shortly after passing through a gate, a footpath crosses the line of the walled lane. Climb over the right-hand wall-stile, then descend to cross the footbridge spanning the juvenile River Kent, some distance above the wooded and very private waterfall **Force Jump**. Advance to the squeeze-stile into a walled lane. Go left, noting the litter of huge boulders that must have frustrated farmers down the ages in the pasture to the right. Go through a gate at Rook Howe, following the lane naturally down to the **church**.

It is interesting to slip through **Kentmere church-yard**. Note the graves of Henry and Edith Marshall (Henry was the generous printer who subsidised Alfred Wainwright's first guide, *The Eastern Fells*). Their son Roger's empty grave lies adjacent; he died climbing on Everest and his body was never found. The family lived at Low Bridge, in the 'lost' Wray Quarter of Kentmere – OS mapping shows the other three Quarters, but omits this one.

Nan Bield Pass, looking towards Mardale

Shipman Knotts,
Kentmere Pike and Harter Fell
from Sadgill

*L*ocked away in the furthest fold of the Far Eastern Fells, Longsleddale embodies all the intrinsic magic of Lakeland and marks its beginning and end. This final walk climbs off the Stile End pass onto the rocky spine of Shipman Knotts, visiting the crest of Goat Scar en route to Kentmere Pike and culminating on Harter Fell, with its commanding view over Haweswater. Running easily down to Gatescarth Pass, it follows the ancient drove-way, later a quarry track, down into the impressively wild upper quarter of Longsleddale.

While the name 'Longsleddale' appears to be geographically descriptive, it actually derives from the traditional 'sled' (pony-drawn sledge) used to haul peat for winter fuel down the valley from the fell-top mires. In this valley the sleds had a longer frame than commonly found elsewhere in the district. Walkers might consider experiencing the valley's greater beauty by starting two miles back from Sadgill, where there is a car park next to the church and community hall (external toilets and interpretative board).

↑ *Ill Bell range from Kentmere Pike*

Distance	13.25km/8¼ miles
Height gain	640m/2100ft
Time	5½ hours
Grade	energetic
Start point	GR483057
Maps	(Harvey Superwalker)
	Lakeland East
	(Ordnance Survey)
	OL5 North-eastern area

After-walk refreshment

Pubs: The Eagle & Child in Staveley and the Plough Inn at Selside. Mags Howe in Green Quarter, Kentmere, for fell walkers' teas (weekends in winter and every afternoon in the summer); or Wilf's Cafe, the Mill Yard, Staveley

The Start

At the Longsleddale road-end beside Sadgill Bridge there is scope for some dozen cars, GR483057, but in this exquisitely confined valley-head setting they are inevitably intrusive, however tidily parked. Alternatively, there is a small car park by the village hall, a 30-minute walk back down the road.

The Route

Cross the sturdy **Sadgill Bridge** following the bridle-way left, signposted 'Kentmere'. Pass up through the gates by Low Sadgill Farm, and at the next gate the lane opens, rising on bedrock. Immediately after the second (fifth all told) gate leave the level track, right. Crossing marshy ground, rise in harmony with the wall, climbing over bedrock steps to the brow. Cross a further marshy patch to rise again close by the wall on a loose stony bed to gain the summit of **Shipman Knotts** 587m/1926ft. Strictly the summit lies over the

Shipman Knotts summit

adjacent wall, but there is no provision for casual access; solace, the view is best on the west.

The ridge path dips and rises to a tall ladder stile. Cross and keep right beside the new fence. At the 'V' corner cross the small stile and venture to the cairn on the crest of **Goat Scar**. Wander a little down the east slope to gain the best of all views of Longsleddale – down-dale, into the craggy fastness at its head – spying the age-old drove lane, the cascading River Sprint (meaning 'the leaping one') and across to Tarn Crag buttressed by Buckbarrow Crag.

Backtrack to the stile and keep right beside the fence. The fence becomes a wall on the easy climb to the top of **Kentmere Pike** 730m/2395ft. Again the summit is over the wall, but here there is provision for anyone to venture to the east side, the location of the stone-built Ordnance Survey pillar (the original reason for the slate wall-stile). But again the best views are on the west side, and the outcropping gives scope for a picnic perch, where you can revel in the lovely view west to the Ill Bell range and beyond into the centre of Lakeland.

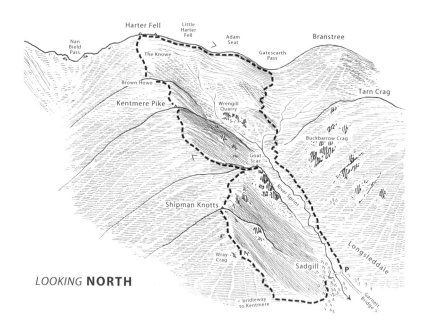

LOOKING **NORTH**

Harter Fell summit looking north-east

Goat Scar and drove lane looking towards the head of Longsleddale

The ridge path continues unhindered on grass, skipping the several eroded peaty areas. The wall gives way to a fence shortly after the first depression, and the fence remains the surest of guides to the plateaued top of **Harter Fell** at 778m/2553ft. The summit cairn is unmistakable, if a trifle odd in composition – the usual gathering of stones laced with sprigs of metal fencing stakes, plucked from the discarded relic of the forerunning fence. The panorama is amazing as one might expect – distanced from the main Lakeland heights, the Ill Bell and High Street ridges hold the main attention. Stride onto the western edge to get the best views down onto Small Water. To the east the long views feature the Cross Fell range, the highest Pennines, the Howgills and Ingleborough.

Continue with the fence, and the next cairn above Harter Crag provides a peach of a view over Mardale Head and Haweswater. The lake name derives from the two high north/south passes ('hawes') above the lake – Nan Bield (meaning 'Anne's shelter') and

Gatescarth (meaning 'goats' enclosure'). The fence continues beside the path until at **Little Harter Fell** it breaks right. They come together again only as the newly structured path meets the ancient bridleway at **Gatescarth Pass**.

Turn right through the gate following the open-tracked Mardale Byway, which duly descends, via zig-zags, and leads past the largely hidden old **Wrengill Quarry** to a padlocked gate (access for off-roading 4x4s is strictly, and rightly, controlled). Cross the stile beside a sheepfold, from where the track continues via a further gate and then becomes a sturdy pitched way, originally set to cope with quarry traffic. Pass down beneath **Buckbarrow Crag** (left) to wind along the attractive walled lane, viewing Goat Scar rising abruptly on the west side of the level strath. The walk ends effectively with the native trees sheltering the farming hamlet of **Sadgill**, derived from the Norse meaning 'streamside hiding-place'.

APPENDIX 1:

Concise Walk Reference and Personal Log

WALK/START	DISTANCE	HEIGHT GAIN	TIME	GRADE	WALKED
1 Lingmoor Fell from Little Langdale	10km/6¼ miles	410m/1350ft	4½ hours	energetic	
2 Pavey Ark and Harrison Stickle from New Dungeon Ghyll	6km/3¾ miles	677m/2220ft	4½ hours	energetic	
3 Loft Crag and Pike o'Stickle from New Dungeon Ghyll	9.25km/5¾ miles	610m/2000ft	5 hours	strenuous	
4 Bowfell and Rossett Pike from Old Dungeon Ghyll	12km/7½ miles	854m/2800ft	7 hours	strenuous	
5 Pike o'Blisco and Crinkle Crags from Old Dungeon Ghyll	13.5km/8½ miles	1158m/3800ft	7 hours	strenuous	
6 Wetherlam from Coniston	13.25km/8¼ miles	924m/3030ft	7 hours	strenuous	
7 Dow Crag and Coniston Old Man from Coniston	8.75km/5½ miles	555m/1820ft	5 hours	energetic	
8 Dow Crag, Brim Fell, Swirl How and Grey Friar from Seathwaite (Duddon)	18km/11¼ miles	1030m/3380ft	8 hours	strenuous	
9 Black Combe from Whicham	11km/8 miles	600m/1960ft	5½ hours	energetic	
10 Harter Fell (Eskdale) and Hard Knott from Brotherilkeld	11.25km/7 miles	732m/2400ft	6 hours	strenuous	
11 Scafell Pike and Esk Pike from Brotherilkeld	19.75km/12½ miles	1146m/3760ft	10 hours	arduous	
12 Scafell and Slight Side from Wha House	13.5km/8½ miles	908m/2980ft	7 hours	strenuous	
13 Illgill Head and Whin Rigg from Wasdale Head	14.75km/9¼ miles	609m/2000ft	6¾ hours	strenuous	
14 Great End, Scafell Pike and Lingmell from Wasdale Head	13.5km/8½ miles	1051m/3450ft	8 hours	strenuous	
15 Pillar, Scoat Fell, Red Pike and Yewbarrow from Wasdale Head	17.5km/11 miles	1117m/3665ft	8½ hours	arduous	
16 Kirk Fell and Great Gable from Wasdale Head	11.25km/7 miles	1012m/3320ft	6½ hours	strenuous	
17 Buckbarrow, Seatallan and Middle Fell from Nether Wasdale	13.5km/8½ miles	808m/2650ft	6 hours	energetic	
18 Crag Fell, Caw Fell and Haycock from Ennerdale Bridge	20km/12½ miles	945m/3100ft	9 hours	strenuous	

WALK/START	DISTANCE	HEIGHT GAIN	TIME	GRADE	WALKED
19 Steeple, Scoat Fell and Pillar from Bowness Knott	21km/13 miles	914m/3000ft	9 hours	arduous	
20 Mellbreak from Lanthwaite Wood	11.5km/7¼ miles	686m/2250ft	4½ hours	energetic	
21 Whiteside, Hopegill Head, Grasmoor, Wandope, Whiteless Pike and Rannerside Knotts from Lanthwaite Green	18.25km/11½ miles	1120m/3675ft	8 hours	strenuous	
22 High Crag, High Stile and Red Pike from Buttermere	8.75km/5½ miles	793m/2600ft	6 hours	strenuous	
23 Haystacks from Buttermere	13km/8¼ miles	518m/1700ft	6 hours	energetic	
24 Fleetwith Pike, Dale Head, Hindscarth and Robinson from Buttermere	16.5km/10¼ miles	1188m/3900ft	7½ hours	strenuous	
25 Green Gable and Great Gable from Seathwaite (Borrowdale)	13.75km/8½ miles	713m/2340ft	7½ hours	strenuous	
26 Rosthwaite Fell and Glaramara from Stonethwaite	10km/6¼ miles	762m/2500ft	6½ hours	strenuous	
27 Eagle Crag, Sergeant's Crag, High Raise and Ullscarf from Stonethwaite	15km/9½ miles	811m/2660ft	6½ hours	strenuous	
28 High Spy, King's How and Brund Fell from Rosthwaite	13 km/8¼ miles	549m/1800ft	6 hours	energetic	
29 Catbells, Maiden Moor, High Spy, Dale Head and Hindscarth from Hawse End	19.25km/12 miles	1052m/3450ft	8 hours	strenuous	
30 Robinson, Knott Rigg and Ard Crags from Rigg Beck	13.5km/8½ miles	924m/3030ft	5½ hours	energetic	
31 Grisedale Pike, Hopegill Head, Eel Crag, Sail, Outerside and Barrow from Braithwaite	16km/10miles	1160m/3806ft	6½ hours	strenuous	
32 Ullock Pike, Long Side, Carl Side, Skiddaw Little Man, Skiddaw and Bakestall from Bassenthwaite	19km/12 miles	1045m/3430ft	9 hours	strenuous	✓
33 Carrock Fell and High Pike from Stone Ends (Mosedale)	10.5km/6½miles	533m/1750ft	4½ hours	energetic	
34 Bowscale Fell, Blencathra and Souther Fell from Mungrisdale	14km/8¾ miles	834m/2736ft	6½ hours	energetic	
35 Blencathra from Threlkeld	7.5km/4¾ miles	732m/2400ft	5 hours	strenuous	

WALK/START	DISTANCE	HEIGHT GAIN	TIME	GRADE	WALKED
36 Clough Head, Great Dodd, Watson's Dodd, Stybarrow Dodd and Hart Side from High Row (Dockray)	18km/11½ miles	1143m/3750ft	8 hours	strenuous	
37 Raise, White Side and Helvellyn from Legburthwaite	14.5km/9 miles	960m/3150ft	7 hours	strenuous	
38 Helm Crag, Gibson Knott, Calf Crag and Sergeant Man from Grasmere	16km/10 miles	808m/2650ft	7 hours	strenuous	
39 Low Pike, High Pike, Dove Crag, Hart Crag, Fairfield, Great Rigg, Heron Pike and Nab Scar from Ambleside	19.5km/12¼ miles	1050m/3443ft	9 hours	strenuous	
40 Red Screes, Little Hart Crag, High Pike and Low Pike from Ambleside	18km/11¼ miles	1000m/3280ft	8½ hours	strenuous	
41 Caudale Moor from Cowbridge	15km/9½ miles	643m/2110ft	5 hours	energetic	
42 Dove Crag, Hart Crag and Hartsop above How from Cowbridge	11.25km/7 miles	823m/2700ft	6½ hours	energetic	
43 Fairfield and St Sunday Crag from Patterdale	17km/10¾ miles	911m/2990ft	8½ hours	strenuous	
44 Dollywaggon Pike, Nethermost Pike, Helvellyn and Catstycam from Patterdale	18.4km/11½ miles	1007m/3230ft	8 hours	strenuous	
45 Birkhouse Moor, Helvellyn, White Side, Raise, Stybarrow Dodd and Sheffield Pike from Glenridding	17km/10½ miles	1340m/4400ft	10 hours	arduous	
46 Place Fell from Patterdale	11km/7 miles	550m/1800ft	4½ hours	energetic	
47 Steel Knotts, High Raise, Rampsgill Head, The Knott, Rest Dodd, Angletarn Pikes and Beda Head from Martindale	19km/12 miles	1012m/3320ft	8 hours	strenuous	
48 High Street, Rampsgill Head and Kidsty Pike from Mardale Head	10.25km/6½ miles	760m/2490ft	5½ hours	energetic	
49 Yoke, Ill Bell, Froswick, Thornthwaite Crag, High Street and Mardale Ill Bell from Kentmere	19km/12 miles	995m/3265ft	8 hours	strenuous	
50 Shipman Knotts, Kentmere Pike and Harter Fell (Mardale) from Sadgill	13.2km/8¼ miles	640m/2100ft	5½ hours	energetic	

APPENDIX 2:

Index of the Fells

APPENDIX 3:

Further Reading

The Central Fells by Mark Richards
ISBN 9781852845407   £12.95

The Near Eastern Fells by Mark Richards
ISBN 9781852845414   £12.95

The Southern Fells by Mark Richards
ISBN 9781852845421   £12.95

The Mid-Western Fells by Mark Richards
ISBN 9781852845438   £14.95

The Western Fells by Mark Richards
ISBN 9781852845445   £14.95

The North-Western Fells by Mark Richards
ISBN 9781852845452   £14.95

The Northern Fells by Mark Richards
ISBN 9781852845469   £14.95

The Far Eastern Fells by Mark Richards
ISBN 9781852845476   £14.95

The Lakeland Fellranger Collection by Mark Richards
ISBN 9781852847487   £119.95

Navigation by Pete Hawkins
ISBN 9781852844905   £8.99

Map and Compass by Pete Hawkins
ISBN 9781852845988   £14.95

The Hillwalker's Manual by Bill Birkett
ISBN 9781852843410   £12.95

The Hillwalker's Guide to Mountaineering
by Terry Adby and Stuart Johnston
ISBN 9781852843939   £14.00

Mountain Weather by David Pedgley
ISBN 9781852844806   £12.95

Pocket First Aid and Wilderness Medicine
by Jim Duff and Peter Gormly
ISBN 9781852847159   £9.99

Outdoor Photography by Jon Sparks and Chiz Dakin
ISBN 9781852846466   £14.95

The Book of the Bivvy by Ronald Turnbull
ISBN 9781852845612   £9.99

Tour of the Lake District by Jim Reid
ISBN 9781852844967   £12.00

GMD and the Lakeland Fellranger series

Great Mountain Days is a distillation of Lakeland's finest fell walks. A more thorough fell-by-fell exposition of the region is to be found in the eight-part Lakeland Fellranger series by the same author. Work on this series began back in 1999, with the first four titles originally published by HarperCollins between 2003 and 2005. Cicerone Press then relaunched the series, with the first two titles published in autumn 2008, the next two in spring 2009, two more in 2011 and the final two in 2013.

The walks in *Great Mountain Days* are distributed among the Lakeland Fellranger series as follows:

> 5 in Far Eastern Fells
> 9 in Near Eastern Fells
> 7 in Central Fells
> 7 in Mid-Western Fells
> 4 in Southern Fells
> 9 in Western Fells
> 5 in North-Western Fells
> 4 in Northern Fells.

Helvellyn muscles into three GMD walks; 22 fells feature on two walks; and 111 fells make solo appearances. The GMDs roam over 133 fells in total – over half the recognised fells in the Lake District National Park.

The precise number of fells within the Lakeland Fellranger series (227) exceeds Wainwright's 214 – not least because the series covers the entire mountain area. The determination of separate fell status is an inexact science. Considerations such as height, bearing, character and summit situation all come into play and everyone and anyone can have a view. There are numerous instances of a summit resting upon a rising ridge to a clearly more substantive height, for instance Nab Scar/Heron Pike and High Hartsop Dodd/Little Hart Crag. Guidebook writers make their own distinctions – some hold to strict rules such as the scrupulous list of 171 Nuttalls; to which when subsidiary tops are added you get a generous 541 Birketts. One might say the rule is that there are no rules.

Scrambles in the Lake District by Brian Evans
vol. 1 (*South*): ISBN 9781852844431   £14.00
vol. 2 (*North*): ISBN 9781852844639   £14.00

Short Walks in Lakeland by Aileen and Brian Evans
vol. 1 (*South*): ISBN 9781852841447   £12.95
vol. 2 (*North*): ISBN 9781852842321   £12.95
vol. 3 (*West*): ISBN 9781852843083   £12.95

Walking – Trekking – Mountaineering – Climbing – Cycling

Over 40 years, Cicerone have built up an outstanding collection of 300 guides, inspiring all sorts of amazing adventures.

Every guide comes from extensive exploration and research by our expert authors, all with a passion for their subjects. They are frequently praised, endorsed and used by clubs, instructors and outdoor organisations.

All our titles can now be bought as **e-books**, **ePubs** and **Kindle** files and we also have an online magazine – **Cicerone Extra** – with features to help cyclists, climbers, walkers and trekkers choose their next adventure, at home or abroad.

Our website shows any **new information** we've had in since a book was published. Please do let us know if you find anything has changed, so that we can publish the latest details. On our **website** you'll also find great ideas and lots of detailed information about what's inside every guide and you can buy **individual routes** from many of them online.

It's easy to keep in touch with what's going on at Cicerone by getting our monthly **free e-newsletter**, which is full of offers, competitions, up-to-date information and topical articles. You can subscribe on our home page and also follow us on **Facebook** and **Twitter** or dip into our **blog**.

Cicerone – the very best guides for exploring the world.

CICERONE

2 Police Square Milnthorpe Cumbria LA7 7PY
Tel: 015395 62069 info@cicerone.co.uk
www.cicerone.co.uk